PENGUIN BOOKS
DON'T GET TAKEN EVERY TIME

A novelist, consumer writer, and commentator, Remar Sutton is also considered one of America's foremost automotive experts. For thirteen years he has directed and participated in a nationwide investigation of selling and leasing techniques used by large and small dealers. He is co-founder with Ralph Nader and President of the national Consumer Task Force for Automotive Issues. The Task Force coordinates some of the auto fraud work of many states' attorneys general, consumer groups, and plaintiff law firms. Sutton has been a consultant and an expert witness on automotive matters for the attorneys general of the states of New York, Illinois, Missouri, and Florida, and in numerous class action lawsuits brought on behalf of consumers. Sutton is also the author of "Car Facts," a member-education program developed to serve the sixty million members of the Credit Union National Association.

His articles on the automotive business and other subjects have appeared in such magazines as *Reader's Digest*, *Family Weekly*, *Sports Illustrated*, and *Credit Union Magazine*. He is a contributor to the Style section of *The Washington Post*.

Sutton is a frequent guest on talk shows such as *20/20*, *Oprah Winfrey*, *Nightline*, *Good Morning America*, *Today*, *Hour Magazine*, National Public Radio's *All Things Considered*, and *ABC Primetime*. He also appears regularly on scores of regional radio shows.

He is the author of *Body Worry* (Penguin), two mystery novels, *Long Lines* and *Boiling Rock*, and is co-author of *The Common Ground Book* with Mary Abbott Waite.

BOOKS BY REMAR SUTTON

NONFICTION
Don't Get Taken Every Time
Body Worry
The Common Ground Book

FICTION
Long Lines
Boiling Rock

DON'T
GET TAKEN
EVERY TIME

*The Insider's Guide to Buying or Leasing
Your Next Car or Truck*

4TH REVISED EDITION

Remar Sutton

PENGUIN BOOKS

PENGUIN BOOKS
Published by the Penguin Group
Penguin Books USA Inc., 375 Hudson Street, New York, New York 10014, U.S.A.
Penguin Books Ltd, 27 Wrights Lane, London W8 5TZ, England
Penguin Books Australia Ltd, Ringwood, Victoria, Australia
Penguin Books Canada Ltd, 10 Alcorn Avenue,
Toronto, Ontario, Canada M4V 3B2
Penguin Books (N.Z.) Ltd, 182–190 Wairau Road, Auckland 10, New Zealand

Penguin Books Ltd, Registered Offices:
Harmondsworth, Middlesex, England

First published in the United States of America by The Viking Press 1982
Published in Penguin Books 1983
First revised edition published 1986
Second revised edition published 1991
Third revised edition published 1994
This fourth revised edition published 1997

10 9 8 7 6 5 4 3 2 1

LIBRARY OF CONGRESS CATALOGING IN PUBLICATION DATA
Sutton, Remar.
    Don't get taken every time: the insider's guide to buying or
leasing your next car or truck/Remar Sutton.—Rev. ed.
    p. cm.
    Includes index.
    ISBN 0 14 02.6670 4
    1. Automobiles—Purchasing. 2. Trucks—Purchasing. I. Title.
TL 162.S96 1997
629.222'029'6—dc21 97–7992

Printed in the United States of America
Set in ITC Cheltenham Book
Designed by Sabrina Bowers

To Dad

Acknowledgments

The passage of time makes this book more accurate. Each year hundreds of people ensure that by sharing with me what has happened to them recently at dealerships.

So, if this book is a good one, the thanks go to editor Mary Abbott Waite, to my staff and the volunteer shoppers across the country who work with us constantly, and to those of you who have written me after using a previous edition of *Don't Get Taken Every Time*.

Contents

Introduction

A DAY IN THE LIFE OF KILLER MONSOON	1
WHAT'S WRONG WITH THE AUTOMOBILE BUSINESS?	9
How Do the Dealers Respond to These Charges?	12

Part I: Forearming

1. What You're Up Against: The World of Sellers and Selling   17

KILLER AND HIS "FAMILY"	17
INSIDE THE FAMILY: DEALERS, SALES MANAGERS, AND SALESMEN	22
First the Good News: They Really Will Sell You a Car for Less	32
Well, Just How Honest Are Car People?	35
The Salesman's Greatest Talent	35
The Salesman's Favorite Targets	37
Profits, Not Profit	38
Supply and Demand	39
So, How Do You Win?	39
KILLER MONSOON'S FAVORITE SELLING TECHNIQUES	40
"Will You Buy a Car Today at Some Price?"	41
"If I Can . . . , Will You . . . ?"	42
The Sincere Salesman-in-a-Contest Ploy	43
The "I'm Salesman of the Month" Routine	43
The "I'm a Trustworthy Salesman" Ploy	43
"Setting You" on a Car: The Demo Ride	44
"We Can Allow You This Much with a Difference of This Much and a Deferred Payment of This Much. Now, Just Sign Here"—The Old Confuse-Them-and-Control-the-Sale Ploy	45

Justifying the Sale   45

"Ah, This Is the Beauty of a Trade-in You Mentioned?"—
    The Ploy of Bringing You to Their Reality   47

The "Other Customer" Ploy   48

The Old (Make That VERY New) "Lease 'Em a Car Instead" Ploy   49

THE SELLING SYSTEMS   50

The T. O. System   50

The Four-Square System   51

The Note System: Killing You with Kindness   52

The Tower System   54

One Price, No Hassle Systems   54

"Spot Delivery" Systems   55

"Credit Doctor" Scams   56

The Advent of Major Automobile Dealerships Designed Solely
    for "Sub-Prime" Borrowers   57

Well, What Should I Do If I Think I Have Credit Problems?
    How Can I Protect Myself?   59

Welcome Centers   59

RUNNING A CREDIT CHECK   60

Getting a Deposit   60

THE RAISE   61

LOWBALLING   62

WELL, WHY DON'T YOU JUST COME OUT WITH IT AND CALL
    ALL THOSE SALESPEOPLE CROOKS?   63

2. A Look in the Mirror: Know Yourself   65

"IN THE BUCKET" AND "DIPPING": THE PROBLEM WITH THE
    CHASES   67

SINGING THE BLUES: THE TROUBLE WITH THE ALLGOODS   70

THE NEWEST TOY: THE PROBLEM WITH THE ESTRUMS   73

FACING OUR FOIBLES: THE PROBLEM WITH ALL CAR BUYERS   75

How Naïve Are You, Really?   75

Impulse Buyers: You're a Favorite   75

WHAT SHOULD YOU BUY?   76

Need vs. Want   76

What Can You Really Afford?   79

New vs. Used   80

American vs. Foreign   86

Trading Down   87

THINGS THAT IMPRESS AND TERRIFY SALESMEN:
TRAITS YOU CAN CULTIVATE 88
   Indecision 89
   Lack of Enthusiasm 89
   Knowledge 90
   Nonromantic Attitudes 91
   Patience 91
   Impatience 91

3. Know Your Present Car   92

THE INSTRUCTIVE TALE OF JIM WRIGHT 92
THE IMPORTANCE OF A CLEAN, SOUND CAR 96
IS IT A POPULAR CAR? 97
WHAT'S THE MILEAGE? 98
COMPUTING YOUR CAR'S DOLLAR VALUE 99
DETERMINING WHOLESALE VALUE 101
WHAT ABOUT "BOOK VALUE"? 104
SHOULD YOU SELL YOUR CAR YOURSELF? 105
   What Should You Sell Your Used Car For? 112
   What's the Best Way to Hawk a Hirohito? 112
   Are You Afraid of the Dickering? 113
   Your Payoff and His Financing 113

4. Dollars and Sense: Know Your Financing (Even If You Pay Cash)   115

WHY SHOP YOUR MONEY BEFORE YOU SHOP YOUR CAR? 119
FINANCING SOURCES 121
   Cash Value in Your Life Insurance 121
   A Home Equity Line of Credit 121
   Credit Unions 122
   Banks 125
   Dealership Financing 126
   Finance Companies 129
   "Buy Here, Pay Here" Lots 129
WHAT TYPE OF BUYER DO THEY THINK YOU ARE? 130
NEW OR USED, HOW MUCH CAR CAN I AFFORD? 132
   Shopping for Rates and Terms 134
   Evaluating "Rate Sale" Gimmicks 137
   So, Where's the Best Place to Finance? 138

How Much Can You Afford to Pay Each Month? How Long
    Will You Pay It?   139
The Concept of Loan Cash—The Soul of This Book   140
Figuring Loan Cash from a Payment   140
Putting the Loan Cash Concept to Work   141
The Concept of Available Cash   143
How Much Money Should You Finance on a Particular Car?   144
Determining Available Cash for Different Buying Situations   146
**USING THE CHART TO DETERMINE PAYMENTS WHEN YOU KNOW
THE LUMP SUM**   151
SHOULD YOU BUY CREDIT LIFE OR DISABILITY INSURANCE?   152
What about Life Insurance from Credit Unions?   154
What about Credit Life Insurance from a Bank?   154
What about Credit Disability Insurance?   154
Can Finance Sources Make You Take Insurance?   156
DETERMINING YOUR BEST LOAN SOURCE OVERALL   156
Comparing Loan Opportunities   157

**5. Big Town, Small Town: How the Boys
Play the Game**   160

FINDING ONE OF THE FEW GOOD DEALERS: WHAT TO LOOK FOR   160
A LOOK AT SELLING SYSTEMS IN THE REAL WORLD   161
Intermission   161

Part II: Battle Time!

6. Some Preliminaries to Shopping   183

DOWN THE ROAD OF GOOD INTENTIONS   183
SOME PRELIMINARIES ON ADVERTISING   185
THE BIG LIE: DEALERSHIP ADVERTISING   187
But What about "Truth in Lending"? How Can They Print
    What's Not the Truth?   187
Dealers' Favorite Advertising Gimmicks Used in Your Hometown   189
Whew! How Can You Find a Rose in All That Garbage?   192
What about Ads from Individuals Selling Their Cars?   193
DO CAR PEOPLE EVER—EVER—REALLY HAVE REAL SALES?   194
IS THERE AN EASIER TIME TO BUY?   195

7. Jumping Into the Fray: Shopping the Right Way   198

   SHOPPING: IF YOU PLAN TO BUY A NEW CAR   207
     What Do Those Pretty Cars Cost the Dealer?   209
     Understanding "Cost," MSRP, and Dealer Stickers   209
     Okay, So What Do Those Pretty Cars Cost, Then?   212
     Other Nice Ways to Be Taken: Car-Buying Services   217
     Ordering a Car   218
     "Demos," Demonstrators, "Executive," or Program Cars   219
   SHOPPING: IF YOU PLAN TO BUY A NEW TRUCK OR
   FULL-SIZED VAN   220
   PUTTING THE INTERNET TO WORK FOR YOU   221
     Just Who's Providing the Auto Information on the Net
       and World Wide Web?   222
     Finding Information on the Net   224
   SHOPPING: IF YOU PLAN TO BUY A USED CAR OR USED TRUCK   225
     Why All This Work Is Worth It   228
     Why It's Harder   228
     The Importance of Loan Value   230
     Used-Vehicle Sources   231
     Locating a Specific Used Car   235
     Checking Out a Used Vehicle   235

8. Leasing a Car the Right Way   238

   HOW LEASES WORK   238
     Who Should Consider Leasing?   239
     Before Choosing a Lease, Understand the Consequences
       of Doing It Wrong   240
     Are There Different Types of Leases?   241
     Who Are the Parties in a Lease?   242
     Who's Making the Big Profits Here? The Leasing Companies
       or the Dealerships?   242
     How Do Leasing Companies Defend Their Services?   244
   UNDERSTANDING THE COMPONENTS OF A LEASE   245
     Important Leasing Terms   245
     Personal Leasing Checklist   247
   LEASING THE RIGHT WAY   250
     Surviving the Minefield at the Dealership   254
     How Do I Negotiate Down the Effective Interest Rate?   256

Why Can't I Save All This Work and Just Lease One of Those
    "$199 a Month" Cars I Always See on Television? 256
What About Leasing Used Cars? 256

9. Negotiating the Sale: Specific Tactics for Specific Buyers 258

WHAT IS A "FAIR" DEAL? 258
HANDLING HIGH-PRESSURE TECHNIQUES 259
DEALING WITH THE FINANCE "MANAGER" 261
    The Toughest Sales Gimmicks at the Dealership 261
    Protection Packages, Warranties: Should You Buy from
        the Dealers at Any Price? 262
    Where You'll Meet the Finance Salesperson (a.k.a., Your
        Friend, The Business Manager or "Financial Counselor") 263
YOUR HOUR UPON THE STAGE: THE IMPORTANCE OF
    PLAY-ACTING 265
STALKING AND THE KILL: THE NEGOTIATIONS 266
    If You Are Financing, Buying a New Car, and Trading the Old 267
    If You Are Financing and Buying a New Car without Trading 271
    If You Are Financing, Buying a Used Car, and Trading the Old 275
    If You Are Financing and Buying a Used Car without Trading 279
    If You Are Paying Cash, Buying a New Car, and Trading the Old 283
    If You Are Paying Cash and Buying a New Car without Trading 287
    If You Are Paying Cash, Buying a Used Car, and Trading the Old 289
    If You Are Paying Cash and Buying a Used Car without Trading 294
WARRANTIES, NEW AND USED 297
    New-Car Warranties 297
    The Biggest Joke: Used-Car Warranties 299
A NOTE ON DEPOSITS 302
SIGNING THINGS 303

10. Lomax 308

Appendix

Checking Out a Used Car or Used Truck 313
THINGS TO CHECK OUT YOURSELF 313

Mechanic's Checklist 321
IN YOUR OPINION 321

What They Cost, Minus the Profit 322
**PERCENTAGE OF PROFIT: CARS AND MINIVANS,
AMERICAN AND IMPORTED** 323
**PERCENTAGE OF PROFIT: VANS, SPORT UTILITY VEHICLES
AND TRUCKS, AMERICAN AND IMPORTED** 328

Chart For Use in Figuring Loan Cash or
Monthly Payments 331

"The Negotiation" in Abbreviated Form 333
**IF YOU ARE FINANCING, BUYING A NEW CAR, AND
TRADING THE OLD** 333
Dealing with the Store— 333
**IF YOU ARE FINANCING AND BUYING A NEW CAR
WITHOUT TRADING** 334
Dealing with the Store— 335
**IF YOU ARE FINANCING, BUYING A USED CAR, AND
TRADING THE OLD** 335
Dealing with the Store— 336
**IF YOU ARE FINANCING AND BUYING A USED CAR
WITHOUT TRADING** 337
Dealing with the Store— 338
**IF YOU ARE PAYING CASH, BUYING A NEW CAR, AND
TRADING THE OLD** 339
Dealing with the Store— 339
**IF YOU ARE PAYING CASH AND BUYING A NEW CAR
WITHOUT TRADING** 340
Dealing with the Store— 340
**IF YOU ARE PAYING CASH, BUYING A USED CAR, AND
TRADING THE OLD** 341
Dealing with the Store— 341
**IF YOU ARE PAYING CASH AND BUYING A USED CAR
WITHOUT TRADING** 342
Dealing with the Store— 343

Glossary 345
Index 349

Introduction

A DAY IN THE LIFE OF KILLER MONSOON

"Killer Monsoon" is late for the sales meeting again, the daily "ream-'em-out-and-charge-'em-up" gathering that begins the day at most automobile dealerships in America. Killer's feeling fine today; he's delivering a new car to that nice old couple who came to the store yesterday. The folks never knew what hit them, either; they paid "full-boat," list price, and they're happy, of course. The buyer's order showed a whopping allowance on their trade, and that's what they wanted. It's Killer's best talent, giving people what they want.

The general manager is running the meeting this morning. When that guy's up this early, it's usually going to be a bad session, Killer thinks. And he's right. J. C. looks angry. Don, one of the sales managers, looks solemn. Killer stands by the door until everyone is seated and then strolls down the aisle, nodding, passing out "good mornings" and "how are yous?" to the forty men settled tentatively in their seats. As he passes J. C. and Don, he turns slightly toward them and curtsies, spreading his imaginary dress with both hands, a thin and innocent smile curving his lips. The rumble of laughter in the room turns to silence quickly as J. C. stands, pulls his belt upward over his belly, and inhales, a snorting sound. Obviously J. C. isn't amused. He walks three heavy steps to the podium, grabs both edges with an intensity escaping no one in the room, and begins to talk in loud sentences.

"Why, boys and girls, are you so screwed up? *Why,* when American cars are finally good, do you quit selling them? We're down in new car sales. We're down in new-car gross. We're down in used-car gross. Financing is down. Rustproofing and warranties are down. We had fifty people on this lot last night. We didn't sell ten cars. We didn't lease five cars. And not a damned one of you T. O.'d a soul. [Lots of terms at car stores are peculiar to the business. The Glossary on p. 345 will help you with those that are unfamiliar to you.] The *next* one of you that lets anybody walk without registering your 'up' or turning them to a manager is going to be on his ass out the door!" J. C. begins to upbraid each salesman individually, saying each name as if it were a command, looking first at the man and then the Perk Board on the wall. The board ranks every salesman on unit sales new and used, "front-end" gross, "back-end" gross, deals financed, deals leased, and bonus cars. Killer is leading in every column; he's not only "Salesman of the Year" again, but the dealership's best closer.

But even the Salesman of the Year isn't immune from a lecture today. Pausing at the end of his roll call, J. C. looks at Killer, who has slipped down in his chair, eyes half closed in boredom. "Hey Killer, wake up!" J. C. slaps the lectern. "This applies to you, too. You may lead the board with two hundred new cars out. But you've been doing too much sleeping. This time last year you had out three hundred new and your average gross was fifty dollars higher. So either you've been dozing or you're over the hill, old man."

"Well, J. C., I guess you better send me to that great car store in the sky. But before you do that, why don't you help us sell some cars? Like, why don't you put a bonus on that beat-up old Lincoln; I get indigestion every time I see it. Maybe it's my age or something." Killer still reclines in his chair, but he's made a smart move. He's changed the subject. He's also changed J. C. into a bear again.

"Killer, you traded the damn thing in," J. C. replies hotly. "But I'm going to be nice today. The first person that brings me a deal, a signed order, on that piece of junk will get a $200 bonus when the S.O.B. drives it off. I'm also paying $100 for each 'up' you switch to leasing from buying *and* $100 for the first one of you to close an extended warranty sale or a protection package sale." The promise of the last spiff brings scattered laughter to the room. More and more customers had been falling for the dealership's favorite new profit gimmicks.

J. C. pauses, looks over the room once more, and brings his fist down hard on the podium. "Now, damn it, I want to see some grosses! Pound those people! Peel 'em off the ceiling! Never give 'em time to think, and *write me some deals!*"

One of the first men out of the room, Killer heads for the employees' lounge. He pours himself a coffee, drops in six sugar cubes, and sits at a small table by the door. Between sips he looks at his bird-dog list. Jerry, his car-queer friend who just loves to trade cars every six months, might have a new prospect, Killer thinks. Jerry is a barber, one of the best bird dogs, a guy who tells everyone sitting in his chair what a good deal he can get them "as long as you deal with Bobby DeMarco." That's Killer's real name. "Killer Monsoon" is what the other guys call him, a good description, too. Killer always squeezes every single ounce of profit from every customer. He's famous for "bumping" one guy, raising him, six times.

By ten in the morning, Killer has made his bird-dog phone calls and is standing close to the main entrance of the showroom. He's hot. All these damn new salesmen, the "floor whores," are grabbing all the "ups" and blowing them off the lot without ever really working them. And nothing ticks Killer off more than people blowing sales. "Those new guys don't know how to control anyone," he's always bitching to J. C., "they're costing you money, man." J. C. knows he's right, too. A salesman who works his own deals always costs the house money. One of these days J. C.'s going to kick ass. But not today. The hangover is bad today.

Killer watches a car pull onto the lot and quickly enters the car's tag number into the computer near the front door. "Good," he mutters, as a file detailing the couple's name, the value of their trade-in, and their credit worthiness pops on the screen. The file also shows this couple has visited two other dealerships, but haven't made an offer on a car yet. Killer glances again at their old buggy. It looks like a clean, nice car, three years old. The people look nice too, a middle-aged couple who obviously don't know what they want, first crawling into a minivan and then a two-door. Killer starts toward them. He needs to set them on that van with the nice bonus. Screw the two-door.

Killer isn't dressed like the hot-shots with their blown hair and snappy shoes. He is a perfect shade of gray in a gray world: slightly rumpled short-sleeved shirt covering an ample belly, a tie that's the wrong width pulled loose at the neck. He needs a haircut—Killer always needs a haircut. He is quiet, almost shy, unassuming in the most disarming way, and friendly without showing his teeth too much. If you met him, you'd instantly feel comfortable and slightly superior.

"Hi, I'm Bob DeMarco; thanks for coming in to see us." He shakes both their hands, paying attention to them equally, watching for the signs that will say which person is the control, the decision-maker of the two. As Killer talks, his eyes constantly move from the couple to their car. "Folks, that's a mighty fine trade-in you have there," he volunteers. "I'll bet it's paid for, too." His observation is an important one. The couple's response will tell Killer what their payment range is if they're still paying. If they say, "Oh, it's paid for, just last month," he'll know the couple has lots of equity, a situation in which good salesmen always make more money. If they say, "We paid cash for it," Killer will know he's dealing with a different type of buyer.

These folks turn out to be the easiest marks, the type who say, "As long as the payment isn't too high, we're not concerned with what the car costs." Killer just loves payment buyers. He'll never mention once during the next hour what the couple's trade-in is worth, or what the difference in the old car and new car will be. He'll just talk payments. "After all, it's the payment that's important, isn't it folks?" They nod yes. "Well, let me ask you then—if I can get the payments to a level that is satisfactory to you, will you buy the car today?" Well, who wouldn't say yes to that?

Now the three of them are sitting in Killer's office, surrounded by "Salesman of the Month" plaques, pictures of the DeMarco children, and several "Appreciation" scrolls from the local YMCA. The computer printout for a pretty silver minivan is lying on the desk right by a pad of buyer's orders and the two Cokes Killer insisted on purchasing. Both people have driven the van—Killer insisted on that. After a few moments of small talk about the price of cars these days, Killer begins his quiet talk, a gentleman speaking to intelligent buyers.

"Now, I know you folks were paying $350 per month on your old car. But the new one lists for several thousand more. You understand, then, that it will cost you a little more per month?" Sure, they understand that. "Mrs. Smith [Killer knows by now that she's the real decision-maker], I think we can have you riding in that van tomorrow. If a payment of $625 sounds okay to you."

The couple's faces turn dove-white. She clears her throat. "Mr. DeMarco, there's just no way we can afford that . . . I don't think."

Killer knew that all along; he was just testing. They're not the bolting type, people who run out, or at least try to. They weren't *that* shocked, either. Killer continues talking, lowering the payment in small amounts, reminding them how much will be saved on maintenance, how much will be saved on gas. "Well, Mrs. Smith, I don't really believe the boss will let me get the payment below $495. If you remember how much more this car costs, it's really an excellent payment. If the house—my bosses—will agree, you will actually be saving $6240, the difference between a payment of $625 and a payment of $495." The two of them like that logic, and they look at each other silently.

"I'll tell you what," Killer adds happily, "I will even *make* the first payment for you. You won't have a payment for two and a half months. I really do want to see you folks satisfied."

And so the Smiths buy the car for $495 per month, and they're happy. The first payment is paid for them, too. Now, what's wrong with this deal? After all, Killer brought the payment down from $625 to $495, plus the Smiths received a free payment.

Everything is wrong. First, Killer knew all along he could sell them the car for $250 per month. And that wasn't a payment pulled out of the air, either. He knew how much $250 per month would buy. Second, Killer didn't lower the payments by cutting his deal. He simply quoted them the first payment based on financing for thirty-six months at the maximum interest rate, where the final payment was based on forty-eight months at the minimum rate. Killer's profit never changed. Third, the couple's car was appraised and had an actual wholesale value of $5000. But these people were not really interested in the value of their trade-in. "After all," the guy had said, "that 'trading' figure always keeps changing at different dealerships; that's why I stick with something that's simple, like my payment." So, is it Killer's fault the couple accepted $4400 for it, instead of $5000?

And finally, there's the "free" payment. In the car business this technique is usually called the "Christmas Club." Killer didn't reach into his pocket and make that payment; he simply added the amount of the payment to the total car price, then financed the $495 in their contract. Killer gave them a check for $495, sure. When he turned his deal into the finance office, he simply attached a note saying, "First payment financed; cut a check to the Smiths." But the Smiths would simply be paying that $495 back over the next forty-eight months, plus interest.

A nice sale like this calls for a celebration, so Killer makes a quick trip to the little food shop next door and downs a quick beer. Yes, sir, this is going to be a fine day.

By twelve-thirty, Killer is sitting up at the used-car department. Most of the regular used-car salesmen go to lunch then, and it's an easy time to catch another "up." The car pulls in before Killer's feet are up on the desk, and a couple jumps out quickly, hurrying around a small used Nissan. These folks are jumping beans, nervous customers convinced they'll be taken wherever they buy. Killer is a master with this type of customer.

"Hi, folks, I'm Bob DeMarco. Boy, I'm glad I saw you! The guys have been trying to sell that car to someone for a month. It's just not a car you would want to own." The people stop walking and look at him. Here is an honest man, just what they've been looking for.

They are a young couple with little credit but a savings account of $2000. The type of car they purchase isn't important, as long as it's a good car with a "drive-out price" of $2000—tax, title, and tag included. And Killer knows just the car to fit their budget: the Lincoln with the $200-dollar bonus.

"Yes, Tommy, it's a better car than the Nissan. It's also a safer car. Did you read the story in the paper about the wife and two kids who were killed in a little car like this?" Killer looks at the Nissan as if it's infected with a dangerous, highly contagious germ. He pulls a copy of the article from his pocket. This article has switched lots of people from small cars.

Killer prices the Lincoln at $2100, even though it's on the books at $1000. As usual, he raises the asking price to fit the sucker's cash. He lets them drive it by themselves; that's against the rules, but Killer isn't worried about things like that. He knows the couple will be impressed with this kind of trusting attitude. They drive the Lincoln back to the new-car showroom and wander inside, looking for him.

Killer's in his office, already filling out the buyer's order, and he barely looks up as they enter. "Folks, sometimes I want to quit this business. Would you believe the boss says I can't sell the car for a dime less than $2100? That guy never gives up; he wants to take advantage of everyone. I'm going to sell it for $2000 anyway. What you had better do, though, is give me a check for the whole amount. It'll give me more ammunition when I'm arguing with the s.o.b." Of course, Killer hasn't seen the manager. But that's not really important. How can these people be so lucky? Killer is actually on their side. They buy the car.

It won't last them a week before conking out on the freeway. Killer earns the $200 bonus, plus his regular commission. The buyers have no recourse when the car breaks down, either. Killer sold it to them "as is," with no warranty. "At this price, we can't give you a warranty," he had told them. "I'm going to be in trouble with the boss as it is."

Killer likes to take a break in the afternoon. Around five each day he checks out with the switchboard. "I've got to show a car across town, honey. I'll be back by seven." He winks at her. That Killer is such a sport.

The Dead End is a noisy bar, and after two Seven-and-Sevens have done their job, Killer barely hears the waitress. "Hey, Killer!" Cherry nudges his shoulder, drawing him from some other world. "They found you. Your boss is on the phone." Mr. DeMarco is not worried, however. When you are the high-gross man, and have been for years, people may yell and scream and threaten, but they do not fire you. It's one of the nicest realities about the car business: Whatever you've done in the past means nothing. It's what you do every day with the ups that makes you good.

A specialist is needed at the store; that's why J. C. called. One of the new boys has spent three hours with a guy who's on a customized sedan, one with extra opera windows and two moon roofs, not the most popular car on the lot. The guy is an "allowance buyer"—all he cares about is how much he's allowed for his trade. The new boy has already given the car away, cut the deal to $200 above invoice, and he still can't sell the car. It's T. O. time.

It takes Killer exactly sixty seconds to sell this man, and the new salesman is even more surprised by Killer's words than the customer.

"Now, how much more do we need to give you for your car?"

"Five hundred dollars and not a dime less!"

Paying that for the trade-in would give the man a deal on the new car that's three hundred dollars *under* what the car cost the dealer. But Killer doesn't blink. "Sir, you are a smart bargainer . . . but we'll do it, under one condition," he says in a slightly defeated tone.

The man sits up. "You will? And what's that condition?"

"That you don't tell a soul what you paid for this car."

The man breaks out in a grin and pokes his spouse in the side. "See, I *told* you!" he says victoriously.

Killer begins to fill out the paperwork as the new salesman watches wide-eyed. "Folks, now, you're going to want that life insurance and accident and health insurance on both of you, aren't you?" Killer chuckles. "I don't even have to ask that, do I? You already know how important that is."

The man nods yes, but a little less assuredly.

"And I suppose you're even going to want the special protection

package—our kryptonic rustproofing and undercoating—at the sale price, too? As a service, we're offering that at $995 this month. And"
—Killer looks at the calendar on the wall—"we've still got the 'Invincible' service agreement on sale until Friday, too. That's normally $1895, including the 24-hour toll-free number." Killer goes ahead and writes $895 on the buyer's order for that, too. The man says nothing. "And what about an alarm system? Did you know your insurance rates will go down a lot with one?" The alarm system is on sale for $695: Boy, is this man lucky! Killer writes the figure on the buyer's order and turns the pad around to the couple.

"Don't you make a lot of money on these . . . these things?" the man says, pointing to the "add-ons" Killer had so convincingly presented.

"Not a dime. Mr. Stevens, they're just here to help you."

The man pauses a minute and then signs the buyer's order. He does not argue when Killer says, "Now, if you can afford it, I need a deposit for $3000." Of course he can afford it. This guy is no idiot.

Sure. The dealership really did lose $300 on the sale of the new car itself. But on the life and accident and health insurance they made $1100; on the rustproofing and undercoating $850. The service agreement gave them a profit of $700 and the alarm system a profit of $500. A total gross profit of *$3150*. Who cares if the dealership lost $300 on the car itself? The net profit was still $2850.

"You see, kid," Killer says as he walks from the sales booth, "it doesn't matter which pocket you take their money from. It just matters that we get in their pocket."

It is a satisfying way to end the evening. Killer walks to the conference room, takes a bright orange piece of chalk, and writes "Killer's O.K. with me—signed Robert DeMarco" across the width of the Perk Board. "Over the hill, hell!" he mutters. Killer walks from the room and heads to his demo. "Just wait until tomorrow."

WHAT'S WRONG WITH THE AUTOMOBILE BUSINESS?

If you find the previous tales of consumers led astray a little hard to believe, you are right. I've deliberately made them gentler than the real thing, and quite frankly I wonder if you would believe many of the true-life situations I encounter daily as I investigate this rather unfortunate business. I say *unfortunate,* because probably no legitimate business in our country takes advantage of the unwary consumer—most particularly the poorer consumer—as does the automobile business.

And each year it gets worse, as you will see. The automobile business has become the master of predatory selling—relentlessly stalking its victims, ruthlessly seeking the weakest prey, and without hesitation or any sense of conscience, devastating them. This business in the process has become so lucrative, the competition so unrelenting, the incentives to mislead so enticing that many of us in the consumer movement are helping to initiate class action lawsuits and regional conferences to deal with dealer excesses.

The abuse centers on six very closely related factors.

1. Chain and Multiple-Car-Line Dealerships. These are the worst new developments in the business, and they are happening in your community right now. Welcome to Friendly Buick-Honda-Jeep-Isuzu, Inc. One of ten (or fifty) dealerships owned by, uh, what's-his-name? The guy who flies in on his jet to load up your money and fly down south with it for a quick cruise on the yacht. The "megadealers"—and they number several hundred—completely control the car business now, enjoy their own closed-circuit television network to share selling techniques quickly, and make millions of dollars each off good, hardworking people. If you don't think the profits are that big, pick up a yachting magazine some time and pick out the professions of many of the top 200 yacht owners.

Or, easier yet, take a look at the stock exchange. Did you know that some national dealer chains are becoming so big they are on the

Board? And do you think those monster chains really care about what happens to an individual customer?

But isn't that what free enterprise is all about? No, it's not. Free enterprise, when it's working right, says both sides have enough information to negotiate sensibly. The megadealer system doesn't agree with that, however. It is designed solely to limit and control the flow of information, to the great detriment of the consumer. Megadealers have taken away any sense of community focus and responsibility and have centralized the selling process in a business office very far from and little concerned with the needs of the individual customer.

Does the salesperson sense that the customer can't afford a certain model? When dealerships were locally owned, the salesperson's conscience could send you on your way. But not now. The megadealer selling system has removed the selling decision from the salesperson. Do you like Hondas as well as Jeeps and plan to play the sellers against each other (real free enterprise at work)? You can't do that when the Honda and Jeep dealer (and the salesperson) is the same person.

Do you live in a smaller town isolated from the big city? Did you know that in many towns like yours, *all* the dealerships are owned by one company or person?

The megadealer system has brought about the dark ages for you, the consumer. The great power of these chains constantly blocks state and federal legislation that would help you, buys politicians with legal donations and free demonstrators, and swallows the few remaining independent dealerships as surely as a hungry dog gulps down the last remaining tidbit of food.

2. The Megadealer Selling Philosophy. You're going to hear about this in detail later, but right now learn the sole objectives of these selling systems. I am sorry to say that virtually every dealership in the country adheres to these objectives, generally in this order, too: *excite the customer, confuse the customer, mislead the customer, pressure the customer, and then take every last dime you can get.* Regardless of the consequence to the customer.

All dealership sales-training programs are based on these tactics, and I have seen dozens of programs. In one way or another, the points are repeated over and over again in training manuals, videos, on the dealer network, and in person by sales managers.

The great irony here, of course, is that dealerships like to tell you they're here to "help" you; like to tell you they just love to cut those profits; get absolutely teary-eyed over their love for you. But while those fine words drip off smooth tongues, they are working to the rhythm of their powerful and private mantra: "excite, confuse, mislead, pressure . . ."

3. Rebates and "Cheap" Financing Rates and Schemes. Zero percent! 2.9 percent! $3000 rebates! While you would think dealerships and their financing sources would be going broke offering these promotions, just the opposite is happening. Their profit per car *and* their financing profits have shot up. Why? The promotions aren't really available for the vast majority of customers who rush in for them. They simply serve as a legal bait and switch: get you to the dealership and then switch you to more profitable financing plans. As we'll see, you'll usually do better to forget special dealership financing and finance your vehicle at a bank or credit union. Which brings us to the fourth megadealer reality.

4. Megadealers Refuse to Let You Compare Their Offer Realistically with Others. I list this point here because it has become the foundation of the dealership selling system. While the dealers like to tell you how helpful they are, they refuse to give you meaningful information to make your comparison shopping easier. Want to take a copy of their figures home with you to think about it? Impossible. Want to copy down the price information from the window sticker? Many dealerships are trying to stop you from even doing that. Want to know what your trade is really worth? Don't think a dealer will tell you.

5. The "After the Sale" Salesperson. This alone is probably the most lucrative refinement in the dealership universe, and boy, will you become familiar with it, even if you are a cash buyer.

After you agree to buy a particular vehicle, after you've agreed to payments, after the transaction should really be completed, dealerships will then *require* you to see their "business manager" or "financial counselor," supposedly to fill out "all that other paperwork, you know." Just someone to help you, right? Unfortunately, no. Whatever you say, you will be required to talk to this very high-pressure salesperson whose only job is to dramatically raise the dealership profit *again*. After you've already agreed to buy the car!

Here you'll be switched to their financing, even if you have the cash on you. Here, like Killer's customer, you'll be talked into their "protection" packages and warranties and alarm systems—all priced dramatically above their real value, as we'll see.

As surely as a salesperson will smile, you will have to waste time with one of these supersalespersons.

6. The Aggressive Leasing Programs by Both the Manufacturers and the Dealers. Leasing, as we'll see later, can be a very smart move for many of you—if it's done right. But unfortunately leasing is seldom done right. For the uninformed, it has become the greatest consumer ripoff of the decade. Just ask your state attorney general.

How Do the Dealers Respond to These Charges?

They first say "Only the other guys do things like that," and then they say "We couldn't stay in business if we did things like that," and then they say "Oh, we're a *profession* now, we don't let our salespeople do things like that," and then they say "What does Remar Sutton know anyway?"

Well, as we've seen, dealerships *are* more professional—in taking your hard-earned money. And not only do they stay in business using these tactics, they thrive, because most customers don't have the slightest idea what has been done to them. Particularly if they are not used to such widespread deception. Are you?

So why don't we ask the dealers to address these specific realities:

1. You, Mr. Dealer, don't *want* to give the lowest-priced deal. You want to make the maximum profit any customer will stand for. What does that make your advertising? Very misleading and probably dishonest.

2. You use selling systems developed either by your dealership or by professional selling services; and your system, like all systems, is designed to control the buyer, play to the buyer's psychological weaknesses, and encourage the buyer to pay more for virtually every product or service you sell than he or she needs to.

3. Your objective isn't to "help" the consumer; it is to make the maximum short-term profit, regardless of the effect on the consumer.

Well, if all these things are true, what chance does a consumer have out there? An excellent one, if you will read on. This book is designed to help you understand every trick in the business. It takes you on the other side—the salesperson's and manager's and dealer's side. It listens in as the road hogs, dip-shop managers, F and I men, skaters, and whores do their magnificent magical acts. Every single portion of the buying and selling and leasing transactions is detailed and explained.

The bad news about the car business is bad indeed: If you don't know what you're doing, even the best dealership will take your last penny.

But the good news is great! *Know what you're doing*, and even the worst dealership will sell you any vehicle for a virtual penny's profit rather than lose a sale.

It's up to you. So, read on and smile. You're in control this time.

WRITE ME

You can help prepare the next edition of this book. After you've shopped, write me about your experiences.

> Remar Sutton
> *Don't Get Taken Every Time*
> P.O. Box 77033
> Atlanta, GA 30357

PART I

Forearming

1

What You're Up Against: The World of Sellers and Selling

KILLER AND HIS "FAMILY"

"I mean to tell you, she was one classy dame, a real lady. And her figure? Oh, God! She had more curves and ripples than a roller coaster!" Killer was talking with his hands more than his mouth, entertaining the guys in their favorite "break room," the clean-up shop located behind the service department. On cold and wet days like this one, everyone seemed to head back there. It was a good place to hide from the boss, J. C. It was also a good place to hide the community bottle. Buzz and Ted, the new guy, were there. Forrest DeLong was there, too. Even Kip had joined the sipping party this day. He was a retired colonel, a quiet type of guy who never really seemed to fit in comfortably with the off-color conversations and endless streams of four-letter words that constitute most in-house discussions at automobile stores.

Ted took the bottle next and sweetened his coffee. He was maybe twenty-two, had moved to town several weeks earlier, and had sold no more than two cars during his first weeks at the store. Ted wiped his lips with his right thumb and began to talk. Maybe it was the juice. Half-and-Half at eleven-thirty would untie any tongue.

"Well, boys, let me tell you something. I don't know whether this business is going to bore me to death or starve me to death. I mean, where are all those big commissions J. C. told me about when he hired me? Hell, I'd do better working for the Boy Scouts or something."

"Ted, from what they tell me at the Dead End, you'd be a better Girl Scout," Killer volunteered. "I understand you chase just about every tail that flies by."

"Hell, yes, I do! After standing around here all day talking with

17

jerks, I've got to have some recreation. How do you guys put up with all the crap around here? If the flakes don't drive you crazy, then it's J. C. or Don. I don't think they know any other words than 'get on the phone, boys,' or 'let me see some deals, boys,' or 'let's get some ups in here, boys'—why don't they just record all that bull, play it over the P. A., and go play golf with Davies?"

"Sure," Kip added. "I don't think Davies even likes to talk with *those* guys. Owners don't want to get their pinkies dirty."

Killer raised his hand. "Now, wait a minute. I don't want to hear any of you damn guys talking about my dealer. I want you to know he talks to *me*. Of course, that was last Christmas. And he called me Bill. Then he got confused and called me Will." Killer started laughing. "Maybe I'll give him one of my cards the next time we meet. As a matter of fact, I think I'll ask him to *pay* for my cards the next time I see him."

Killer had hit a nerve. Forrest spoke first. "Hey, Killer, I was going to ask you that. I don't mind paying for my cards, but, hell, I hear we're going to be paying more again for our demos. Don even told me that we're going to have to sell them before we get another one, too. And drive junkers from the used-car lot until they're sold."

Killer was high man on the pole at Davies Motors, and he liked that. Everyone came to him for the real scoop on what was happening at the store. "Yeah," he said, "Davies says we've got too many demos in service, and he's also yelling about the money. Within the month, I'll bet we'll all be paying at least two hundred bucks for our cars. But that isn't the worst of it. They're raising the pack on all the new cars again, and they're cutting our percentage on financing to three percent."

Killer's words seemed to light a very short fuse in each of the guys, and Forrest was the hottest. "Like hell he is! I'll be damned if I'm going to hang around this place and put up with that. Hell, there are a lot of other stores in this town." His outburst brought a laugh. Gary Oliver Davies owned many of the town's dealerships. Forrest's hot head was probably one of the reasons he was a vagabond in the business, spending one or two months at one dealership and then lighting across town to some other. But he wouldn't be missed. There would probably be a hundred DeLongs at Davies Motors in the next twenty-four months. The Forrest DeLongs of the world may make up the vast majority of automobile salesmen, and they may sell lots of cars in the aggregate, but they are always the low men on the scale of respect.

At the opposite end of the scale was Kip, the Colonel. Kip had been at the store for five years, running the fleet operation, and was never a part of the pack. He rarely took a drink with the guys, either. But, at this particular moment, he served a really important function at this meeting of the Half-and-Half Club. He heard the door open as they were talking, quickly silenced the group with a "shhh," then walked quietly around the corner. He returned double-speed, looking like some kid caught in the closet with his sister. "It's J. C.!" he whispered. Everyone quickly lit up cigarettes, hoping perhaps the smoke would cover up the smell of Jim Beam, or maybe even throw a wall to make them invisible. J. C. sauntered around the corner and ambled toward them, as if he were simply taking a Sunday stroll. No one spoke as they stood there, waiting for the explosion.

J. C. just looked at them, his lips moving apart enough to make a smacking sound—like some wild animal's anticipation of the bite to come. "Well, boys." J. C. looked from man to man, no expression betraying his thoughts. He looked at Killer last. "I sure could use some Half-and-Half—my coffee's cold."

It was an unexpected comment. But that's why most of the guys liked him. J. C. was a real bastard at times, but just as the guys were ready to write him off, he would say or do something like that. No one could really figure J. C. out. No one cared to at the moment, though. They all sat on the floor, their feet pulled up, bodies in a semicircle.

Buzz broke the ice. "Well, J. C., if you'd send someone for marshmallows, we could have a campfire." His comment broke them up.

"Hell, yes," J. C. said. "I tell you what, we could get a van and go to my cabin. We'd probably sell as many cars there as here today." J. C.'s statement didn't really seem like a cut—it sounded more like the truth. Business had been lousy, real lousy, for the past two weeks, and no one had gotten more heat than J. C. "Boys, I'll tell you what. I think all the ups have just packed up and left town. I talked with some of the other stores a while ago, and none of them are doing any business."

It's the damnedest thing about the car business. Customers either come in in droves, filings to the magnet, or they don't come in at all. After a few years, people in the business accept that fact. Or, at least, the employees do. The dealers of the world never accept it, and that's where the heat always comes from first.

The coffee thermos was sitting on empty and the Jim Beam down to a third when the real war stories began. The new kid, Ted, started them rolling. "J. C., I don't mean this to sound bad or anything, but doesn't anything exciting ever happen in this business? I thought selling clothes was bad, but, unless you sell someone, the days get awful long."

"Hey, J. C., Ted doesn't know about the Smith thing. And from what I hear, he'd *better* know about it." Mention of the "thing" didn't bring a smile to anyone's face. It had made headlines around the country, really big headlines in the scandal rags, and no one felt it was typical of the business. But God, had it thrown a wrench in the operation of All-City Motors, a well-respected and successful dealership in a neighboring state.

J. C. didn't look at any of them as he began to talk but quietly laid out the story, as if he were reading some bedtime story to a group of kids. "It was bad, real bad." He stopped just long enough to take one final sip. "A new salesman, the guy had been at All-City maybe three months, was sitting in the lounge when he got a page to the showroom. His name was Ed Vista. There was a man waiting there to see him—from what everyone said, he was a real nice person, too, real friendly. Well, anyway, Ed thought the guy wanted to buy a car, and he took him into a big closing office just off the showroom, one with glass partitions. Shirley Kubek in the office was standing outside and just happened to be looking at Ed's face when he turned snow-white and started to stand up. The guy sitting across from him stood up first, and Shirley said, just as Ed raised his hand, the guy raised a gun and shot him in the head." J. C. looked around the room and continued. "Then the guy just sat down. All hell broke loose; the place went crazy. Joe Weeks, the owner, heard it and came down there, but the guy was still holding the gun, so he cleared out the showroom and waited on the police. The guy was so damned calm, he introduced himself to the cops and even tried to shake hands with them."

J. C. had a manner, a certain way of sounding and gesturing in some enormously kind fashion whenever he talked about bad things, and as he continued, his face and arms seemed to evoke the senselessness of this incident better than the words. "The guy finally told the police Ed was having an affair with his wife. No one knows if that's true or not; she won't say. But, hell, the salesman may have been a little crazy, but he had a wife, too. He also had a son not much younger than my youngest." He shook his head. "I mean to tell you, this is a crazy world." J. C. sat there, scratching the back of his neck, twisting his head as if to loosen the very tight screws that seemed to push into every nerve.

"J. C.?" Ted broke the quiet. "I was telling the guys what a hard time I'm having making any money. At the rate I'm going I'll be dead and gone to hell before I see one of those W-2s you told me about— you know, the $40,000 years?"

J. C. grinned and reached over to Ted, grabbing him around the neck in a bear hug. "Son, be patient. Why, you're sitting in the room with one of those guys right now. Killer, tell him what you made last year."

Killer blushed just enough to look modest and stretched his arms out. "Hell, J. C., I've had better years than the last one. But I made $100,000, which isn't bad, I guess." You can bet your B. P. on that statement. Killer was in the top tenth of one percent in the country last year. He continued to talk. "But, hell, it took me fifteen years and a lot of work to get to that. And I spend nearly $10,000 a year on things for my regular customers, too. Plus, I really do work, you know." He smiled, and started to speak again before any of the guys could stop him. "And yes, I do sell *lots* of cars at the Dead End. Who ever said drinkers don't buy cars, anyway?"

Smart move. Killer's visits to the favorite automobile watering hole were one of the worst-kept secrets in the business. But Killer really didn't want the conversation changed to that subject. He had just started a tale about how the business *really* used to be when Don Burns, one of the new-car managers, came walking around the corner.

Don showed no surprise but started talking quickly. "Excuse me, fellows, but there are some ups on the lot and, J. C., Davies is on the phone. I told him you were in the closing booth with some customers." It was a good breaking point in the camp meeting, and the group stood up and, almost in unison, reached in their pockets for the nice little bottles of Binaca Mouth Freshener. J. C. started laughing as he pushed down the little nozzle and closed the meeting between sprays. "Well, boys, if you'll excuse me, I've got to call my broker. It looks like Binaca stock is going up again."

It had been a nice morning, and the guys headed back to the showroom single-file. "Hey, Buzz." Don Burns walked up behind him, pulling him back a little as the others went on. "Buzz, I hate to tell you this, but there's another process server in the showroom. I told the man you were out, but he says he's going to wait for you. Since J. C.'s in a good mood, do you want me to ask him to talk to the man? If he can't put him off, maybe he'll pay him."

Buzz looked just a tad upset—nothing really monumental in a process server, he thought. Car people were pretty used to those people. As a group, car salesmen aren't exactly known for their good credit ratings. "No, but thanks," he said. "Hell, I might just as well add his to the pile. Thank God, J. C. doesn't care, though. I'll go see him now. At least it's in the family."

Buzz was right, too. It's one big family.

INSIDE THE FAMILY: DEALERS, SALES MANAGERS, AND SALESMEN

Like any business, the automobile business is its own little world, populated by folks who live and work in a rigid pecking order: first, the salesmen, who come and go just as quickly as a week of twelve-hour days; then the sales managers, guys who crack the emotional whip to keep the sellers working; and then general managers, who feed and tend to the crops of money that flow quickly in and out of parts departments, body shops, finance and insurance offices, and new, used, and wholesale car and truck sales. At the top of the whole pecking order is the dealer, usually a self-made man who grew up in the days when the automobile business made the Mafia pale in the depths of its dishonesty. If you're over sixty, you probably have your own memories of keys thrown on the roof at your friendly neighborhood car store—a nice technique to keep you there—or of new cars with no price stickers, or ads with prominently displayed "caveat emptor" notations, or a used-car lot filled with cars showing suspiciously low mileage.

During the late fifties and early sixties, many of those practices supposedly began to change. Federal law made it a crime to turn back speedometers, and mileage statements provided some measure of accountability for each car's mileage. The manufacturers finally succumbed to pressure and began placing "suggested retail price" stickers on most cars. In the seventies, consumer complaints about auto sales techniques in general began to mount. By the eighties, thousands of lawsuits began to challenge auto fraud. As important, buyers simply began to revolt against the more obvious sales techniques. By 1990, the sales techniques were much less obvious, but still there—simply hidden in very sophisticated selling systems. While dealerships and manufacturers crowed very loudly over their new-found "professional" selling status, the number of lawsuits against them mounted.

During all these years, however, as the car business has developed more sophisticated methods for taking you, one thing has remained constant, and that is the absolute ignorance of the average car buyer. The customer's knowledge of how dealerships function, of financing, of dollar value has remained back in the Dark Ages. Sure, car people want your mind back there and certainly aren't concerned with your proper education, but that's not the problem. The average customer either thinks the whole car-buying process is too difficult to master or else feels that perhaps too much knowledge will take the romance from what has always been regarded as a mystical process. Unfortunately, the only really mystical event is how quickly your money disappears. The automobile business is a magnificent money machine; it eats every cent you have, puts you in debt just long enough to require another chariot, and then eats again. And if you are going to have some chance of muzzling the beast, you will need to understand the opposition.

Who are you dealing with? On the salesman level, you are basically dealing with three types of people. Most stores have a few old-timers, the guys who were selling cars back in the days when list price was any figure the salesman wanted to create. These guys have dealt with every type of customer: the easy ones, the suspicious ones, and the crooked ones. They are professionals in the sense that years of selling have provided them a steady flow of repeat customers who have always dealt with them and always will.

Hanging around in the corners of every showroom and lot are the young eager beavers, the "floor whores," who pounce on the first person that walks in cold, just hoping the poor sucker really wants to buy and has the credit to do so. The next floor whore who waits on you could be a college kid passing his time waiting on a good job or an ex-con. One of the nicest things about the car business is its ability to forgive the past. If you want to be a salesman, your past doesn't matter; as a matter of fact, it really doesn't matter if you drink too much, or are hiding from the police, or have a couple of wives. All that matters is how efficiently you can sell cars. Most of the floor whores have shallow roots, popping up at different stores every few months. To them the particular business is unimportant.

Many dealerships also have their share of former colonels and captains and noncoms, folks who have retired from the service and enjoy the freedom of being in business for themselves. Although the business was once the most male-oriented in America, dealerships are now employing more women. Grandmotherly types are popular.

Regardless of the type of salesman who is waiting on you, he's probably not getting rich selling you or anyone else a car. Most dealerships pay their salesmen twenty to thirty percent of the "front-end gross," the actual profit on the sale of the new car. Or, rather, they pay them twenty or thirty percent of the profit above the "pack." Let's say the actual cost to the dealer of your average Expenso Gargantula is $12,000. But when the dealership's title clerk prepares a computerized stock card on that particular car, the invoice price is coded as $12,500. This "pack" is supposed to help the dealer pay his overhead. In reality it's just another way to keep from paying the salesman his due. Incidentally, many dealerships encourage their salesmen to show this pack figure to recalcitrant customers. "Here, Mr. Jones, that's the actual cost of the car. If you will pay me a $400 profit over that figure, the car is yours." Presto, the house has just made $900. Most dealerships also pay their salesmen a small percentage of the profits from the sale of financing and life and accident and health insurance. Some pay a little on warranties, too. And virtually all pay "spiffs" (or cash bonuses) for every customer switched to leasing from buying.

The average car salesman sells six or seven cars a month. He averages $125 per car in commissions, if he's lucky. But on those six or seven cars, the house—the dealer—has grossed $5000 to $7000. But whoever said life was fair?

Another factor that tends to shorten the careers of salesmen is the tremendous pressure to succeed each hour of each day, a success measured on only one scale—selling. Because the average car salesman, especially the new-car salesman, is invariably on the downside of the income scale, this pressure to sell is not something solely manufactured by dealerships, either. If anyone other than the customer is "worked," milked of more than his fair share of money in the car business, it would be that fellow waiting on you. As a matter of fact, if anyone is more ignorant than the customer of the many ways people are taken in the car business, it's the salesman.

The house, the dealer, does its best to keep the boys working the front line from knowing about things like factory incentives: "write-downs"—used cars that have been lowered in value because of their condition or time on the lot; and "holdbacks"—extra profit built into each car invoice but not considered "cost" by the dealer. Dealers seem to think of their salesmen as cheap things to replace. They may smile at them, give them a bonus for Christmas, and occasionally visit a sales meeting, but most dealers hold the men who make them money in disdainful contempt.

Take Gary Oliver Davies, Killer's big boss. Sure, he started in the business as a lot boy, someone who serves as the dealership "gofer." Sure, he sold cars for a few years. But Mr. Davies doesn't think he has anything in common with the boys who work for him, managers included. "Hell, I'm smarter than those bastards—that's why I'm the boss," Davies likes to tell folks. If a psychiatrist were really to look into the head of Davies—probably many dealers—I would suspect that he would find lots of contempt piled up there. Contempt for the salesmen and other employees, contempt for the customers, and contempt for the whole messy world of cars. Maybe the money makes them that way.

Gary Oliver Davies was reviewing his monthly Dealer's Financial Statement, the total summary of his store's performance that must be sent to the factory each month. It's a complicated form, encompassing hundreds of figures and percentages on everything, from "selling gross, new and used"—the amount of the monthly gross from new and used departments left after paying variable expenses such as advertising, used cars, repairs, and commissions—to "service sales per service order." Davies was feeling pretty good. Though the year had not been a record one, his store was showing in this ninth month a net profit just in excess of $1,000,000. The statement showed average new-car sales of one hundred fifty units per month, year-to-date, and average used-car sales of three hundred units. His year-to-date profit also showed a tidy contribution from the parts department. Parts was paying the majority of the fixed overhead on his whole store. His average new-car gross per unit was $1600.

Davies paused at that figure. "Hell—$1600—*that's* the real problem," he reflected. "You just can't make real money in years like this." Davies was thinking about the last really good year—the year his store had a net profit before write-downs of $2,000,000. Now *that* was nice. It was a time when the general population seemed to have a severe case of car fever. Once some customers came in and looked at a $24,000 car with a $4,000 profit margin. In slow times Davies would have happily had his managers accept a $800 profit on that car. But in good times? Killer had been waiting on the couple. When the man had asked, "Well, what is the least you will take for that car?" Killer had looked the guy in the eye and said, "$24,000." The guy had started to object, but his wife yelled, "Shut up, Henry, I want that car." Davies just loved that memory.

Davies's eyes continued down the statement. The leasing department's gross was way up to over $4400 per car from an old average of $2800. He smiled. Leasing had become the dealership's big money-maker in the past few years, and just by switching leasing companies Davies had raised the profit per lease again. The new company would let him add an additional $2000 in profit onto every lease deal. Very nice. "Thank you, suckers," he said quietly under his breath. Just about every one of those fat lease profits was made on people who would have paid hardly any profit if they'd bought the same cars rather than leased them. It wasn't Davies's fault customers didn't know how to negotiate leases.

Then Davies looked at the used-car numbers. Grosses were really high—they always were when new cars weren't hot—but he saw a figure that drew his hand to the phone, something really bad. He paged Timothy Raxalt, the used-car manager.

Raxalt was in his office quickly. As a matter of fact, whenever the employees heard Davies paging, they always dropped whatever they were doing. He didn't page people often, and when he did, the reason was invariably unpleasant. There were no pleasantries during this meeting, either. Davies was talking before Raxalt had a chance to sit. "How many times do I have to tell you about ninety-day cars? I want you to look at every one of the used cars over ninety days and write them down again. Then, get some wholesalers in here, match up some of the lead with a few good cars, and get that junk out of here. I don't want any ninety-day cars on this lot next week." Davies was hot as he talked; his statement showed over $100,000 tied up in cars that were over ninety days old. That money wasn't working for him. Idle money is dead money in the car business, and there would be no dead money at this dealership.

Raxalt didn't argue. It didn't matter that virtually every one of these cars was still on the lot because of Davies, that Davies had insisted on their high appraisals. It didn't matter that most of the cars were trade-ins of Davies's pals—sailing buddies and bankers and a couple of local pro football players. "Look," Davies continued, "I pay you to do your job. And *this*"—he pointed to the statement—"isn't doing your job."

Raxalt left without saying a word. He wasn't particularly upset, either. I mean, it's what you expect from the boss. He's smarter. Or at least that's what he says.

Gary Davies *is* a smart man, and there are many dealers out there like him who make money regardless of the temperament of the car-buying public. When new-car sales are down, they push leasing, service, parts, and used cars. When new-car sales are hot, they push their men to raise the gross. These dealers will survive handsomely. They will weather any bad year the car business can bring. As a matter of fact, the bad years brought on by the great gas scare of the midseventies were really the birthday of the megadealer system. Poorly run dealerships (i.e., those that gave the customer a chance) were gobbled up by those with strong management (i.e., those that don't give the customer a chance).

And that's the key: though Davies doesn't like to admit it, his best talent is hiring the best managers. Like J. C. Hollins. J. C. is really an odd type to be in the car business, especially as a general manager. He is college-educated, from a family of professionals, and much more sophisticated in his personal tastes than most managers. He is also a good man, the type of person who thinks nothing of lending his men money, even a guy he's fired for one thing or the other. J. C. is comfortable with people outside the car fraternity, mixing well with just about anyone. He belongs to Rotary, coaches his youngest son's Little League team, and goes to church, too. But in the car business, J. C. is known for one talent: he is a trouble-shooter. That's why Davies hired him away from another dealership eight years ago, in the midst of a recession.

J. C. was used to people like Davies calling him in the slow times. He'd also heard the same sob story over and over again: a small dealer who grew rich, started to play, and forgot to tend his store. Hell, J. C. had known the problems before he'd asked the questions, but he had asked them anyway.

"Well, Gary, you say there's water on your used-car lot. Just how much?"

"Hell, I don't know—I just know that we can't wholesale a damn one of our cars." Davies had approximately $500,000 worth of used cars at his store—the actual dollar amount his people figured the cars were worth when they traded for them. If those cars can be wholesaled for only $460,000, he's got $40,000 in water. Water is an obsession with dealers—it's lost money just as surely as if someone took the same amount of money from their pockets. The problem develops when appraisers put more than wholesale in a trade—or when someone's hand is in the till.

"Well, what about your R.O.s? If you're losing a lot of money in the body shop, have you checked the R.O.s?"

No, Davies didn't have the time to have someone pull through old repair orders. "No one would be stealing in the body shop, anyway. The manager back there is an old friend of mine."

J. C. would want to know more about that later, but right then he wanted to know a little bit more about the used-car operation. "Gary, I know you say you've got water, but are your people wholesaling cars anyway? Are they even breaking out of any of them?"

"Hell, no! Every used car we wholesale is at a loss. I think we sold three cars last month at what we had in them. The rest were all losses."

The phone conversation had lasted no more than twenty minutes, but J. C. smelled at least two rats. He was also very interested in the dealership's deposit procedure when new cars were sold. "Tell me, what type of receipts do you give your customers after the business office is closed?" Davies wasn't sure but believed that the night manager simply wrote them out a receipt. "Gary, there's just one thing more. How did you hire your present general manager, did you know him, or what?"

"Listen, the guy is not a crook. He just doesn't seem to know what's going on around here," Davies retorted.

J. C. thanked the man for the call, and added, "Oh, Gary, I want to tell you one thing. I don't think your general manager is the only one who doesn't know what's going on. And if you hire me, you can be damn well sure I'm going to fire whoever needs firing—including your buddy in the body shop. Now, do you want to do business on that basis?''

His last comments are probably the reason that J. C. and Davies aren't friends but, rather, business associates. Davies really didn't have a choice in that conversation, however, for the waters at his store covered more than the used-car lot. Mr. Davies had made two classic mistakes as he climbed quickly up the dealer's ladder: he had hired friends and at the same time stepped away from the daily operations of his business.

When J. C. took over the Davies store, it took him less than a week to find three sets of sticky fingers. His first morning there, he'd invited the used-car manager out for a cup of coffee. The guy was too nervous in the beginning, and J. C. noticed that the nervousness increased considerably when he casually mentioned, "You know, I noticed that you wholesale a lot of cars to the same people regularly. I sure would like to meet those people." The guy's nervousness turned quickly to physical shaking. J. C. just smiled at him. "And I also noticed that you sell a lot of trades to some of the salesmen every now and then. I didn't know Mr. Davies allowed any curbing here." Curbing refers to the practice of salesmen buying nice trade-ins from their own stores and then selling them privately. It's a nice way to make a few bucks.

The guy just sat there, his hand over the coffee cup and eyes any-place but on J. C., who continued. "You know, I once had a guy working for me that you might be interested in. This S.O.B. would have a nice used car come on the lot, maybe a car that was worth $3000. Nine times out of ten it would be a real pretty car, too, one that makes a nice resale piece. But, no, this guy would call up some wholesaler —as a matter of fact, he would usually call up the *same* wholesaler— and he'd sell it to the man for $3000. But—damn, this was a funny thing—he would always tell the man to give him a check for $2700 and the rest in cash. I never could figure out where that $300 went to, either." J. C. paused just long enough for the words to press down on the guy a little more. "And, do you know what else he'd do?—I guess he did this just because he was generous or something—well, that same wholesaler would come by the used-car lot with some sled worth $1000. The hog would want to sell it to us for about a thousand, too, but my friend would pay him $1400 for it. Hell, we'd be stuck with the tub *and* $400 in water. Well, anyway, one day I talked to the whole-saler myself, and do you know what? The bastard said *he* only got $1200 of that money—he'd given the rest to my friend."

J. C. didn't say anything after finishing that little story. Instead he just sat there drinking his coffee. In a couple of minutes, the man sitting across from him simply said, "Well, what do you want me to do now? I've already spent the money." He had, too. All $125,000.

The body-shop skim was just as easy to find. When a body-shop foreman needs parts to repair a car, he simply fills out a parts ticket and sends that ticket over to the parts department. Each part is "charged out" to the ticket. The part is also listed on the repair order attached to the windshield of whatever car is being repaired. In theory, the parts listed on the R.O. should always be on a parts ticket also. But Mr. Davies's old friend the body-shop foreman had a much better idea: he would contract for private repair work at his house, check the parts out from the dealership, list them on a legitimate repair order in the shop, and then have free parts for his home repair work. J. C. caught that quickly, just by comparing the new parts on a few repaired cars with the parts listed on the car's R.O. He readily found a car with an old windshield that should have had a new one.

Another nice way some folks try to make money on the sly is simply to tear up repair orders. J. C. had that problem at another store he'd managed. It was a real sweet operation. The service cashier would wait for some customer to pay cash for repair work, then put the cash in her pocket rather than the register and quickly destroy the repair order.

All of these little tricks are not too hard to catch in a tight store operation. But that had been the problem with Mr. Davies's store—nothing had been tight. J. C. was one of the best specialists in the business because he never trusted a soul and always watched the little things. "I'll tell you what," he was fond of saying, "if you watch the little things, the big things will take care of themselves."

Management in the car business is a "closed thing"—you won't find, for instance, the sales manager from an insurance company hired to be the sales manager of a car store, and for good reason. There are few businesses in the world as complicated as the car business. A good general manager or sales manager at a car store needs years of on-the-job training simply to understand what is happening at his store. And J. C. Hollins is a good example of a good general sales manager. He understands that a store is like a giant sieve: regardless of how much is poured into it, there are literally hundreds of little places where profits can be drained away. There's the salesman who promises a set of floor mats to close a deal and neglects to tell his manager. That's $30 off the top. Or the lot boy neglects to check the coolant in a nice trade-in, and a $4000 piece of merchandise quickly needs a $300 engine overhaul. These all add up.

And then there's the cash flow problem. Even in the most profitable dealerships, cash flow is a daily challenge and headache. Like the Wade deal. The Wades paid $17,300 for a hardtop that cost the dealership $16,000, a nice profit. But the Wades had a one-year-old trade-in that was worth $9000 in real cash. After subtracting that $9000 from the dealership's selling price of $17,300, the dealership received a check from the Wades for $8300. The dealership then had to pay off the "floor plan" on the new car, $16,000. On paper, the store made a $1300 profit, sure. But in cash-flow terms, they had to pay out the difference between $8300 and the $16,000 owed on the car's floor plan. Until the Wades' trade-in is sold, the dealership will have a net cash *loss* of $7700. There's an old axiom in the car business that selling lots of cars with trade-ins can break a dealership.

And finally, there's the personnel problem. After the experience of running a staff of car salesmen most sales managers and general managers can relate really well to the den mother of a Cub Scout pack or, more appropriately, to the house mother at the Lotsa Whoopee Fraternity house, just down the road from Worldly Wise U. Most car salesmen end up working in car stores by happenstance rather than career planning. Because they sell under tremendous pressure and get the smallest cut of the profits, it's no wonder these stepchildren have a short tenure. This stepchild attitude also accounts partially for the rambunctious nature of salesmen as a group. J. C., for instance, has received more than one call from the local gendarmes to bail out a salesman. He's always firing guys for not selling or for "skating," stealing another salesman's customer.

J. C. doesn't resent all these problems, either, because they are a given in his job. A general manager in most stores doesn't have the luxury of stepping back from his business as his boss does. He is on the front line each day, taking flack from the dealer, the customers, the guys in the service and parts departments, and the new- and used-car sales boys. He's dealing with the factory, trying to resist their rep's weekly cajoling to buy a few more of this or that slow-moving car, to order more tilt steering wheels, and to shape up things like the restrooms and the general condition of the used cars. He's worried about the "floor-planners," the guys who come by without notice to be sure each new car's "mortgage" is paid on the day the car is sold. Automobile lending institutions, the guys who loan dealers money to floor-plan their stock, don't like dealers who sell their collateral—the cars—but neglect to pay off their loans.

Each moment of his waking day, the general manager is also watching the sales board. Dealers don't want success every month or quarter; they demand success—selling—every hour. J. C. knows this and doesn't begin to smile inside himself until the customers' names start going up on that tote board each morning. If by noon the list isn't long, he begins to growl to the sales manager. If by two the list is still short, he'll call a special sales meeting. If by five the deals are still short, he'll call another meeting. "Now, God damn it, *no one* is leaving this place until I see some paper," he'll tell the guys.

It's the J. C.s who make a car store tick. You may not see them much, may never meet one, but they are there, pulling the strings, orchestrating the four-wheeled ballet of buyers and sellers. And that's where you, the buyer, enter the picture.

First the Good News: They Really Will Sell You a Car for Less

In combativeness and in pure, raw competition, the automobile business makes the forces of Attila the Hun look like a group of butterfly collectors running through the fields in their safari shorts, squealing, "It bit me, it bit me!" Salesmen froth at the mouth each time some customer says, "Well, there's a car just like your car just down the road," and sales managers age quickly each time they see a customer's pocket filled with cards from dealerships selling the very same merchandise. Everyone in the store knows that the fickle nature of the customer rivals any teenybopper's loyalty to her latest beau. Some customers have actually bought cars at below cost thanks to this rivalry between brothers.

Car dealerships survive this siege mentality by adhering closely to the "bird-in-hand" theory: a definite $200 profit, right now, today, is much better than some vague chance of selling the car to someone for a $500 profit tomorrow. The theory is gospel even in a strong "seller's" market. The dealers don't *like* it, though. They continually cry that the government has begun to legislate dealers right out of the business or that customers "come into dealerships expecting us to practically give away a new car, and we're not going to do that." These last sentiments, which belong to Joseph Ricci, president of a Grosse Pointe car store, are echoed by the vast majority of dealerships around the country, and the sentiment is a valid one. After years of believing that car stores are the closest thing to some shill game on Forty-second Street, the car-buying public has finally decided to fight back.

Unfortunately, the confrontation is not productive for either party. Dealerships lose sales every day simply because their customers are too paranoid and uninformed to accept legitimate buys-of-a-lifetime. And customers are taken every day because salesmen feel some desperate need to rip off easy marks for all they're worth, as some form of retribution against all the nonbelievers who won't believe the truth under any circumstances.

These realities may not be pleasant, but they do present the informed car buyer with the best opportunity to buy or lease a new car at the lowest possible price. That fact in itself is not the answer you need, however. Dealerships do not survive, much less prosper, by selling new cars. The new car is simply one of the first steps in a multi-step transaction of churning money, and you will be lost from the moment you set foot on any lot in America unless you understand each step.

But let's not complicate the most important fact: Virtually every dealership in America will sell you a car for less. They will give you maximum dollar for your trade, if you want to trade. All you have to do is ask. And know a few things in the process, like how to handle salesmen.

Take the Webbs. They could have purchased a car very cheaply—*if* they had managed their salesman correctly. The Webbs had been to three other stores, writing down carefully each discount and list price on the three cars that interested them. They really liked the one Forrest DeLong was showing them now, too.

"Forrest, if you'll sell me that car for $11,500, we'll buy it," Carl Webb spouted out. "We're tired of looking and I'm tired of dickering. I am going to buy a car today."

Forrest looked at the price code on his stock card and figured the guy's offer as a $100 deal. There was no trade to sweeten the deal. He didn't really like the couple; they were too sure of what they wanted and what they would pay. Why the hell should he sell a car and make twenty-five bucks, his share of the $100? "Carl, you may buy a car today, but you're not going to buy it for $11,500, at least not this car."

Forrest just sat there, a bundle of frustration and impatience. The Webbs didn't know enough to insist their offer be submitted, and they left the showroom, walking past J. C. as they headed to their car. Oh God, Forrest thought, *that* was a mistake. I should have T.O.'d them. He was right. J. C. was at his desk in a second.

"Why the hell are those people leaving without talking to someone else!" J. C.'s tone wasn't that of a question, and Forrest backed up two steps. J. C.'s words betrayed a hotness all the guys knew too well.

"The guy wouldn't pay anything over a hundred dollars, and I knew you wouldn't take that, J. C."

"How did you know that? You don't know *what* I'll take. Did you hear what I said about letting people walk?" DeLong shifted his weight to his right leg, but said nothing. "Son, you're not long for this world if you keep that up," J. C. said as he walked away. He was right, too.

DeLong won't last long in the car business—he's too independent, likes to work his own deals, decide for himself when the profit is right. You may have met his type before, the guy who never has a boss. Car stores don't want this kind of person working for them for a simple reason. If your salesman is bossing his own deal, then he is your adversary, the person you must conquer in the battle for money. However, in the eighties, almost all dealerships refined a nice psychological ploy to remove this adversary relationship from salesman and customer. The technique involved large doses of the words "they" and "we." "They" represents the house, the bosses, the greedy people who must approve a salesman's deal. If Forrest DeLong had been using this system in dealing with the Webbs, he would have said, "Mr. Webb, I don't think *they* will accept $11,500 for the car, but why don't *we* write it up at $11,500, and then I'll go in there and fight for *us*. Remember, I don't make any money if you don't buy a car."

The Webbs now have a friend, someone on their side against the house. It's a nice system, and while no dealership likes to sell cars for a $100 profit, they will probably do that *if* the customer can't be raised. There is one small catch to this system, though: Would you know a small profit if it bit you? Perhaps you could just ask your salesman, "Am I really getting the best price?" while at the same time gazing with trust into his eyes. That would probably be as safe as entrusting your goldfish to the cat.

Well, Just How Honest Are Car People?

If you define honesty as telling the simple truth—for instance, a "yes" or "no" answer to a question about car safety or mechanical reliability or profit—I'm sorry to say you won't find it in the car business. If a dealership sells a car that is ranked lowest on a safety scale, you can't expect the dealership to pass along that little tidbit. (Would you if you had to make your living selling it?) If you expect statements such as "Folks, we have another customer on this car if you don't take it now" to be truthful, you're going to be disappointed.

Honesty in the car business is always defined like this: "What answer will give us the biggest profit right now?" If a seller has to bend the absolute truth a little, that's just fine if the profit rises.

I call this little trait "convenient truth," and it generally precludes any chance of a dealership giving you a helpful answer about anything unless that answer helps the seller.

The sin of omission also makes most dealerships the house of the one-sided truth. Why tell a direct lie when you can simply leave out the bad part?

"How is the transmission in that used car?"

"Oh, fine," says the salesperson—the truth. But since you didn't ask if the air conditioner worked, the salesperson certainly doesn't volunteer that it's broken.

And what responsibility does all this depressing news place on you? The responsibility to know the answer to every question before you even think about approaching a dealership. And if you don't know the answer? Find an independent way to verify any dealership statement. We show you how at various steps in the process.

The Salesman's Greatest Talent

Killer was back in the service department, standing next to the young kid who spent his days taking care of the used cars. The kid was removing a worn tire from the left rear wheel of a car Killer had sold the night before. Killer had taken the car to the state inspection station just an hour earlier; he'd promised his customer the car would pass inspection, and the damn thing had failed because of that tire.

The kid slipped it off the car and jacked up the left front wheel of another used car, removing the tire and transferring it to Killer's car. It was a good tire, one that would pass inspection quickly. And it would just as quickly be replaced with the worn tire once it was time for Killer's delivery. Killer smiled. Those damned inspection people were just too picky, he thought. And not nearly as smart as they thought. He walked toward the showroom, stopping in the customers' lounge for a Coke, barely noticing the old man sitting right by the machine.

"Hey, DeMarco, what are you doing back here!" the man said enthusiastically. He was an old customer of Killer's who had purchased his last new car over four years ago and was sitting in the lounge waiting for the guys to finish a quick tuneup.

Killer smiled again—the customers' lounge had always brought him luck. He grabbed the guy by the arm and said, "Hey, Loren, come with me. I want you to feel something sexy." The two of them walked back to the employees' parking lot, and Killer opened the door to his new demo.

"Loren, just rub your hand over this carpet and tell me what that reminds you of." Killer walked around to the other side of the car and sat in the front seat. Loren was already sitting in the driver's seat and took the keys without a second thought.

"Here, feel the padding over your head," Killer said, as both men pressed their hands hard against the ceiling. "And Loren, push that button by the door and lean back."

Loren stretched his body as the seat automatically reclined, his eyes closed, a relaxed "ahhh" exiting his mouth. "You know, Bob, all I need is a TV and a beer!"

Killer laughed. "Hell, Loren, you've got those at home! What you need is this car. Now, get up and let's take a drive." Killer sold Loren the demo in thirty minutes, traded in his car without once driving it, and waved as he drove off.

It is the car salesman's greatest talent: titillation. Any good car salesman is the master of tactile excitement, the mark of a good pimp. Salesmen are incessantly drilled in the power of tactile selling, and for good reason. You, for instance, may enjoy looking at *Playboy* or *Playgirl*, but wouldn't you have more fun if those pictures were replaced by real people? A smart pimp knows that. Sure, you like the pictures, but put you next to the real thing—let you smell the heavenly scents and touch that supple skin in person—and reason flies out the window, along with your pocketbook.

Smart car salesmen use tactile excitement in many ways. They want you to feel the padding under that $500 vinyl roof, caress the leather, slam the doors; they want you to do anything that will make you fall physically in love with one specific car. Privately, the salesmen and managers take a slightly less romantic view. Cars are referred to as hunks of meat, lead, potatoes. They serve only one purpose: as decoys for the ducks, the surest lure for monetary reward. And you've seldom met a more proficient marksman than a good car salesman, either.

The Salesman's Favorite Targets

The nice old lady drove up in a plain brown sedan. A widow who had never purchased a car before without her husband, the woman was nervous. She had a right to be, too. Women and older people are usually easy business for any car salesman.

Buzz was the first person to reach her. "Hello, ma'am, I'm Peter Kiever. People call me Buzz—short for Buzzard." He smiled. "Thanks for coming in to see us."

The woman was smiling by then and quickly fell under the spell of this "nice man," as she referred to him. Buzz was patient. He spent two hours with the lady, never pressuring, the "ma'ams" flowing from his mouth like honey from a bear's lips. He could afford to spend time with her. After all, Buzz knew that ladies, particularly old ladies, don't like to argue, want to believe that niceness is honesty, and invariably buy cars from people who *are* nice.

Women and older people are just two favorite types of customers. First-time buyers are really popular, too, especially the young first-time buyer, a person who breathes the heaviest when first sitting behind the wheel of a car. Innocence, enthusiasm, and a trusting nature make the selling process so simple. Many poor people, black and white, are also favorite targets—people who actually feel inferior the moment they walk on the lot. "What do these folks know about wheeling and dealing?" is the car salesman's attitude. And then there are the people who think their credit is marginal. It may not be, but if

you're one of these types, keep thinking negatively, please. Your salesman will sense that your main concern is not getting a good deal but
getting financed. Car salesmen make much more money on you,
thanks to that.

But who's the best target? *Anyone who makes the assumption that
nice people will sell you a car for less.* Next to a water moccasin, a nice
friendly car salesman is probably the most dangerous thing in the
world *because* it's so easy to trust him. And trusting just about anybody in the business of buying and selling cars will cost you money.

Profits, Not Profit

The actual negotiation for the sale or trade of an automobile is one
of many ways dealerships have of fleecing you honestly, though many
times it is the least profitable part of the transaction for the dealer.
Killer knows that better than most salesmen, and therefore he likens
an automobile dealership's need for other profit sources to a rapidly
flowing river. The river is never filled by the random raindrops that
fall every now and then, but rather by the small streams of water that
pour into larger streams, each one adding to the massive flow of the
river. So the dealership fills with money.

If you prefer, think of your friendly dealer as playing an enormous
game of "Gotcha." Lurking around every corner, in each innocent
statement of the smiling salesman, is some thing or service that will
grab just a little more money for the dealership. Virtually all of these
extra dealer-profit sources are not presented to you until you've
signed your name on that buyer's order—your salesman probably
just asked you to "Okay these figures," which sounds much better
than "sign the binding contract here, sir."

Consider, for instance, the "protection" packages we mentioned
earlier. The package usually includes rustproofing and undercoating,
"glazing," and "fabric protection," and is usually sold by the "business manager" or "financial counselor"—you know, that extra salesperson they're going to make you see.

The products themselves are cheap. Rustproofing and undercoating usually cost the dealer no more than $75. Fabric conditioning
about $5. Glazing about $5. But what do the dealers want? We've
tracked dealers who regularly charge *$3000* for this package. And we

haven't even addressed the fact that you probably don't need this extra "protection" at any price.

And then there are the extended warranties or service agreements. You probably don't need these, either (more on that later), and you certainly don't need them at ripoff prices. Most cost a dealer under $200, and most dealers try to sell them for *$600* to *$1800*.

Just remember what Killer said: "It doesn't matter which pocket you take their money from. It just matters that we get in their pocket."

Aren't these guys nice?

Supply and Demand

This old bugbear of the economics student is the reason the identical car can vary in selling price from store to store. If a dealer has only one of the hottest-selling cars on his lot, you won't buy that car cheaply. If the same dealer has fifty slow-selling models, he'll give them away at cost, if need be. The law of supply and demand is probably the nemesis of the car business, because the lead time required for supply to follow demand is a long one, and invariably, the moment supply has been adjusted, demand will have changed again.

So, How Do You Win?

In order to win, you really need to understand what's ticking inside the head of every person at the dealership. You need to understand why they think and react as they do. This book takes you inside that world and exposes the way it works. But even so, it will still be up to you to act on that information. As you read, you would do well to remember that the moment you walk into a dealership, it's a war for your pocketbook. Make it a gentlemanly thing. Have a good time visiting with that nice young salesman. Drink lots of coffee, or let the guy buy you a Coke. But don't forget that it's going to be a war. To win, you will need to know what is happening in each and every part of the buying and selling transaction.

KILLER MONSOON'S FAVORITE
SELLING TECHNIQUES

It was Saturday night, the last night of the store's "Beat the Clock" sale, and Killer picked up one of the last cold chicken legs on the table at the end of the showroom floor. A few customers were still sitting in front of the big board that listed every single car on the lot. Each hour for the past twenty-four, one of the salesmen had been assigned the honor of "marking down" the cars $100. Many of the cars still listed on the board had bright red stars beside them, indicating "bonus cars"—"Beat the clock, and buy a bonus car, and we'll give you a free color TV!" the radio and television ads said.

People actually believe that crap, Killer thought, as he watched a man who had been sitting in front of the board hour after hour finally jump and yell, "I'll take that one, the one with the $3000 discount!" Killer burped. Chicken sales weren't his idea of selling cars. Sure, it was a good technique for the suckers, but anyone can sell a car to a sucker.

J. C. walked up to the board and taped a "sold" sign by stock number 224. Killer laughed to himself. Not one single customer in the room knew that the car wasn't sold—J. C. just didn't want to sell it at such a big discount. During the entire twenty-four hours, no one had received a TV, either. The salesmen would say, "I'm sorry, folks, but at *that* price, we just can't sell you a car and give you a TV." The line worked every time, for every "giveaway"—bicycles, toasters, vacations. During Killer's thirty-five years in the business, he took pride in having never given away a single premium yet. Screw the show biz, Killer thought, as he slipped out the service door and headed to the Dead End.

Have you ever driven by an automobile dealership and seen a giant "tent sale" in progress, balloons flying high in the air and clowns running around pinching all the nice customers' kids? All car stores like to create a carnival atmosphere, promising fun and prizes, and generally intoxicating the customers with an air of excitement. And why shouldn't they? Car people have learned from experience that the average customer doesn't want too serious an environment during car negotiations. Customers seem to revert to a childlike attitude when they think about cars—to suspend reason and judgment. You would do well to resist this urge to return to the crib, for while you are giggling away, smart car people are using very effective psychological techniques to lower your defenses even further. Have you ever been the victim of any of the following techniques?

"Will You Buy a Car Today at Some Price?"

It's a salesman's most important question. It tells him whether or not you are going to be an easy sale. If you say "yes," the guy will probably start salivating, especially if you're in heat over one particular car. If you say "maybe," he'll be extra nice and probably even volunteer to show you his "best deal" of the day. As he talks to you, the guy will be looking for your "button"—the one psychological element he can push that will turn you into a buyer today. If you say, "No, I'm not buying today at any price," the guy will in all likelihood put you out on a "ball," an impossibly low price, on the one car you've shown interest in. You would be surprised how many people come back in, too, and then let that same salesman raise them another $2000 for the same car.

Be honest when someone asks you this question, but couch your honesty in self-protective terms if you are dead set on buying a car, a specific car, that day. Try something like this: "Yes, I may buy a car today. But I am going to buy it from the dealership that lets me determine how we negotiate."

One of the most important defensive techniques you can learn to use with car people is the ability to be negative in a nice way. Don't let that thought make you uncomfortable, either. Would you be passive and mushy if someone were lifting your wallet? Of course not. Yet some customers actually seem to feel that any indication of disagreement with a salesman will bring immediate expulsion from the dealership, as if they're being banished from heaven. Don't forget that every dealership in America survives on all of us. Each and every one will not only sell you a car if you are strong and demanding—they will respect you for it, in their own convoluted way.

One quick warning here: **Don't *ever* buy a car on your first visit to a dealership, even if the dealership offers to give it to you. Boy, will you be taken if you break this rule.**

"If I Can . . . , Will You . . . ?"

The Fillmores were walking around the new-car lot with Killer, past the plush, expensive models and the stingy little sedans, too. They had asked for Killer, because Mr. Fillmore worked with one of Killer's bird-dogs.

"Mr. DeMarco, these are all pretty cars, and I'd be lying if I said I didn't want to own one, but all of these things are too rich for my blood. I'm a poor man, you understand."

Killer chuckled, looking straight into Fillmore's eyes. "Why, of course you are. And I appreciate your concern. It's ridiculous how much cars cost these days. But let me ask you something. If I can sell you this car right here [it was one of the most expensive sedans on the lot] for a price and payment that is reasonable to you—if I can give you more than you think would be fair on your trade—Mr. Fillmore, if I can do that, will you buy it today?"

How do you answer Killer's question? Of course, most of us would buy a car if the payment was reasonable and if we felt we were getting more than our trade was worth.

"If I can . . . , will you . . . ?" however, is not a fair question, because normally if you will, they won't. The question is simply a nice way to confirm to any salesman that you will buy a car if you *think* you are getting more than your due. The question can also lead you into deep waters quickly. For instance, once a salesman has determined that you don't want to pay over $300 a month for a car, and that you consider $275 per month an easy payment to make, he automatically knows you are a buyer if he can find a car you like that will fit that payment. So why shouldn't you be happy if he can? Because you might be able to buy that same car for $225 a month, if you bargain.

The Sincere Salesman-in-a-Contest Ploy

If every car salesman went on a winning trip each time he said "Ma'am, this car will send me over the top," there would be no more car salesmen in America—they'd all be away on trips. Sure, there are contests, many of them. Dealerships place bonuses for salesmen on the most new or used cars sold or leased, the largest gross (profit) per car, the most rustproofings sold, the highest number of financed cars. Dealerships and manufacturers also employ contests to sell slow-moving cars. But these contests and bonuses don't necessarily mean you're going to receive a better deal. Don't fall for the sympathy routine; negotiate even harder with these contest fellows. After all, if they are really going to win a trip or extra money, they can afford to make a little less on you.

The "I'm Salesman of the Month" Routine

Do you think that nice salesman with his picture on the wall was picked for his service to humanity? No, he probably was picked because he makes more *profit* for the dealer than the other guys. Sure, the nice salesman can afford to be relaxed, to laugh, smile, and act like St. Francis of Assisi—after all, would a saint take you? You bet he would. Do not forget that this is a business transaction, not evening prayers.

The "I'm a Trustworthy Salesman" Ploy

Because most customers are naturally suspicious of car salesmen, smart guys know that they *must* gain your respect if they're going to sell you a car. There are lots of techniques for doing this, too. If Killer is talking with a customer who seems determined not to buy a car that moment, he'll look the person straight in the eye and say, "You know, I'm really glad you're not buying today. Quite honestly, the house is holding out for too much profit today. I can save you a lot of money if you'll come back tomorrow."

Sometimes Killer will close a deal with a large front end (the profit on the new car) by telling the customer, "Folks, don't ever quote me on this or the boss will can me, but you *will* get a little better financing rate if you go directly to the bank down the street. I'll be happy to call the loan officer for you." Isn't that nice of Killer? What he doesn't tell the folks about is *his* relationship with the loan officer—Killer gets paid a fee for each person he refers.

And then, there's Killer's best line for used-car buyers. You're looking at a used Toyota when he walks up and says, "Sir, I wouldn't recommend that car to you. It really isn't a very good car. Let me show you something else." What do you think of Killer? Do you instinctively trust him? After all, he *was* being honest with you. Perhaps. He may be telling the truth, but because he is so well trained in a favorite technique of used-car selling, he is usually simply gaining your confidence for the kill: that six-month-old clunker with a cracked head sitting in the back lot with a bonus on it.

"Setting You" on a Car: The Demo Ride

A good salesman will always insist that you drive the car you like best. That's the salesman's most important job, getting you behind the wheel of that car. He'll probably insist that the whole family go, too—kids and a spouse can quickly become a salesman's best friends.

By all means, drive the car you like. Play with all the buttons, feel the nice seats, and enjoy the ride. But don't let your adrenaline take control: be cool, be objective. Don't fall prey to the guy's spiel, and for God's sake, don't let him "reinforce" you. That's a nice technique that goes something like this: "How does the ride compare to your present car, Mr. Smith? . . . It's a quiet car, isn't it? . . . How do the seats feel, aren't they comfortable, just like an armchair?" The salesman saw you drive in, the smoke belching from the rear of your rusting GM diesel. He *knows* you've got to like the scent of new plush, and he *hopes* your reason will be smothered under all this beauty and comfort. A new car is never as nice after a week or two, especially if you've learned how much money you wasted.

"We Can Allow You This Much with a Difference of This Much and a Deferred Payment of This Much. Now, Just Sign Here"— The Old Confuse-Them-and-Control-the-Sale Ploy

Confusion is the salesman's best friend. Most folks after a day's shopping at several different dealerships hardly remember their own name, much less understand the offers and counteroffers whisked before them. Salesmen use confusion to keep you from buying a car at another dealership. They *imply* that enormous savings are waiting for you on your return. They tell you about the customer who has been waiting for a trade-in just like yours, hoping you'll fall for that classic line.

Confusion is also used in more specific ways. For instance, if you are a "payment buyer," smart salesmen will continually quote you only payments, conveniently forgetting to mention the trade-in allowance or discount. If you are a "difference buyer" (if you care only how much difference you must pay between your old car and their new car), salesmen will try to convince you that "allowance" (how much they *say* they are actually giving you for your trade) is more important than difference.

Don't tell a salesman that you only care about your payment. Don't tell him you only care about the difference in price between your old car and that pretty new four-footed thing. Those are expensive ways to deal, since you'll be lost in the confusion. The only things that count are what your car is really worth in wholesale dollars, what their car actually costs, how much profit you are willing to pay, and which financing costs the least.

Justifying the Sale

These days, all of the major automobile manufacturers have videotape presentations designed to teach salesmen how to overcome customer objections. One good series is called "Justifying the Sale," a nice euphemism for making nickels look like quarters. A new salesman at the dealership, a nice kid who enjoys talking with Killer, Robbie Miers, is sitting at the feet of the master, Coke in hand, listening to war stories. The topic is overcoming objections.

"I remember the time this smart-ass came into the dealership so set on exactly what he wanted on a car that the other salesmen gave up," Killer said with a smirk. "I bet four of them twenty each I could sell the guy, and I did."

Robbie sat there in anticipation. Killer just looked off in space. "Well, come on, what did you do?" the kid asked.

Killer started laughing, a belly laugh. "Hell, I did just the opposite of what I'd done with the customer before him! God, this business is fun. Well, anyway, the first guy had wanted a specific car, but with a vinyl roof. I convinced him that vinyl roofs allow moisture to build up and cause serious rust. He also didn't really like the car being red, so I just put him on the phone with the used-car department—the guys up there told him red is the most popular resale color and would bring him more money in trade. Then, this second jackass came in, the one none of the guys could sell, and he just wouldn't have a vinyl roof and definitely had to have some light-colored car. I showed him the used-car book—the place where you add on for vinyl roofs in figuring the value of a trade—told him how much quieter cars are with vinyl, and convinced him that the roof insulated the car so much he'd save a gallon a mile on air-conditioning! Then I told him how much light colors rust, and that black cars had less rust than any, and he bought it all!" Robbie smiled. Killer was better than any videotaped spiel.

Killer was not lying to either one of those customers, just telling the selective truth. Bright colors are more popular at resale time. Some vinyl roofs do encourage rust but at the same time provide deadening and insulation. Black cars do rust less than light-colored cars. As a matter of fact, most of the techniques used by salesmen do have some ring of truth in them. For instance: "Do you think it's too expensive? Just think what you'll save on repair bills." "You don't want to finance for sixty months? Why not, you can pay the loan off earlier if you want to." "You want to think about it until tomorrow? Why? You said you liked the car and the payment. If you buy the car today, I'll even give you a free undercoating."

So how in God's name do you make any sound judgment with all these semblances of truth flying around? It's easy. If you need to justify what you are spending or what you are choosing, if you have doubts about what you are doing: STOP THE TRANSACTION. Go home and defuse. Don't try to think in the midst of confusion.

"Ah, This Is the Beauty of a Trade-in You Mentioned?"—The Ploy of Bringing You to Their Reality

Killer was standing by an up's trade-in. The man had ridden to the store that morning with a friend. It was a cool Saturday in October, one of those days that seem to draw every looker in the world to car stores, and the two men had planned to kill a few hours looking over all the new models sitting proudly in front of their temporary homes. Killer normally has little patience with these "bumblebees," the people who light at one store just long enough to draw a salesman from the showroom, waste fifteen minutes of his time, and then fly off to the next candy store. As a matter of fact, he never paid any attention to the type. But Gary Oliver Davies had been on the warpath that week and had passed down that damn edict from whatever particular cloud he was nesting on at that moment. "I want a salesman at every single up's car before the door is open," he'd yelled. "Hell," Killer mused, "I guess his damn boat needs a new set of sails." It was common knowledge at the store that Mr. Davies's fifty-foot sailboat was regularly maintained at dealership expense.

These two guys had been nice enough, though, and one of them even exhibited a reasonably serious case of car fever, enough to garner Killer's attention. It was this man, Tommy Hines, who had now returned to the store with his trade-in. But Mr. Hines's battle-worn car looked nothing like the glowing description presented to Killer that morning. "Mr. DeMarco, I want to tell you my car is one of the prettiest four-year-old Chevys this side of Detroit!" he had said with obvious enthusiasm. Killer was used to statements like that. Everybody who came in the store seemed to have no problem at all believing their trades were things of beauty, even if fenders were missing, seats were torn, and large pools of oil formed quickly on the pavement each time the junkers rolled to a stop. But over the years Killer had developed a really nice technique for handling this "blind love." And he was just about to unleash it on Mr. Tommy Hines.

"Tommy, this does look like a mighty nice car. You know, I remember when I had one pretty much like it. . . ." Killer continued to talk and started working his way slowly down one side of the car, something like two steps, before stopping to continue his story. Each time he stopped he'd look at the car again. If a small dent was within reach, Killer would simply rub his hand over it and continue walking, talking all the time. When he was standing by the hood, he pulled out a large handkerchief and vigorously rubbed the worst area of faded paint; then Killer ran his finger along the windshield molding, right to the large rust bubble in the corner. Tommy, of course, was seeing these little problems for the first time. Like most of us, he'd become used to the pimples. But Killer never once mentioned the little problems with the car as he stood by the driver's door.

"Hey, Tommy, you know, I may have a customer for your car. Why don't we take a spin around the block?" Tommy didn't really like the idea—the brakes weren't too good really, something he'd kept meaning to fix, and the worn-out shocks bounced the car up and down in a good imitation of a camel loping across the desert. But how could he say no? After all, this was supposed to be a really "nice" car. They headed down the road, Killer jabbering away, seemingly not in the least aware of the lope or the brakes. He did run his hand over the torn armrest and do his best to push the ashtray in—the damn thing kept falling down, as if it were trying to talk—but words weren't really necessary. Tommy was getting the message by osmosis. The dreamboat just wasn't that great, after all.

Or that's at least what Killer wanted him to think. Smart car people will do their best to "educate" you about the value of your trade before they try to sell you a car. It's a smart move, one you can't refute very easily. If you don't know the real value of your trade *before* you drive on the lot, you will lower its value in your own mind every time a salesman points out its weaknesses.

The "Other Customer" Ploy

You're sitting in the salesman's office, and you want to think about his offer until tomorrow. "Sir," he says, "there *is* someone else interested in that car; the people are expected back here at five. If you really like that car, why don't you just give me a small deposit to hold it for you?" Don't do it, even if your spouse threatens to cut you off. Clear that glaze from your eyes and say no. You are spending thousands of dollars, and there are thousands of cars out there, too. You will invariably get a better deal and be more comfortable with your purchase if you wait a day.

But let's assume you follow this advice, only to return the next day and find your dreamboat gone. Don't be upset; car people know the disappointment you feel usually means you won't buy anything from them, and so they'll bend over backwards to make you an even better offer on another car. Some smart buyers use this technique deliberately; they pick out a car and wait for it to be sold to someone else, when they really wanted some other car on the lot.

The Old (Make That VERY New) "Lease 'Em a Car Instead" Ploy

Salespersons use this ploy invariably because they can't make enough money on you at a certain price, and know for sure they'll make a lot more if you can be switched to leasing. Your response should be quick and friendly, but firm, unless you've studied our sections on leasing: "I'm not leasing a car today, period."

"Lease 'em rather than sell 'em" in its honest guise is bad enough. But, unfortunately, its dishonest version is much more prevalent, and has become the subject of state attorney general investigations and thousands of lawsuits. This version would be better called "Lease 'em a car and let them think they're buying it." It's used particularly with older folks already confused, exhausted, and devastated by dealership tactics, and also with others who seem like easy marks. The salesperson simply begins to discuss leasing terms without calling them that, has a contract drawn that says it's a lease, but quickly rushes the exhausted customer through the signing process. What makes this particularly cruel and obnoxious is the first thing the buyers are usually asked to sign: a sheet saying "I have read all of these pieces of paper, and understand them."

This tactic is used thousands of times each month in America, and many consumers don't know they've leased rather than bought for months. And unfortunately, even if they discover the switch in a day, there has been little recourse to have it overturned: they've signed the papers. But you will be happy to know that this tactic may be changing as lawsuits are filed again and again.

So what do you do if you find a dealership has pulled this ploy on you? If you discover it before you sign anything, get out of there. Don't buy a free cup of water from them. And tell your friends to stay away, too. If you've already signed the papers, but haven't left the dealership yet, don't leave. Force them to revoke the contract that day. Then leave. If they won't cancel it, call an attorney, or your local help lines, from the dealership.

But since you're reading this book so carefully, none of those bad things can happen to you, can they?

THE SELLING SYSTEMS

Earlier I told you about the "adversarial" selling approach used by virtually all dealers, in which the salesperson is positioned as your friend against the nasty bad guys, the salesperson's boss. The general system itself is dishonest because the salespeople are pretending, of course. They are taught to *appear* to be on your side and to use that appearance against you.

In the past few years, the megadealers have really refined the adversarial selling system and continue to do so now. Here's a look at the most popular systems. At times dealerships *combine* systems, too.

The T. O. System

The gold standard, it's been around for two decades and is still the most popular way to take your money with a smile and an unhealthy dose of confusion and exhaustion.

Let's say you've spent two hours at a dealership. You've found the car you like, one of those special-edition Expenso Gargantula Majesty

Hardtops you have always yearned for. Your trade-in has been appraised, and though you are not really sure what they want to pay for it, you think their offer sounds pretty good. Or at least the salesman thinks it's pretty good, since you've noticed that he giggles every time the figure is mentioned.

The monthly payment they've quoted you doesn't seem that bad, either. Sure, it's twice what you pay now, but the finance manager, who came into the office with the salesman, showed you how much lower it is. "Yes, it's $6 a day more, but that's only twenty-five cents an hour. And you'll probably save that on gas, once gas gets up to $3 a gallon." You know, *that* type of logic.

However, you are tired and a bit confused, and you have been trying to leave for a little R & R. The salesman has even lowered the price to keep you there; he's also told you about his children and his sick mother. ("She's a real saint, I tell you.") But still you want to leave. The salesman excuses himself and returns with his sales manager, who wants to dicker some more. Still you resist. Pretty soon, he leaves, and now the general manager drops in. He wants to dicker a little more. You buy the car. After all, you had to, just to get out of there. You have been the victim of the T. O., the "fresh face can do miracles" theory. *Don't* put up with that. Don't feel guilty for leaving —it's not really a prison bust-out, though you may feel that way. Smile, shake hands, and say goodbye until tomorrow.

The Four-Square System

If you go to a dealership that uses this system, leave. In my opinion, there is no more deliberately unfair way to sell a vehicle, because this system is designed to confuse you completely. Why deal with a dealership this sleazy?

Four-square works like this: the salesperson draws a cross on a blank sheet of paper, creating four squares. The salesperson then asks what payment you want to make a month for a car and writes that figure in the top left square without arguing. You feel pretty good.

Then the salesperson asks how much you want for your old car. You know it's worth a thousand, but you say five thousand. That figure is put without argument in the top right square. You're beginning to feel real good.

Then the salesperson asks what you want to pay for the car itself. The window sticker says $20,000, and you, as a joke, say $10,000. The figure goes in the bottom left square. Your heart skips a few beats. Are you a tough negotiator, or what?

And then the salesperson asks you to sign that simple piece of paper and fork over a fat deposit, which you promptly do. Who wants to miss a deal like this? You sit back and smile. The salesperson disappears for a few minutes.

When the salesperson returns, the fun begins as you are "worked" on each square *as if they are not interrelated.* You wanted to pay $200 a month? They scratch through that and put $600. You jump. They scratch through that and put $525. You jump, they scratch through the latest figure until you quiveringly agree to a payment.

Then they begin to work you on the value of your trade. You said $5000, but they scratch through it and put $200—scratch, change, mess up that simple piece of paper, confuse . . . and then they do the same thing with the total price of the vehicle you're looking at.

Who can make sense out of all that chicken scratching? No one. That's the point. Why does the four-square system always come back and ask for an impossibly large amount of money—or offer you virtually nothing for your trade? To *condition* you. If a payment should be $200, but the seller keeps asking for $600, then a little less, then $545, you'll feel pretty good when they get down to $245, won't you? But on a 60-month contract, you'll have just paid an additional $2400 in profit. Thank you very much.

Some four-square dealerships will keep you there for hours playing this game, and worse. At a dealership in Texas, the staff kept a deaf-mute customer at the dealership for eleven hours playing hardball. The customer eventually sued the dealership for mental anguish. And do you know what the dealership's defense was? If you think *that* salesman and manager were tough, you should see our really tough guys in action! Makes you want to buy a car from these folks, doesn't it? Oh, the customer was awarded six million dollars by a jury.

The Note System: Killing You with Kindness

Many people have caught on to the T. O. and four-square systems. The moment another smiling person enters the office to ask for more money or the moment the square appears, they become more savvy consumers. That, of course, won't do.

Enter the latest slick and misleading sales ploy. Rather than send other salespeople in to talk with you, the note system simply sends personalized notes to you from the sales manager. Usually five notes. All very friendly. And though each note asks for more money, their wording is so sincere it's hard to argue. For instance, note 1:

"Dear Mr. and Mrs. Smith, thanks for coming in, but we unfortunately can't meet your price. If we come down $500 could you come up $500 and let's meet in the middle?"

You agree, and note 2 appears: "Dear Mr. and Mrs. Smith, thanks so much. We appreciate your help, but the customer we had for your old car? They've already bought something else. Can you help us another $300? We hate to ask, but some folks are coming to see that car within the hour." You pay.

And note 3 appears: "Dear Tom and Sally (the invisible man is now your friend), we are so close. We're going to have to call the boss on this one, but if we move a little, could you help us just a little? Sam."

You give. These people seem so sincere. And the fourth note comes: "Tom and Sally, just another $21.63 and we can do it! Sam."

Why, of course you pay. Boy, can you drive a bargain. And then the fifth note arrives. "Now, just remember you can't tell anyone what you paid." Right. You'll tell everyone, won't you?

The note system seems so nice, but it has a couple of problems. First, the notes weren't written for you. The wording was taken out of a notebook, and the notes themselves were probably written up en masse at the sales meeting. Only your name had to be added.

Second, a salesperson is required to give you all five notes *even if you agree to pay the highest maximum profit before you get the first note!* The salesperson still must try to raise you again and again.

And the last two notes? The one asking for $21.63 is simply to make you *think* you're bargaining (more on that in a minute), and the final "don't tell your friends" note is designed to make you do just that.

What's the gist of the note system? *It's fantasy. Don't fall for it.*

The Tower System

Generally used at very large dealerships and always used in conjunction with another system, the tower system intimidates the salesperson more than the customer but still provides maximum control over you. At these dealerships, a "control tower"—it can be an actual tower, like an airport control tower, or simply a centrally located platform area—houses managers whose only job is *to watch* you from the moment you arrive on the lot. At times with binoculars. If a salesperson doesn't reach your car immediately, a walkie-talkie dispatches one; if you start walking toward your car to leave, a walkie-talkie dispatches a "runner" to stop you. Tower systems are based on physical intimidation and control and are becoming awfully popular these days. If you find yourself confronted with one, be prepared for a battle or get out of there. If they'll let you leave.

One Price, No Hassle Systems

"No hassle" or "no dicker" dealerships are the tidal wave of the future in the rocky business of cars. They're wildly popular, touted in the press, and pointed to by dealers as a sign that the car business is becoming a friendly, downright pleasant racket—er, business.

And in theory, one-price dealerships should work: you walk in and either like the price of the car and buy it, or don't. What can go wrong? Well, where shall we start? To begin, this gimmick—and that's all it is—takes away your natural defense mechanisms. Since there's no hassling, you relax and enjoy your visit for a change. Dealerships know your guard is down. And in predatory selling, that's when you always strike. First, they make a nice profit on the new vehicle itself. That's not really that bad, either. So what if you pay a measly $500 to $1000 more for the car than if you had carefully bargained for it?

But then the fun begins. Next they steal your trade from you. They look you in the eye and say, "Hey, we don't hassle you, remember? That's what it's worth, friend." You say yes and, bam, accept $4000, let's say, for your car rather than the $5000 it's worth. You've now paid $2000 more than you would at a "normal" dealer where your guard and trading skills are up.

And then they take you to the finance office to talk financing and add-ons. All done without a bit of negotiating and lots of laughter on both sides. In the finance office they put you on a high rate, laughingly talk you into double insurance, and tack on $35 a month for their "environmental package," perhaps. That's usually a wax job. Let's see, they made an extra $1700 on the financing and $2700 on the add-ons. In total that brings their profit on one sale up to a little over $6000 if my math is right.

Do you see why dealers like "no hassle" selling? And do you understand that dealerships using it are generally making a dramatically higher profit per customer? *That's* why they switched to this system, not to be nice to you. And not, as some dealerships are saying, because their manufacturers require them to; they don't.

The system you're learning here will defeat that system, however, if you'll just keep on reading.

"Spot Delivery" Systems

You're going to face this latest, highly deceptive scam, and if you fall for it, you could be in real financial trouble: the salesperson looks you in the eye and points to your old car as he talks. You half listen as you watch dealership personnel moving all your belongings from your beat-up old bucket to that glimmering coupe you just drove.

"Folks, we know you," the salesperson says—(of course, he doesn't say "we know you because we ran an unauthorized credit check on you")—"and we're letting you take that car home right now! We're drawing up the contracts right now, too, *at the figures you wanted!*"

Well, what is wrong with that? Your kids agree, too, as they promise to wash the dishes for two years. So you start signing papers, laugh at the salesperson's final joke, and drive home happy in your dream machine. You stay happy, too, until the phone rings in about a week: "We've got a little problem," the sales manager invariably says. "We couldn't get you financed for the full amount (or, we made a mistake on our paperwork)—but don't worry. All we need is another $3500. And we need it today." You notice the edge to the manager's voice.

Well, what do you do? You don't have the money, so you nervously tell the manager you'll bring the car back and get your old car back.

"Oh, you can't do that," the manager says, "we sold your old car. Now, when are you going to bring us the money? Have it here in twenty-four hours." His tone is a little colder.

"Uh, well, I can't get the money. And it's the dealership's fault, anyway," you say. They told you the loan was approved. And if they made a mistake, whose fault is that?

Completely your fault, in both cases. "Hey, didn't you read our recission and mistake release?" the guy says—you know, the fifteenth thing they asked you to sign, the page in ant-sized print filled with confusing legalese.

"Uh, no, I didn't read that very carefully. The salesperson said it was a formality."

"Well, I'm sorry you didn't read it. We'll need that money by tomorrow or I'm afraid we'll have to report this car as stolen."

What do you do? Don't worry! The dealership has a plan to save you. They'll borrow you the money from a small loan house, or borrow you a bigger down payment from a bank, or help you call your favorite uncle. And when you go to sign all the new paperwork on your new loan, you'll notice the interest rate is up and the months you'll pay are longer. What you won't see directly is the dramatic increase in profit on your deal for the dealership.

All that happened because you fell for "spot" delivery. So, how do you stop that? *Never* take delivery on a vehicle when you're financing at the dealership if you are asked to sign *any* documents which imply your deal isn't absolutely final. And if you're smart, you simply won't take delivery on the day you negotiate under any circumstances. More on this later.

"Credit Doctor" Scams

Ever worried a bit about your credit worthiness? Been late for a payment or two? Ever had a real credit problem? If you have (and most of us have at one time or the other), you've probably been drawn to the enthusiastic ads which invariably say "No Credit? Bad Credit? *No problem!* Come see us: The Credit Doctor!" Just about every dealership, big and small, is running a version of this ad.

Though the dealers would like you to think their "credit doctor" promotions verge on public service—you know, helping out those who've had problems—the truth is unfortunately exactly the opposite. Dealerships have learned that people who worry about their credit don't argue about their deal: the more you worry, the less you argue, and the less you argue, the more the dealership makes. And where the profits are, the dealership sales machine is always relentless at work, regardless of the damage to the customer.

That's why dealerships have developed special sales techniques and assign full-time "credit doctor" sales personnel to those of you who have or think you *may* have a credit problem. Let's say you've had late payments once or twice. Being late a few times normally doesn't impact your credit, but nonetheless you're worried and ask for the credit doctor when you arrive at the dealership. This person is going to help you find the best car for the least money, right? Wrong.

Instead that friendly "doctor" targets you for the worst predatory sales techniques, starting with a vicious little game called *maxing out:* "What is the maximum amount of profit we can squeeze from this sucker? Can we get some money from a credit card? Can we get an uncle or friend to borrow from a small loan house? Can we 'fluff' their credit statement (lie on it)?" The credit doctor never thinks of your credit or your budget, only of profit.

And then you're pushed toward the "old maid" cars that no one else wants to buy, or worse, to the junkers; you're put on the highest interest rates, even though you qualify for a lower rate; you're sold the "sucker" options or services that no one should buy.

Can anything get worse than this? There is something. The real, ugly underbelly of the American automobile business.

The Advent of Major Automobile Dealerships Designed Solely for "Sub-Prime" Borrowers

For decades every town has had "buy here, pay here" lots, usually sleazy, run-down lots that make you want to wash your hands before you even touch the front doorknob. Only the most desperate buyers went to these places. But in the early nineties, both major automobile dealership chains and major lending institutions began to look at the profits made by some of these fleabag operations. The dealers and lenders were also smacking their lips at the profits made off the unfortunate customers who had fallen for their "credit doctor" scams. "How," they thought, "can we make more money like this?"

One solution was the creation of used-car chains with snappy names like "C*A*R*S, Y*O*U *B*E*T!" or "WHEELS FOR YOU!," clean, handsome showrooms, and clean-cut, apparently helpful sales personnel. From the look of it, a poor consumer had found a good place to do business.

But how deceiving those looks were. While there are some dealerships and sub-prime financing companies that actually strive to help the poorer customer, the consumer movement, through involvement in many class action lawsuits, is getting below the well-scrubbed surface of these chains and lenders and finding a messy reality:

➤ Many of these chains simply serve as "dumping grounds" for a new car dealership's junkers. Cars placed on these lots receive cosmetic work to make them look good, but virtually no mechanical repair. "If the cars were any good," one person said in a deposition, "we were told to put them in the shop and then put them on our regular used-car lot; if they were junkers, we were told to drive them directly to the junk chain."

➤ $500 cars are being sold for $7000 without any warranty.

➤ Some of these chains won't even tell you the price of a car.

➤ Some of these chains are targeting African Americans and other minorities for especially tough sales tactics.

➤ Customers are seldom allowed to drive the vehicles. "Oh, we don't have insurance for that," the sales personnel are trained to say.

➤ Major financing companies are charging two to three times more interest on these exorbitant prices than even the worst customer may need to pay.

➤ Many of these cars don't run a *single week* without breaking down. Since they don't have warranties and since the customers have already had every penny taken from them in the negotiating process, customers are unable either to repair their vehicles or to continue making payments. Their cars are immediately repossessed and resold. Some of these vehicles are being sold, repossessed, and resold *six times in one year*.

➤ The unfortunate consumers are being sued for astounding "deficiencies": one junker car worth $500 was sold four times in a single month; each sale was $7000. Every time the vehicle was repossessed, the unfortunate owner of the moment, though he had driven the car less than a week, was sued for the full $7000 of the original loan. In less than a month, a $500 junk vehicle had returned a *$28,000 profit for the dealer.*

Well, What Should I Do If I Think I Have Credit Problems? How Can I Protect Myself?

First, stay away from "credit doctors" and "Cars, You Bet!" type dealerships. Find out your true credit situation before going any further. If you have a banking relationship, talk to a banker and ask him or her to pull your credit report and evaluate it for you. If you belong to a credit union, ask them to do the same thing. If you have credit problems, *slow down.* Talk to a credit counseling service. Your city or county probably has a free one.

Bad credit or no credit, you have a right to sensible advice and a good deal. Just don't listen to the "good deal" boys at the dealerships.

Welcome Centers

This is another technique now used with all of the very tough selling systems. The moment you arrive on the lot you're escorted to the "welcome center," where a very nice person asks for your vital statistics—name, address, phone, *social security number, and driver's license number*—all the information they need to run an unauthorized credit check on you and call you day and night if you, by some miracle, aren't forced to buy that day.

Later, before you go shopping, I'll ask you to come back and read this section again. Right now, let's continue your education by looking at a few more favorite pressure sales techniques.

RUNNING A CREDIT CHECK

Getting a Deposit

"Folks, I just need to get that deposit to show my boss that you're serious." You'll hear that line at most dealerships, and it's about as honest as "the check is in the mail." Every vehicle salesperson, regardless of the system, lives for the moment you pull out a roll of bills or your checkbook or (their current favorite deposit) your credit cards and driver's license. But the significance of paying a deposit is not what you think it is. To you, it is an agreement to buy at a certain price. To the sellers, it simply means you can't leave as they begin to pressure you, confuse you, raise you.

And these days they don't ask for a $50 deposit, either. Most dealerships ask for *thousands.* Do they think most people will actually pay it? No. But if they ask for $3000 they know you'll be embarrassed to offer $50. And, of course, the more of your money they have, the less likely you will be to leave.

Some dealerships have become laughingly creative in their references to deposit and even monthly payments, referring to deposits as "initial investments" and to monthly payments as "monthly investments." But whatever the name, cash isn't the most dangerous deposit you can give a dealership.

If a salesperson asks for your social security number or your driver's license or your credit cards before you have agreed to buy a car, he generally has a little surprise for you. The dealership is pulling a "short form" credit report on you without your knowledge and is planning the profit they'll make based on your credit. After pulling the credit report, the dealership actually fills out a loan application in your name and faxes it to many different loan sources—banks, GMAC, and so forth. And then *those* loan sources pull a credit report on you. All without your knowledge.

Isn't this a little illegal or something? It certainly should be, since the mere fact of all these credit inquiries actually lowers your credit rating with lending sources. A bank, for instance, is suspicious when they see a potential borrower has applied for loans all over town—and they see that when they pull your credit report. But this underhanded dealer trick probably isn't illegal. Though credit information isn't supposed to be given to others without the consumer's knowledge, credit rating services say that by simply handing over your driver's license number and social security number, you're giving permission for a credit check.

Killer has many standard lines in situations like these. "Folks, I need your social security numbers for insurance purposes." Or "Folks, I'll need to show those credit cards to my boss to show him you're who you say you are."

Well, what do you do when all this happens? Say no. Never give your social security number, a deposit, your driver's license number, or your credit card numbers to any salesperson or manager until *a manager has approved your offer on a car in writing.* Don't give deposits of any sort until the seller has agreed to sell.

How will dealerships react to this? Since most selling systems rely upon the trickery of deposits, many dealerships will say they won't sell you a car if you don't do it their way. *Don't give in.* Stick to your guns, and leave the dealership if necessary. Tell your friends to stay away, too.

But do you know what will usually happen when you stand up for your rights? The dealership will back down and do it your way.

Deposits are designed to control you. If you're going to win, you have to control the dealership. Don't fall for this shill game.

THE RAISE

All systems use the raise, too, and if you've shopped for a car in the last five years, you've been a victim. The philosophy here is simple: always get more money. Even if the customer can't afford it. Always ask for a *lot* more than you think you will get, too. If you want another $200, ask for at least twice as much.

We mentioned the odd-raise earlier: you sign an order, give the salesman all your credit cards, and sit there while he goes off to "fight for you." Of course, the guy really just goes for a Coke—he doesn't bother the manager—and returns with a smile on his face.

"Folks, we're so close! If you can just help me a little bit, $135.39, the boss'll go for it." Well, of course you'll do that. These guys are down to the pennies. And the guy's salesman of the month, anyway.

Smart salespeople almost never ask for even amounts of money; they ask for those odd amounts that imply (falsely) a good deal. Don't fall for it.

There is a catch-22 in the whole "bumping" syndrome. Some customers actually want to be "bumped," or raised. If the house should take their offer without arguing, the customers feel they must have made a bad deal. Yet many dealerships won't try to bump people who have agreed to very *low grosses;* a customer that *close in his offer* may leave if he's bumped. One thing is sure, though. Dealerships just love to bump people who are on *high-profit* deals on the first offer. Why? Managers feel that anyone dumb enough to agree to a high profit will probably be dumb enough to be bumped.

Do not be patient with raises. Tell your salesperson you won't budge when he goes to get your offer approved. Look him in the eye when you say it and don't smile—even grimace a little. Threaten to leave if your deal's not approved; he will get the message.

LOWBALLING

Let's say that you've held out against the system. Perhaps you have not been able to get your offer approved or perhaps you simply don't want to make an offer on the Expenso today. As you're walking from the showroom, the salesperson makes one last try. "If you will come back tomorrow, I'll try to get that car for $500 less than the figure you mentioned." Or he says, "I think I can get you $500 more for your trade-in if you come in tomorrow."

Don't go home and celebrate. You've just been lowballed—"put out" on a price they just know will bring you back tomorrow. Most people who are "put out on a ball" will invariably spend hours arguing with salespeople at other dealerships, saying "But the other guys have said they will give me $500 more." They exhaust themselves trying to buy a car from a ball figure and finally return to the first dealer the next day, only to be told, "Gosh, I'm sorry, we had a customer on your trade-in that would have allowed us to give you $500 more, but he bought something else just before you got here." And would you believe that most people, from pure frustration, will actually pay the $500 simply to end it all?

Why not take the offensive with the salesperson who makes you a ball offer? If what he proposed really would be a fantastic deal, grab him by the arm and drag him to his sales manager. Tell them both you'll buy the car right then and there for that figure, and if you can't, you'll never darken their door again. You will either buy a car very reasonably that day, or else your body will be found floating in some muddy river.

WELL, WHY DON'T YOU JUST COME OUT WITH IT AND CALL ALL THOSE SALESPEOPLE CROOKS?

Because most of them aren't. They just can't help what they do, and neither could you if you worked at a dealership. As a matter of fact, what would you do in these situations?

You're about to be fired, and your sales manager gives you one more day to sell a car. Just as the dealership is closing, a couple walks in and falls in love with a specific used car and offers to buy it. Trouble is, you know the car has lots of mechanical problems. But the folks don't ask a single question about the car and pull out their cash. Then, just as the wife starts to sign the contract, she says, "Will this be a good car for us?" What would you say?

You've bought a dealership with friends, and are determined to be honest and up-front. But the day the dealership opens, you turn on the radio and hear the National Highway Traffic Safety Administration presenting a study that shows you sell the most dangerous vehicles in America. Would you stop your sales, and make sure all your customers read that report?

You've got a chance to make a $50 bonus on a car nobody wants. The boss says, "Sell it at invoice, and you get fifty in walking money." But a customer comes in and falls in love with the car. He offers you a $2400 profit. Your commission would be $600. Would you say, "Oh, we're not taking $2400 profits on this car today, but I'll be happy to sell it to you for cost"?

Do you see the problem? Dealerships just weren't designed for straight answers. That's why you need straight facts.

2

A Look in the Mirror:
Know Yourself

The Allen Chases live north of town in one of those new subdivisions with big artificial security gates that are supposed to look imposing but in reality seem pretentious. The Chases are not wealthy, but they would like people to think that at least they're getting there. Their home, though small, has two large stone urns by the front door. The flowers that used to bloom well there have slowly withered from neglect. "Honey, I've just been *so* busy," Allie continually tells her husband. Allison Chase is very involved in the lesser social scene—you know the type.

"Well, damn it, what do you think I do? Whose work is it that lets you be that busy?" Allen invariably snaps back. The Chases fight quite a lot, usually over money. As a matter of fact, they seem to spend what little time they have together either fighting or silently watching their new giant, rear-projection-screen television. It's financed, too, like most things they "own." They drive two cars: one a three-year-old recreational vehicle, the type predominant in the suburbs these days; the other a large, very clean, high-mileage luxury hardtop, one of those cars that seem to blink "we are rich" while passing lesser cars and people. Both cars are financed, but Al Chase has determined that, yes, he can trade in the hardtop for one of those new sporty Gargantulas, the type that is supposed to improve your sex life. They will buy that car and receive an excellent deal in *anyone's* book. They will receive excellent financing rates, too. But that new Gargantula will spell the end of the Chases' solvency not too far down the road. They don't know that yet, though; they won't, until it's too late.

Buck and Carolyn Allgood pulled back onto the expressway, one of those perimeter highways that ring large cities and seem to sprout automobile dealerships on any unoccupied parcels of land. Carolyn was writing on a note pad.

"You know, I really liked that minivan and think it was just about the right list price. The seats were good, too, high enough for me, and practical with the kids. And I like the way that man didn't try to pressure us. His sales manager was nice, too."

Buck nodded his head, biting on the end of his pipe in some salute that seemed to signify yes more than the nod. "Yeah, you're right," he added in midpuff, "and I think the fifteen percent discount was good. *Consumer Reports* said those smaller vans have about an eighteen percent markup. Three percent profit would seem fair to me." He looked in the mirror twice, turned his head just to make sure the lane was clear, and headed slowly up the ramp to the next dealership on their list.

Buck and Carolyn Allgood are careful buyers. He is the comptroller of a small company located just twenty miles from the city. Carolyn teaches school, the second grade. They are thoughtful, nonemotional buyers who trade cars only when the repair bills come too quickly and irregularly on their present car. They are not in the least in love with automobiles. Their Saturday visits to four dealerships have been preceded by several weeks of careful study. The make and model van they hope to purchase is no casual choice. Their shopping method is good, too: find several specific vans, drive them, discuss price, and then go home for the night to think objectively over the individual deals. Neither of these people feels that any salesman or dealer can pull the wool over his or her eyes. Both are wrong.

The Estrums, the youngest of our couples, seem to possess qualities of both the Chases and the Allgoods. They are upwardly mobile, solvent, happy with each other, and in love with those physical possessions they honestly can afford to pay for. The Estrums usually trade cars every year, in the midst of new-car introduction time, or perhaps a month after that time. "I always wait until they've dropped their prices some," Phil tells his admiring neighbors as they inspect his latest purchase, "and, do you know what: our payments didn't go up a *nickel* the last time we traded!" The Estrums are proud of their car-trading ability and of the new car that reigns proudly in their driveway. "We never spend a dime on repairs, either. I tell you it pays to trade every year." This nice couple can afford to trade cars every year. In the course of their lifetime, however, they will throw away

$40 a month, year in and year out, because they buy when and as they do.

"IN THE BUCKET" AND "DIPPING": THE PROBLEM WITH THE CHASES

The guys were flipping pennies for Cokes, four of them standing around the Coke machine, one of the few machines that still dispensed bottled pop, not cans. Davies thought the old-fashioned machine conveyed a down-home image to customers. "Heads," called Killer as Ronnie Cheatum, the store's "business manager"—i.e., finance, insurance, warranty, and add-on salesman—tossed the coin into the air and snagged it.

"Tails." Cheatum grinned as he lifted his palm from the back of his hand. "You buy."

"You bastard," Killer said, dropping coins into the machine as the other guys grinned. "At least you owe me a favor now, Ronnie. Get that Chase deal bought. I got no gross, but I know you'll take care of that, if you can get the guy financed." Everyone chuckled, a respectful laugh of sorts. All the guys liked Ronnie—they called him "Magic." He was a miracle worker who could get just about anybody financed, and he would put half of them on "the chart," a nice high interest with lots of insurance added on. But Ronnie had a problem with the Chase deal; the guy was in the bucket. He had a trade-in worth $6000, but he owed $8000 on it. Sure, his credit was okay, but the guy was a "hand-to-mouth"—every cent he made each month was already obligated to payments, like that big rear-screen television—and he didn't have a cent of the $2000 "down stroke," the cash that would be needed to make up the difference between the $16,000 the finance company had agreed to finance on the new car and the $18,000 Chase would owe on the new car.

"Killer," Ronnie said, "I tell you what, if I get him dipped today, you buy me a drink tonight."

Killer put his hand on Ronnie's shoulder. "You get him dipped today, and I'll buy you *two* drinks, my friend."

The dip will be the proverbial straw to Al Chase. When he comes into the store to pick up that shiny new car, Killer will have him sign the normal papers and contract obligating him to forty-eight payments at $440. He will then put him in that car and ride him to the local easy-loan store down the street. Mr. Chase will sign papers there for an additional $2000, pick up the check, and immediately sign it over to the dealership. He has been dipped. He now owes $16,000 plus interest on one new contract for a car that will be worth $13,000 tomorrow. He also owes $2000 plus interest on the few pieces of household goods that weren't already mortgaged. With interest, Mr. Chase owes over $22,000 on that car. He is paying $65 per month for double life and double accident and health insurance. In four months when the sap realizes he can't handle those payments, he will come back into the dealership and ask them to buy his car back.

Sure, they'll buy it back—for $11,000. And since the payoff, the net amount owed on that car, will be nearly the same amount he financed, since the payoff on the dip is still the same amount, Mr. Chase won't be able to sell his car. Or rather, if he sells it, he'll have to pay the dealership the difference between its $11,000 value and the $16,000 payoff. He'll still have the $2000 loan, too.

But why would the payoff on both loans be almost the total amount financed if Chase has made four payments on each? Surprise: the first year or so payments don't reduce the loan much, they reduce the *interest*. This is especially true of dealership captive financing sources and small loan houses—the sources of Mr. Chase's loans—which compute the interest on any loan prepaid before its maturity date by using the "Rule of 78s." Though we'll go into the effect of the Rule of 78s in detail when we discuss how to shop for your financing, briefly, the rule benefits the lenders by assuming that all the interest contracted will be paid and loading the payback of that interest onto the front of the loan. Credit unions, many banks, and some dealerships use a fairer method, called the declining balance or actuarial method, to compute their paybacks.

So, let's look at Mr. Chase's plight. The total interest on the $16,000 loan for the 48 months is $5120. If he made ten payments on his car at $440 a month, he would *still* owe approximately $14,000 on his car. Isn't that nice?

Since financing institutions are going to rip your knickers anyway, don't fall for the dip routines, even though car salesmen have such wonderful ways to make them sound sensible. Listen to Killer as he sets up a nice old couple for the kill: "Mr. and Mrs. Carnes, as I told you, the payment on the car will be $225 a month. But what I didn't tell you is that you will pay $225 for only two years. The remaining two years, you'll pay only $175 per month."

Killer smiles, and the couple smiles, too. "Mr. DeMarco, that sounds just fine, but how do you do that?"

Killer smiles again. What a helpful guy. "Folks, what we are going to do is borrow you $1500 from one company for two years, and only finance $5000 through the other company. Then, if you get some extra money, you can pay off the small loan sooner. I like to do this for people because it means they owe less on their car. And it's no trouble, really. You'll just need two stamps each month, rather than one."

Are you laughing at these suckers? Are you saying to yourself, "Hell, I'm not in the bucket, no one will ever dip me?" Don't laugh until you check your payoff. If you are like the vast majority of people, you will probably find out you owe more on your car than the actual wholesale value of the car. Even if you owe a couple of hundred less, don't smile. Unless you owe at least five or six hundred less than your car's wholesale value, you, friend, are sitting in the bottom of that wet, slimy bucket.

Exactly how does a car store know how much to dip you? What determines the amount of money financed on any car, new or used? On a new car, it's simple. If you are reasonably strong, if you have a good credit record, virtually all financing institutions will loan you the invoice price of any new car. For instance, Al Chase did appear to be a good credit risk, since he had met all those payments on TV, furniture, and his other cars on time. The invoice price on the Expenso was $16,000, and the dealer's financing source agreed to loan that much. Mr. Chase was also trading his old car. That car had a real cash value of $6000. That $6000 is deducted from the $16,000 invoice price, leaving $10,000. But Mr. Chase owed $8000 on his old car. Add that figure to the $10,000, and you now have the total amount that needs to be financed, $18,000. The dip is the difference between the invoice cost, $16,000, and the $18,000.

On a used car, financial institutions will normally lend you no more than the "loan value" of the particular car you want to purchase. In the used-car section, we discuss loan value in detail. But for now, whether you plan to purchase a new or used vehicle, remember that financing a car at invoice or loan value is the way everyone gets in the bucket in the first place. As we discuss later, you will always want to finance less on any car—less than the financing source will lend you. If you do that, you really will be able to laugh at all the other suckers.

SINGING THE BLUES: THE TROUBLE WITH THE ALLGOODS

Just about the time that Killer delivered the Chases' car, Buck and Carolyn opened the door to their car and headed to the showroom. The Allgoods had made their decision: they would buy here, and they would buy today. Killer walked up to them. "Hi, folks, can I help you?"

"Yes, we'd like to see Mr. DeLong. We told him we'd be back today." My God, Killer thought. Some "be-backs" that actually came back.

"Ma'am, I'm sorry, Forrest is off this afternoon. But I'd be glad to help you. Of course should you buy a car, the credit would go to Forrest." The Allgoods looked at each other. Well, at least they'd asked for the guy; it wasn't their fault he took the day off. Sure, Mr. DeMarco could wait on them.

You must remember that the Allgoods are the careful shoppers. The previous night, they had figured out to the penny the cost of the van sitting just outside the showroom door. This morning, before driving to the dealership, they had called their bank and checked on the latest financing rates. They had also asked the loan officer to check in the bank's blue book again. "Now, you're sure that $2200 is the average wholesale on our car, aren't you?" Mr. Allgood had said.

"Yes, sir, and this is the latest book, too."

"Good. Then you can expect to see us later in the afternoon. We'll be putting $2000 down and only want to finance the van for twenty-four months." Allgood placed the receiver down, feeling just fine.

Their budget would be a little strained with the short payment period, but it would be worth it—think of the interest they would save.

Killer had the Allgoods in his office. He liked these people, and he talked at length to them about the careless types who bought so many cars. "Yes, let me tell you. It's refreshing to see people who are thoughtful buyers." Killer took the keys to their trade and excused himself. "Folks, I'll be back in just a few minutes."

He drove their car behind the used-car offices and yelled to Timothy Raxalt, the used-car manager. "Hey, Rax! Come take a look at this car, will you?"

The two of them looked over every inch of the car. Each part of it was clean, and the trunk was cleaner than most front seats. Sure, there were a lot of "nickels," small dents from rocks, but for a five-year-old car, this one was a cherry.

"Well, what do you think, Rax? It's a hell of a lot more than an average car." Killer was beginning to work the guy. Good salesmen also work the used-car department.

"Yeah. These things are real hot this month," Rax said. "I'll tell you what, see if you can trade for it for a quarter [$2500]. If you get close, call me, and maybe I can stretch it a little."

Killer looked shocked. "What do you mean a quarter? You couldn't buy a car like this at the sale for $2800 if you tried all day."

Rax walked around it again. Without saying a word, he walked inside and picked up the phone. Within a minute he was back outside. "Killer, if you can trade for the car at $2800, trade for it. Bobby says it's worth it." Bobby was a road hog, a wholesaler who goes from dealership to dealership, whose specialty was cars like this.

Mr. Allgood had his pad, filled with notations, lying out on the desk when Killer returned. "Mr. DeMarco, so that we won't waste your time or ours, let me review the figures that will be acceptable to my wife and me." Killer sat down and listened thoughtfully. "We have figured the cost of your new van at $9500. We think a three percent profit would be fair to both of us. And I know that my car is worth $2500. Can you sell us the van with those figures in mind?"

Killer's expression was solemn. "Mr. and Mrs. Allgood, I believe the manager would agree to a three percent profit on this van; that may not be a problem. But I'm sorry, your trade-in is nice for its age but it's not worth $2500. We have been trading in cars like it for around $2000."

"Only $2000!" Allgood was angry. "I know my car's worth more than that. The bank said at least $2200."

That's what Killer wanted to hear—what the guy really thought he would get for the car. "Mr. and Mrs. Allgood, let me explain the problem. Your car is five years old. Since you are familiar with financing, I'm sure you know that five-year-old cars cannot be financed at most institutions. Even if they can, twelve months would probably be the maximum time it could be financed. That makes it very hard for us to sell the car, since most folks don't pay cash when they buy." Allgood nodded. That made sense.

"Let me do this, Mr. Allgood. Let me take your car back up to the boys once more. Maybe they'll help us a little," Killer volunteered.

"Good, good, I appreciate your help," Allgood said. At least the guy seemed to be on their side.

Rax watched Killer driving up again. Hell, he needs more money, the used-car manager said to himself. And I'll be damned if I'll give him a cent.

"Hey, Rax, I am so close to a deal. Listen, if you'll give me two more, I'll do it. Man, we need this car, I've got someone that will buy it in a minute." Rax started to object. "Wait a minute! If you don't want to put the money in it, just let me take it around town a little. I know I can get $3000 for it. Rax, you can't put too much money in a car like this."

Killer was right, and the guy knew it. "Okay," Rax said. "But I want you to dehorse the guy. Send him home in your demo tonight. Tell him we need to have the car right now." Rax didn't need to tell Killer that. He never lets people ride when the deal is sweet; they might decide to shop some more.

The Allgoods were still sitting there, and both of them watched Killer as he entered the office. He had a smile on his face. "Folks, we did it! I told that guy we needed help, and he finally agreed. I've got you $2100 for the car!" The couple shifted in their seats, looked at each other, and then said yes.

The Allgoods paid their three percent profit. Plus they gave away their $3000 car for $2100. Killer's total gross on the deal was the three percent—$285 plus the $900 in gross his deal gained by underallowing on their trade.

What did these people do wrong? They believed in a book to determine the value of their car. The only way to really know the value of your trade is to shop it. Chapter 4, Know Your Present Car, tells you *how* to shop it.

THE NEWEST TOY: THE PROBLEM WITH THE ESTRUMS

Many people just love to buy a new car at intro time. They rush to the closest car store on show day and invariably pay hundreds of dollars more for the honor of being the first kid on the block to own the latest version of the ultimate car.

Take Mr. Estrum, for instance. Phil Estrum barely graduated from high school, but he was smart and ambitious. He entered the insurance field when he was twenty-five; he studied, listened, polished that smooth tongue of his, and became a successful salesman in five years. He's proud of his profession, too, not something, he felt, that many car salesmen would honestly say. Phil began trading cars every year his third year in the business, and the new one he bought this fall was his tenth.

And of course, Phil had dealt with Killer each of those previous years. After all, he knew from friends that Mr. DeMarco was the top salesman at the store, and Phil likes to deal with the top people in everything. The Estrums had an appointment with Killer one night, eight o'clock. Killer was coming in on his day off, something he made sure the Estrums knew. He even had a little present for Mrs. Estrum, one of those spray bottles of Chanel, which he planned to give to her before talking about the new car. Killer knows his psychology—he also knows that other salesmen are always very easy prey for car people, especially when they are "peacocks," the first-kid-on-the-block-with-the-new-toy type of folk. And the Chanel only cost Killer a buck, anyway—it pays to have friends in the "independent gift" business.

Their meeting evoked one of those reunions of long-lost brothers and sisters, Killer kissing Sue and grabbing Phil's hand in a double grasp. "Come on!" he yelled. "I've got the car over here." It was sitting by itself, away from the other cars and any other distractions that might lessen the moment of unveiling. The car was newly serviced, polished to mirror brightness. The engine was warm; Killer had personally let it stand at idle for five minutes. The interior lights were left on, too, spreading a nice friendly glow over the contours of velour and leather.

The Estrums drove off alone in that pretty thing. Killer told them to take a nice long cruise, even stop for a drink or two on the way back. He would have the papers together when they returned; he'd "even have all the figures filled in, that's okay, isn't it, Phil?"

Phil laughed, a repeat of last year's laugh, and the year before that. "Sure, Bob! Why don't we not argue this year!"

"Phil, don't be so rough on me this time! I nearly got fired last year when you finished with me!" Right. Instead of heading back into the dealership as they drove away, Killer quickly slipped into his demo and swung out toward the Dead End. After all, it was his day off. And it was going to be a day to celebrate, too.

Phil Estrum does negotiate each time he buys a car, and he got a good deal. He also received a fair price for his trade. Two things, however, were working against him, as always. Because he just must drive one of the first cars out each year, he's accepted the fact he'll pay some premium for that honor. Killer has reinforced that thought many times, too, reminding Phil that "these cars are impossible to get at intro time, you know that. And don't forget that you will be driving a current-year model for twelve months, not just the seven or eight months you'll have if you wait. Your car will be worth more when you trade." The logic is fragile at best, but it works every time on people who want to be convinced. If Phil is determined to trade cars each year, it doesn't matter *when* he trades; it does matter that he trade at the same time each year. Phil could buy the same car in January and normally save $1500 to $3000 over an intro deal. His trade wouldn't be worth less the next time around, either, *if* he traded in January again.

Phil's other problem is his own ego, his sure-fire conviction that "any man who is good at dickering over life insurance is good at dickering over cars." Phil has forgotten that he always oversells insurance to car salesmen *because* of that same logic: car salesmen are just so sure of themselves as negotiators that they think *they* know how to wheel and deal with their local insurance salesmen. Maybe Killer and Phil deserve each other, after all.

FACING OUR FOIBLES: THE PROBLEM WITH ALL CAR BUYERS

Maybe you've glimpsed yourself in some action of the Chases, All-goods, or Estrums. Maybe not. Different personalities, they make different mistakes. But they share one failing: they don't know their own weaknesses. They haven't explored all the important questions. We will.

How Naïve Are You, Really?

A customer's false pride is a salesman's best friend. The Chases thought they could afford a newer, sportier car, but failed to understand their financial situation. The Allgoods were *sure* they knew how to get the best price for their trade-in. Phil Estrum just had to have a new car at showtime and really believed *any* good salesman could handle car hacks. Car people just love customers like these folks; they feign respect for them and laugh with them, and then laugh *at* them when the commission slips are handed out. You will be richer if you know your limitations in the automobile arena.

Impulse Buyers: You're a Favorite

Several years ago, a carrier truck was unloading a bright red $30,000 sports car in front of the largest Gargantula dealership in town. A lady screeched to the curb in her equally elegant sedan. "I want it! I want it!" she screamed. The salesmen fought among themselves for five minutes, trying to decide who would "help" this lady. Finally a slightly bloodied young man made his way to her side and walked her into the office. The lady wanted a discount of $1000, and the salesman said no. She agreed on the spot to pay the full price. She then decided to trade in her car. It was appraised at a true value of $9000. The salesman offered her $7000, and she said no. The salesman left the office, supposedly to show the car to someone else, and the lady ran—*ran* after him. "I'll pay it!" she yelled.

It's a true story. The lady paid $4000 more than she needed to for that car because she had given away her bargaining power. Now we all know you are not going to be that dumb. You never let your enthusiasm show, never say things like, "It's just what we've been looking for." You don't do that, do you?

WHAT SHOULD YOU BUY?

Need vs. Want

The people came into the store a little after six in the afternoon. They had just finished their shift at one of those local doughnut shops that make their fare from scratch, and the salesman didn't have to look too hard to see the light touches of flour on their clothes, the tired eyes, and the strained smiles of folks who work hard for a living. Two jobs, really. They both worked at the doughnut shop from ten A.M. to six P.M., and then worked as security guards from midnight to four A.M. Killer was off that day, and one of the new guys just happened to be walking on the lot as they drove up. Their car was old and as tired as they were. And they were nervous. It was a fortunate thing that an inexperienced salesman was waiting on them—at least it was a fortunate thing for Davies Motors—because these two very poor-looking folks wanted to look at an expensive and sporty car. Any experienced salesman would have asked them a few qualifying questions and quickly left them to walk along. After all, how many doughnut people can buy a car that costs twice their yearly income?

Ted, the new boy, hadn't learned to be that sophisticated in his questions, though, and he happily showed them the deep silver and burgundy coupé that stretched low and sleek by the showroom. The Nelsons had never owned a new car. They had four children of their own and a couple of kids no one else would adopt because of their color. They had a nice, very small house back in the woods. "It's not very fancy, but we're proud of it," they told Ted, the hesitant and defensive nature of their words betraying great discomfort merely at standing on a lot filled with $30,000 cars.

Ted came into Don Burns's office quite casually. "Hey, Don, I've got a deal on these folks." For a new salesman he was a very thorough fellow, and he handed Don a neatly filled out buyer's order, showing a $3400 profit and an equally neat credit application outlining the financial life of the couple. It all looked just too nice: the only people who let themselves be taken this badly were always people with bad credit. Don walked back into the closing booth with Ted and struck up a nice, friendly conversation with the Nelsons. "Mr. Nelson! I wanted to personally thank you for coming into the dealership today. And I compliment you on your taste in cars—I drive one just like it. By the way, don't you folks work at the doughnut place just down from the courthouse?" Of course they did, Mr. Nelson happily volunteered. "And I noticed on your credit application that your last car was financed with the Beach Bank. Do you by any chance know Sid Oliver, the chief loan officer?" Yes, they knew him well, Mr. Nelson volunteered with enthusiasm. That was a good sign. People with bad credit don't act enthusiastic when they talk about their loans.

"Well, Mr. Nelson, since this is a pretty expensive car, though it's worth every penny, I think it will help your loan application if we indicate that both of you would like life *and* accident and health insurance on the full amount of the loan. And I think we'd better call this to our *own* financing source. They're much more used to handling cars like this." Why, of course they wanted the insurance. And Don could finance the car wherever the dealership wanted.

The next morning Don personally called the Nelsons' deal into the house financing institution. By three that afternoon the manager called back, hesitating just slightly as he spoke. "Don, I know I should turn this deal down. These people have never had a payment this large in their life. But they pay everything like clockwork. And the bank does anything they want. I guess we'll go with the deal. By the way, do you really want to put all that insurance on them?" Why, of course. A $3400 profit was nice on the deal, but the F and I (finance and insurance) profit would be nearly that large. "And besides," Don volunteered, "anyone that works that much might get sick. You need the protection, too." His source said yes to the insurance, too.

The Nelsons loved that car, caressed it daily, and drove it proudly to work for seven months. But in the first week of that month, Mr. Nelson had appendicitis and missed his paycheck for two weeks. The insurance Don had so happily sold them didn't cover that gap in their income, either, since the insurance didn't begin to pay until the fifteenth day of any illness. Mrs. Nelson came down with ulcers the next week and had to miss work for two weeks, too. Ted, the salesman, brought them both to Don's office shortly after that. "Don, we really appreciate all you did for us. But finances are a little tight right now, and we were wondering if you could buy our car back. We'll buy something else from you, of course, that's a little bit more reasonable."

Don shifted in his chair. How could he buy it back? They owed $6500 more than it was worth. He found some quick way to hedge. "Luxury cars have really dropped in value, you know," and excused himself.

Within two weeks they were back again. "Don, please help us. We just can't make the payments. Please do something."

Don Burns was not totally devoid of heart. Behind the dealership, close to the garbage dump, was a nine-year-old station wagon with a broken windshield. The car had been sitting on the lot for over three years, slowly dying. Besides the broken windshield, the block was cracked a little, and three of the tires were flat. The paint had turned one of those gray-brown colors that is the sign of many years of neglect, and dust had settled comfortably on the seats and dash. That car had been written down to nothing; each ninety days its economic worth lowered, until the moment the comptroller had walked into J. C.'s office and said, "Well, you've got one free now, J. C."

But the wagon did have some value to a small loan house. Those people will loan money on just about anything, so Don placed a call to the local office of a favorite dip house and quickly arranged a loan for $3000. He also called the loan manager at the Nelsons' bank and borrowed them another $2000 on their signature. Banks are very lenient with their regular customers and seldom check credit bureaus or automobile lending institutions if a person pays them regularly. He called another dip house and borrowed the Nelsons $1500 on their household goods. Most of those goods were already mortgaged, but dip houses don't really care about that, and they listed a couple of bicycles, the old furniture on the back of their porch, and their clothes as collateral.

Don and Ted also worked on that station wagon for the Nelsons— put tubes in the tires, replaced the windshield, and actually replaced the block. The car is still running now, and the Nelsons are maybe a little bit happier. Their payment is lower, too. That nice luxury coupé cost them $445 a month. They pay $250 on the nine-year-old wagon —the total of their three payments.

If trading cars is something you don't *have* to do, don't do it, unless you know you can always sell your car for more than you owe. If you can afford the nicest, smartest car on the block, by all means, buy it, if it gives you pleasure. Just make sure then that you're strong enough to pay for the damage up front, not down the road.

What Can You Really Afford?

If you are the type of person who just must have car payments to be happy, your most important decision before visiting showrooms is the amount of that payment. Can you afford a higher payment? In all honesty, would a lower payment, maybe just $30 or $40 lower, support your habit? Car people will tell you "inflation" means you have to pay more, an American tradition, or something like that. Sure. They'll also tell you cars are a good investment, an equally funny statement.

You need to budget your car payment just as you do your food purchases. For instance, do you blow your whole week's food money on Kobe beef just because it's on sale this week for $22 a pound? No, you control your spending on food, because you plan before you shop. Do that with your car purchase. If you follow the steps outlined in the rest of this book, you will have a lower payment than folks who don't buy cars carefully. And if you're really smart, you'll perhaps have a payment lower than your present one. Even though your method of buying is payments, you must consider every single part of your transaction as if you were paying cash.

New vs. Used

The Johnsons had come to the dealership planning to buy a $7000 used car. They had always purchased cars that were a few years old, usually nice, simple, mid-sized sedans. Normally they paid $1000 down, too. The Johnsons are in their sixties: sensible folks who seldom do rash or wasteful things. However, their rational thinking was disturbed that day because there was a sales contest in progress for the new-car guys, and Killer needed just one more new car to be on top again. This time the prize was a trip to Las Vegas.

Of course, Killer didn't get these folks by accident. Though he's primarily a new-car salesman, Killer considers just about anyone on the used-car lot a prospect for a new car. Good salesmen always believe to some degree what they say, however contorted the logic, and Mr. DeMarco felt very strongly that the Johnsons should be driving a new car. He met them at their car, parked just between the new-car storage lot and the used-car lot, and quietly started laying out his most effective new-car sales pitch.

"Mr. and Mrs. Johnson, we do have some mighty nice sedans up there on the used lot. But let me ask you something," he said, while walking slowly toward the new sedans. Killer knew the people would walk with him; they always did. After all, who wants to appear rude? "Would you consider buying a new car, one with a warranty, one that no one has abused and that will be much more economical to operate? Would you consider that, if you could drive the new car with no more debt than a used one and with a payment that's even lower than a used one?"

Both of the Johnsons had started to interrupt Killer the moment he mentioned a new car, but he just kept talking. By the time he'd presented his irresistible logic, they'd stopped walking and looked at each other. "Mr. DeMarco, just how are you going to do that?" Johnson had an amused smile on his face.

Killer laughed. "Now, Mr. Johnson, I can do it, but that wasn't the question. Would you consider a new car under those circumstances?"

"Well, if you're telling me I'll owe less on a new car than a used one, and that my payments will be less, I guess I'd be interested. I don't think you can do that, though." Mr. Johnson's tone was both skeptical and hopeful—who wouldn't rather drive a new car? He'd really wanted one all along.

Killer unlocked the driver's door of a baby-blue sedan—the Johnsons were driving a light-colored car, a good indication they didn't like dark ones—and sat down, reaching in one movement to the passenger door, pushing it open. "Mr. Johnson, sit down for a moment and let me show you a few things. Could you get the back door for the missus?"

The Johnsons without thinking got in the car—it's a nice psychological trick: Don't ask people to do things, *assume* they'll do them—and Killer pumped the pedal twice, starting the air-conditioning at the same time, talking quietly as he sat there. Other than air, the car was completely stripped. But it was very ritzy to the Johnsons.

Mrs. Johnson made the first really positive statement. "My, it smells so good. Why does it?" She was giving the first buying signal, and Killer looked at Mr. Johnson's shirt pocket—there were no cigarettes there.

"That's the smell of a car with no cigarette smoke, or spilled beer on the seats, Mrs. Johnson."

"Oh, really, I like that; you know we never let people smoke in our cars."

"That's a mighty good thing, ma'am—you just wouldn't believe the things our used-car people have to do to make some cars clean." Both the Johnsons nodded without knowing it. "Mr. Johnson, do you know a road around here that's really rutted and bumpy?" They were pulling out of the lot as Killer spoke. He hadn't asked them if they wanted to go for a ride; he'd just assumed they would.

"Well, there's that road that goes out to the mill—it's closed now, you know, but it surely is a bad one." Killer was conveniently already heading in that direction as Mr. Johnson opened the glove box, then ran his hand down the side of the seat.

Killer said, "You know, these new seats are orthopedically designed, and the rear seat has been angled differently this year—better support there, too. Mrs. Johnson, how does it feel?"

She laughed. "Well, I'll tell you one thing, it's more comfortable than *our* back seat!" This was another buying signal.

As Killer headed down the road, he suddenly steered the right wheels off the road, two wheels traveling on the pavement and two along a rutty embankment. The Johnsons were shocked for a second but then smiled. "How do you like *this* for a nice ride—I'll bet you couldn't do it in your car."

"That's really something. Do you do this with everyone?" Killer always does. It's not that a new car really rides better than an older one, however, but that normal people don't drive off the road too much. The Johnsons weren't thinking that, of course; they were just impressed with the ride.

The sedan stopped before the Johnsons knew it, and Killer walked around to the passenger side and opened the door. "Mr. Johnson, I thought *I'd* ride a little, if you don't mind." The man probably didn't want to drive the car, but what was he going to do, tell Killer to walk back around? Getting Johnson into the driver's seat was the most important thing Killer needed to accomplish to sell that car—even more than money. Very few of us can resist the exhilarating pleasure of driving a new car, especially when quietly thinking in the back of your head, This car can be mine for less money than a used one. It's not a logical statement, is it? Read on.

Killer normally doesn't take people to his office when he's planning to show them a lot of figures; he takes them to the small conference room with the window overlooking the lot. The Johnsons were sitting on both sides of him facing that window, the new powder-blue sedan conveniently visible through the glass. "Before we talk figures, Mr. and Mrs. Johnson, I want to ask you just one thing. Do you really like that car? Do you like it better than any used car you've ever owned?"

"Yes, we like it very much, but there's the money problem," Mr. Johnson said.

"Well, then, let me ask you this: Will you buy it if it makes financial sense to buy it?" The technique is called an "early close"—a "yes" means the car is sold, and the Johnsons said "yes."

Killer drew a vertical line down a sheet of paper, putting the list price of the new car, $12,800, in one column and the "asking price" of a three-year-old sedan in the other column. The asking price was a mythical figure—that three-year-old sedan was on the books at $8800, and the dealership would sell it for $6200. But Killer's asking price on paper was $10,800. He then deducted $4000 from both figures. "Let's just assume that your trade is worth this, folks; it's what cars like yours have been coming in for."

Killer paused for a minute for any reaction, but there was none. Good, he thought. We won't have to argue about their trade. It was a very safe way to find out what Mr. Johnson thought his car was worth. If he'd jumped, Killer would have said, "Now, Mr. Johnson, that's what the *average* car like yours has been bringing. I'm sure when we have it appraised, yours will be worth more."

"Now, just for comparison's sake, we're going to forget that you owe anything on your present car. I believe you said the payoff was $800, and since you are paying $1000 down, we don't really need to be concerned with your payoff." That sounded logical, Mr. Johnson thought.

"Now, we have a balance on the new car of $8800 and on the used car of $6800. Used cars, as you know, especially when they're three years old, can only be financed for two years. *And* the law says they *have* to be financed at a higher interest rate, too. If you were to finance $3800 on the used car for two years, your payments would be . . ." Killer factored out their payment on the highest interest rate, the one that was really never used, then picked up an insurance book and tabulated their monthly insurance premium ". . . about $375 a month." The Johnsons, stunned, said nothing.

Killer continued talking. "As you know, there really are no inexpensive used cars anymore. Now, on the new car, we have a balance of $8800. We usually finance new cars on forty-eight months, and of course, finance them at a lower rate. Let's see what your payment would be." This time Killer figured the payment on the "discount rate"—what the dealership actually paid for money. He seldom sold cars at that rate, but this time he was taking no chances. Killer conveniently neglected to add insurance to the payment. "There! Your payments on the new car will be only $225 per month."

"Yes," Mr. Johnson said quickly, "but we're paying two more years than on the used car."

"That's right. But look at this for a moment. The twenty-four payments on the old car would total $9000. The forty-eight payments on the new car would total about $10,800." Killer wrote both figures down, then pulled his used-car "blue book" from his pocket, flipping quickly to the middle of the book.

"Sure, you've paid $1800 more for the new car, but what is it going to be worth in four years?" His finger stopped on the line for sedans just like the new one outside the window, and he quickly wrote down the wholesale figure for "extra clean" models. It's a column in the blue book that is seldom used, since very few cars are extra clean. "Look here"—he pointed to the figure as he spoke—"a four-year-old one like this is going to be worth $6000. Sure, you will have paid $10,800 in payments, but when you finish paying, you have an asset worth $6000. So let's deduct that $6000 from the $10,800. If this book is right, and it's what all the banks use, you'll have a real investment in the new car of the difference, only $4800.

"Now, let's look at the used car. Twenty-four payments is $9000. Now, in four years, that car will be seven years old. Let's look at the value of a seven-year-old sedan." Killer flipped the page and held the book up for them to see—there was no category for seven-year-old cars in the book. "Mr. and Mrs. Johnson, a seven-year-old car is really worth nothing. You might get a few hundred for it, but just for the sake of discussion let's say that you get $1000 for it. That would still mean, if you deduct the $1000 from the $9000, that you have an investment in the used car of $8000. You would have $3200 more in it than the new one, and you would also have all those repair bills that older cars seem to incur."

The Johnsons took delivery on their new car in two days. The payment was just a little higher than the $225 figure that had been discussed, however. "Folks, I'm embarrassed to tell you this, but I completely forgot to figure your life and health insurance payment when we were talking. It's my fault, and I'll understand if you don't want to take the car." He wasn't worried, though—this little bit of reverse psychology always worked. The Johnsons argued not a whit at the $35.00-per-month addition to their payment. Killer gave Mrs. Johnson one of those bottles of Chanel, too. It was a nice exchange for the free trip to Vegas.

It would be easy for most of us to listen to the logic of Mr. DeMarco and drive off in a new car. And, quite honestly, the logic is correct. Killer didn't lie directly to the folks, either. But if he had sold them the three-year-old car for $6200 minus $3000, the actual value of their trade, if he'd quoted them a payment on a normal interest rate for thirty-six months—of course, you can finance three-year-old cars for thirty-six months, if you want to—the Johnsons could have bought that car for under $150 a month. If he'd quoted them payments on the same amount of money for twenty-four months, the Johnsons would have paid less than $175.

What happened? First the Johnsons fell prey to the logic of numbers that lie too easily. Then they accepted Killer's figures on that nice used car without once questioning their accuracy. And then they believed the wrong columns in the used-car book. The Johnsons' new car is not going to be worth $6000 in four years. They'll be lucky if it's worth $3500. But don't think these folks are unhappy with their new powder-blue sedan, because they are not. Would it be too trite to say it? Ignorance is bliss, especially for these folks.

Unless you plan, and I mean are sure, to keep a car for a long time, a new car is probably one of the worst investments in the world. As a matter of fact, ninety-nine out of a hundred will drop *forty percent* in value the day they're driven home. For instance, let's say you buy a $10,000 Minutula, the cheapest car in the Expenso line. That car cost the dealer $7800 minus the "dealer holdback," the two or three percent of the profit Expenso Manufacturing Company "holds back" from the dealer. The dealer conveniently considers this a *cost,* since he actually pays the manufacturer this money. However, every three months or so, the Expenso Manufacturing Company sends the dealer a check for all those two and three percents. Let's say our $10,000 Minutula had a holdback of $300. The $10,000 car now costs the dealer $7500. Included in that figure, however, is "freight," what the dealer actually was charged for shipping the car. On our Minutula, the freight is $300. Now our value is down to $7200. Now, take from that figure the $50 or so manufacturers charge dealers for "preparation"; the charge for gas, $10 to $29; the advertising allowance, $50 to $100. The remainder is the true cost of the car to the dealer: $7090, taking low figures.

But after a week, if you drive back into the lot to trade in your new Minutula, the dealer is not going to give you $7090 for it because he would then have to sell it for as much money as a new car, if he's going to make money. So, what will he give you? Try $6000 or less.

But there is some *good news* in all this. There are actually people out there who are dumb enough to trade in brand-new cars, and if you can find one of those cars, it can be a very cheap buy. A car that is one month or nine months old can be as good as new and cost you thousands less.

We've said little here about how to appraise a used car should you decide to buy one, but the chapter on shopping will tell you how.

American vs. Foreign

Foreign cars have for years now prevailed on our highways and in our consciousness as the best chariots available. While that hasn't changed completely, it has changed enough for you to consider an American car for a change, if your dollars mean a lot to you. I'm not waving a flag here, either: I have little sympathy for the general stupidity of American manufacturers, and I certainly don't think they're making the best products they can. But I do believe that the myth of foreign superiority is just that now.

American manufacturers have finally been to the mountain—Japan—and learned how to build cars better and more efficiently. And—important for you—they are building many cars in *partnership* with their Japanese counterparts, something akin to a bank hiring the men who rob it. Detroit's concern for quality, from the designers to the assembly-line workers, to the enormous number of robots, is real and ever present.

But there is still a little kink in the American manufacturers' plans to capitalize on the foreign myth. The consumer's positive *perception* of American quality hasn't grown at the same pace as quality has increased. That means an American version of a Toyota or any other American "twin" of a foreign-made vehicle—virtually the same quality—sells for less. That's great for the buyer.

There's another reason to consider American-made vehicles, too, for those of you who believe in just deserts. During all those years when foreign cars were the only answer for many sensible people, the import manufacturers and dealers were ripping off your pocketbook on a scale greater than anything Detroit would ever attempt. They saw no reason to ever—ever—give the customer a break. Most of the really popular foreign cars were sold for *more* than list price. A $15,000 car, for instance, would have a little item like this added to the "Dealer" sticker (more on that later):

Added Value Package $1500

Do you know what's included in that package? *Nothing.* The dealer has just decided that his car is worth an extra $1500.

The practice of inflating the already handsome asking price of certain cars has become so widespread that many consumer groups are bringing suits against individual dealers and distributors.

But for now, don't automatically feed that greedy monster. Bargain carefully, and get a car just about as good as any built anywhere, and get it for thousands less.

Trading Down

This doesn't mean buying a car from a dealer located on the wrong side of the tracks. "Trading down" is a term used when buyers either want to trade their newer car for an older one or want to trade their very expensive luxury car for a stripped one. It can also refer to buyers trading very big cars for very small ones. Regardless of what it refers to, the process is always expensive.

People who want to trade a newer car for an older one usually can't afford their current monthly payments. They're paying dearly for showroom fever. The same is true for people who want to trade down to a less luxurious car. Both of you face the same obstacles. First, because your newer or more luxurious car was so expensive when you bought it, your payoff on the car is usually very high. This hurts you, but more important, it hurts the dealer, since it usually requires a dealer to pay cash from *his* pocket to deal with you. For instance, let's say you want to trade in a car worth $15,000 and that you actually owe only $15,000. You want to buy a new car that cost the dealer $10,000. In order to trade with you, the dealer will have to stock a car in his used-car inventory worth $5000 *more* than his new car; that means $5000 in *cash flow* has disappeared until the used car is sold. Dealers don't like to lower their cash flow like that; they therefore give you much less for your trade to make the inconvenience worthwhile.

Second, your newer car always depreciates the most in the first two years; dealers know you are going to expect thousands more than it's worth, and therefore are going to be hard to trade with and much harder to make a nice profit on. You're not a popular customer in this instance, either.

And then there's the most obvious and depressing reason, the one that causes salespeople to wince when a customer mentions trading down. For most of you, it means you're in the bucket, you owe more than your car is worth. As we have discussed, you have a problem.

Before you decide to trade down, read carefully the section on *selling your own car.* Your best chance in a trade-down situation is just that.

Trading down generally means you made a mistake when you originally bought your vehicle, but you won't be making that mistake if you just keep on reading.

THINGS THAT IMPRESS AND TERRIFY SALESMEN: TRAITS YOU CAN CULTIVATE

Forrest DeLong was losing patience again. The lady he'd spent the past two hours walking around the lot was just too damned flighty: liking a small car and then a large car, in love one minute with four doors and then wanting to drive a coupé. And now she was trying to change her mind again, just as he laid the buyer's order in front of her. Bitch. This type of bird was even worse than the other one he'd had that morning—the one that didn't like anything, never once showed an ounce of enthusiasm for anything on the lot. At least *that* guy had bought a car from him. It wasn't much of a deal, less than $200, but, hell, Forrest didn't think the guy was even interested. And the guy had made it damn clear that he didn't really need to buy a car from here, anyway. "At least it was a sale"—Forrest kept repeating that.

It must have been the moon, for Killer was having trouble that day, too. His first customer, sent to him by a bird dog, was nice enough but just wouldn't fall for any line Killer threw out. "Now, Mr. DeMarco, let's just keep this sweet and simple. If you want to sell me a car, and I am really going to buy one in the next two days, let's get my car appraised before we go any further."

"I'm afraid I can't tell you what it's worth until we know what you're trading for," Killer said with an amused smile. But his ploy didn't work. The man raised his hand in a "stop" gesture and continued:

"That won't work with me, Mr. DeMarco. I've already shopped my car at three places and know pretty much what it's worth. And I'll be *real* interested in seeing how close your guys are."

Under protest, Killer drove the car to the used-car department and nearly dropped his teeth when the guys there said they'd already put a figure on the car the day before, a strong one.

And after agreeing to the trade figure (how could Killer argue?), the man then proceeded to bargain like *he knew what he was doing.* Killer was on the phone to Allen, his bird dog, as soon as the guy drove out. "Hey, Allen, do me a favor and send that type of guy to someone else, okay?"

Some people get good deals on cars by accident. Some get them by design. Forrest DeLong's lady customer did buy a car that day, a quick, easy deal, because she was the indecisive type. Killer's man got a good deal because he'd certainly done his groundwork. You need to know the things that really impress and terrify car sales-people.

Indecision

If you are the indecisive type, you may be a lucky car shopper and a very lucky car buyer. Salesmen are not interested in long-term rela-tionships; they need to sell you right then, when you're first on their lot. Always be indecisive, even after you sign a buyer's order, and you'll make those guys sweat every minute they work you.

Indecision to a salesman means you may not buy, or worse, may back out of the deal you've already agreed to. If you're lukewarm until the moment you drive out, your car will be polished to perfection, the service manager will probably have personally driven it, and vir-tually no hanky-panky will take place. They don't want to lose you.

Lack of Enthusiasm

You are standing by the one and only new car you think you love in the whole world. It's the perfect color, it has all the right options, including the digital ashtray, and your instinct is to kiss it right then and there. Don't. Don't even look at it, unless you frown. Tell your salesman how much better you like some other car down the road. Lack of enthusiasm is one of the easiest things you can do in a car negotiation. Put yourself in a salesman's place for a moment. There he is, spending his days talking to countless people who take up his time and then smile, shake hands, and say, "Thanks very much, we'll be back." These "be-backs" are the bane of car salesmen; they're perhaps the most frustrating aspect of the business. Why? Nine out of ten times a "be-back" won't ever be back: He'll end up buying a car from a dealership down the road. It's very important, then, for a salesman to sell you the first time you step foot on his lot. That's why virtually all dealerships these days have specific, tough procedures to make sure you don't leave the dealership too quickly. *All* training manuals for sales staffs make that point vehemently, and I quote from one: "Customers will not be *allowed* to leave without talking to management" (my emphasis). Most salesmen are also told that breaking this commandment will cost them their jobs.

So, how does a salesman feel if you're not enthusiastic, if you can't find one single car you really like, if you do nothing but talk about the *really* nice car you saw down the road, and the really nice price they gave you to boot? He is honestly going to be scared. He'll do anything to keep you there, including offering a price cut or two. One of the first quaint slogans every car salesman learns is "Be-backs won't make you any greenbacks." There is nothing stronger in your favor than that fear.

Knowledge

Car salesmen are so used to blind, deaf, and dumb customers that if you cannot be flustered by their tactics, cannot fall prey to their hypnotic spiels, you will save money and gain the respect of your salesman.

Nonromantic Attitudes

However hard you work, you know that you are going to lose money, so why should your eyelids flutter with the romance of it all? Let the salesman know you consider a car a necessary evil, not your paramour. Let him know you have better things to do with your time. Tell him straight out your romantic qualities concern your pocketbook only.

Patience

Patience is sort of a summary trait, isn't it? But even if you haven't done your homework, and even if you forgot to hide your enthusiasm and let "well, I really do like it" slip out of your mouth before you can catch the words and pull them back, patience will save you. There's one rule here: Never buy a car on the first visit—under any circumstance. Prices drop faster than you blink when you leave a dealership.

Impatience

How much you'll need this trait, too. The worst dealer sales tactics survive because of the niceness and timidity of customers. Dealers use your good manners against you. Nice people just don't get up and walk out, do they?

Yes, they do. As we say many times, if you feel pressure, if you become confused, if you are simply tired of the runaround, *get out of there.* And tell every single one of your friends about your experience, too.

3

Know Your Present Car

THE INSTRUCTIVE TALE OF JIM WRIGHT

Jim Wright was a young person back in the sixties, when new cars were cheap, fancy, three-tone paint jobs were the rage, and the automobile business was in its first "gold rush" era. Though dealerships back then never approached the profits of today's megadealers, they were still better than panning for those little nuggets and slivers tumbling through some mountain stream. It was a time when everyone was in love with cars, and few people had the vaguest idea of what mystical formulas constituted the buying and selling process. But, who cared? It was certainly a more informal business then. Cars didn't have "sticker prices," and one moment that pretty pink-and-cream Bel Aire Delux might have a list price of $2000, the next a price of $3000.

Financing was downright fun during those years, too. Virtually all stores were "recourse" operations: Each dealer would have to guarantee payments to lending institutions on every car sold. If you lived in a small town and happened to know someone who worked at a dealership, credit applications just didn't exist. A quick call, saying, "Yes, these folks are good people," carried much more weight than any impersonal sheet of paper that bared your soul to the world.

The fifties and sixties were also a time when used cars were the stepchildren of the automobile business. Dealerships would take your car in trade if you insisted, but would just as quickly whisk that old thing off to some used-car lot down on the other side of the tracks. Or they'd sell it to a "road hog," one of the supposedly untrustworthy vagabonds who seemed to travel the countryside, peddling junky cars to "white trash" and the like. No self-respecting person would sell one of those things, much less *buy* one. Most folks put used cars in the same category as that old piece of furniture sitting on the back porch, the chair with the heart-shaped back, carved rose crown, and scalloped legs: Who would want something like that when "modern" furniture was the rage, sleek things with toothpick legs and blue-knit backs your spouse had purchased. Proud chairs, these that sat in front of your new twenty-four-inch TV screen.

Jim Wright was eighteen then, the year his father gave him a car. It was a regulation black English Ford, one of the few small cars sold in America, and it was not the type of car any self-respecting young man would claim as his own. During a time when cars were flashy, longer than high, and trimmed in "real double-dipped chrome moldings," when "fluid drive" automatic transmissions and "Crown Royal Coupés" ruled the road, Jim Wright just didn't feel comfortable in something with turn signals that didn't blink, but rather two red little "wings" that unfolded themselves from the columns between the doors, pointing left or right like some dog's stunted leg stretched in the wind. Jim would keep that car far away from fire hydrants, for sure.

One day, not too long after meeting a young lady named Gloria, Jim decided to get himself a proper car for courting. He didn't really have the money for a new car, or at least that's what he thought, but Jim got in that English Ford and drove down to the Chevrolet dealership, the one with the fancy new showroom overlooking the intersection of every important road leading to town. The new Chevys were lined up in front of that showroom like a chorus line of pretty girls all dressed up in pink and cream, and there wasn't a black car in sight, much less anything square with little wings. And dancing at the very center of that line was just about the most beautiful thing Jim had ever seen: a candy-apple-red, two-door coupé trimmed completely in a thin stripe of white that seemed to follow each curve of metal and chrome. Now, here was the car for a young man.

Jim was surprised at how easily that car became his, too. The man who talked with him never once looked at or mentioned the Ford; he gave him $700 "in trade," whatever that meant, told Jim his payments would be $50 a month "with a balloon," and also talked him out of $400 in cash—Jim's only savings.

That candy-apple-red Chevrolet was the beginning of Jim Wright's education in the car business. About six weeks later, a young couple on Elm Street bought a Chevy just like it and just happened to mention to Jim's folks that "actually, $2800 isn't much money for something like this." Mr. Wright looked at them for a second before speaking. "You say $2800? Well, it can't really be the same car as my son's— he paid $3500 for it." Not too many days later, Jim saw his old English Ford sitting outside Black's Pharmacy on the square. Some sixteen-year-old kid had bought it—for $100. How could the Chevy place do that, sell a $700 car for $100? And then there was the "balloon." Jim's dad was the one who saw it on the contract. Twenty-four payments of $50. And one final payment of $1200.

He kept the car for exactly twenty-three months and then had to sell it to the dealership for a $600 loss. He had no choice. Neither he nor his dad could afford the balloon payment. The salesman who had waited on him originally did offer him a piece of advice when he took the Chevy back, however. Maybe the guy was feeling guilty, or maybe he knew Wright was getting married that month to Gloria. For whatever reason, the salesman sent Jim to a road hog. "He will sell you something used," the guy had said. "We don't keep any of that used stuff here." Jim bought an old car from one of the hogs. He also spent a good deal of time with the guy, listening to every bit of knowledge, every funny story which seemed to spout automatically from the guy's head.

In four years, on his twenty-fourth birthday, Wright bought his second new car. He didn't trade his old car this time, either, but sold it to a road hog. He and Gloria spent two days driving to different dealerships in neighboring towns, asking each salesman the cash price on "real stripped-down Bel Aires." Regardless of what any previous dealership had said, Jim told them, one and all, "Your price is too high." The Wrights finally bought a car from a dealership two towns away from theirs. They didn't finance at that store, either, but took one more day from work to arrange financing at their local bank. This time the new Chevy would remain theirs. Their love of cars would stay the same, too. Jim Wright had simply made a decision to understand the car-buying process. He used that knowledge on his second purchase. And he used it from then on, as we'll see.

All the previous sections of this book haven't exactly added to the romance and mystique of car buying. As a matter of fact, I would hope that they have made you a little wary. But the intention of everything presented so far is not to take away any joy from those of you who look forward to your regular dickerings. I have not meant to portray car people as the only salespeople who use ignorance and psychological warfare, either. Most of the same techniques and half-truths are used by anyone who sells, whether an insurance man or a furniture man.

It's really hard, however, for an insurance man to inflict great damage on your pocketbook, since most insurance companies' policies are reasonably competitive in their cost. Sure, some guy may sell you more insurance than you need, but for some reason our natural defense mechanisms protect us more from the overenthusiastic insurance man than from even a lukewarm car man. Have you ever turned to your spouse and said, "Honey, let's go driving this afternoon and visit a few insurance salesmen! I hear that there are some mighty ritzy new policies out this year"?

Every illustration in this book is designed to help you do one thing: come out a little better the next time your natural urge compels a trip to the local car store. You can do that, if you follow carefully the information in the remaining chapters. After all, if the Wrights, now a middle-aged couple with two grown kids, can learn the tricks of the car game, you can, too. Hell, Gloria Wright can't even balance her checkbook, and Jim wouldn't know how to play a good hand of poker if he were holding a Royal Flush. He'd probably fold. But the Wrights do know how to buy cars. Just last week, they took delivery on a really nice Gargantula fastback and they were just as excited about driving into the store to pick up that shiny beauty as anyone in the world. What's even nicer is the Wrights' feeling about that car right now. They haven't had a moment of buyer's remorse. Not a second of doubt has plagued them, and I daresay none will. These people love cars in the most irrational way, but they have learned to keep that emotion far away from any decision-making process. The Wrights by lucky trial and error have learned just what *you* need to know.

Like the Wrights you must know the answer to the four most important questions if you're going to be a smart car buyer: what does their car cost, what is your car worth in actual wholesale dollars, what is a fair profit, and what is the cheapest and most advantageous financing. One thing is sure, however: Your car will always be worth more than anyone will offer you. That value is not determined by any book, either. And the value should certainly not be determined by the dealer you are buying from. Instead, several things will determine the answer to this most important question—the value of your car: its overall condition, popularity, mileage, and the current local wholesale and retail market.

THE IMPORTANCE OF
A CLEAN, SOUND CAR

Love them though they may, the Wrights aren't exactly fastidious keepers of cars. Under the front seat, for instance, is a vintage collection of crumpled Big Mac containers, one coat hanger, a couple of pens, two unsmoked cigarettes, one sock, half of an AAA "Southeastern United States" road map, a toll receipt from the Florida turnpike, matches, and a very dirty dishrag used frequently to wipe condensation from the windshield. On the whole, a good imitation of the city dump. The dashboard is littered with the everyday needs of busy people, and the trunk contains enough forgotten merchandise to supply at least half of the Salvation Army's annual Christmas drive.

"Christ! Gloria, will you look at this!" Jim had been pulling all the nice things from under the seat, when something soft and mushy stuck in the springs caught the attention of his hand. It was a baked potato. "I *knew* we'd ordered four potatoes! Now how in God's name did it get under there?"

"Who knows; I guess the seat was hungry, or something." Gloria was standing by the back door counting the change, over $3 worth of nickels, quarters, and pennies. "You know, I think money multiplies back there. We should pull this seat out more often."

The Wrights' cleaning exercise was not a frequent ritual, but it was a regular one. Every few years at car trading time, they would spend a day working on every inch of the car—a task they aptly referred to as "sending the car to the beauty parlor." Jim would remove the ashtrays and soak them, then he would use a brush on every single piece of chrome, including the ones most people don't look at too often, such as the ones around each wheel opening. He would also use up nearly a can of lighter fluid in removing the hundreds of little road tar specks that dotted the entire bottom third of the car.

They also used a brush on the grill. The damn thing was always a final resting place for careless bugs, many of them "love bugs," those little creatures that come to a crushing end in one final moment of ecstasy. Every single inch of the car's interior was scrubbed with a brush, too, including the headliner. Then all four doors were left open for hours. All in all, the Wrights' cleaning job would rival any scrub nurse's efforts at the local hospital. But was it worth it? After all, can a clean car really be worth more than a dirty one?

A good impression never hurts. More important, however, a clean car implies something much more important: Car people, like most of us, assume that a person who really takes care of the way his car looks also takes care of it mechanically. That is a very dangerous assumption, but use it to your advantage. Whether you are planning to sell your car or trade it, spend hours polishing and scrubbing the thing, saying nice things to it as you work. Clean the doorjambs and under the hood. Make the trunk spotless. If you have a little tear in the back seat, fix it yourself, or throw a pair of very dirty socks on it. Either technique seems to work well. Are there minor mechanical things wrong with it? Does the air-conditioning not work because the fuse is blown? Replace the fuse. Used-car appraisers can be very lazy, and they may assume your compressor is bad, regardless of what you tell them. A fifty-cent fuse can cost you $300 at appraisal time.

Don't repaint your car if the paint is dull or scratched, though. Appraisers and potential customers always believe freshly painted used cars have been in fender-benders. That new paint job could cost you $500 or $1000. Do touch up nicks if you have a properly matching paint. Do buff dull paint with oxidizing compound and wax—those few hours can earn you money.

IS IT A POPULAR CAR?

Do you own one of those older, very underpowered, four-cylinder American cars or some other very unpopular model? If you do, prepare yourself for some hard realities. But should you own a nice medium-sized family car, minivan, or sport utility, you really own the most sought-after car in America. Most of us cannot afford new ones like that and will fight to buy yours. Whichever type car you own, its popularity will directly determine how much it's worth in hard cash.

But how do you know if your current wheels are hot or cold? The most direct way would be to drive into your nearest used-car lot. If the boys clap, you're in luck. If they throw rocks, drive out quickly and minimize the damage. Beyond that, unless you are involved in the day-to-day business of trading cars, you have few guidelines to help you. Generally, the sales of new cars like your older one are the most important determinant of popularity. For instance, when small new cars are selling briskly, small used cars are too. Generally, two-door cars and fastbacks are more popular than sedans or station wagons, bright-colored cars more popular than dark ones.

A little later in this chapter we'll be showing you how to determine the true wholesale value of your car. This answer—the value of your particular car—is obviously what's important. For if you receive the *maximum* dollar for your particular car, regardless of its popularity, you will be faring better than most folks. Car people say it a little more succinctly: "There's an ass for every seat." For now, just remember to be realistic when looking at your car. Sure, you love it and have all those great memories about the trip to Niagara Falls. But it's just a commodity to other people.

WHAT'S THE MILEAGE?

Killer remembers fondly those years way back when there were no cars with high mileage. When some nice customer would present Killer with a car showing sixty or seventy thousand miles, he would quickly drive it back to the service department, singing all the way, and yell out, "Hey, Harry! This damn thing has a broken clock!" Within the hour the car would reappear showing 12,841 miles.

Used-car sellers will tell you the introduction of federal mileage statements brought an end to the friendly old clock-fixer's occupation. But, unfortunately, that is *not* the case. More and more megadealers are "fixing clocks," and many of them are also constantly purchasing cars *that have been clocked* from auctions and individual wholesalers.

Electronic odometers unfortunately make it easier for the very large numbers of crooks out there to alter mileage. Changing one computer chip does it. As we discuss later, you can help stop the clocking and help catch the offenders by making sure that the correct mileage on your car is recorded on a mileage statement at trade-in time. Keep a copy of that statement. Should your trade-in's mileage be altered by a wholesaler or any subsequent owner, your copy of that statement can help trace the guilty party—as well as protect *you* from any future liability.

It's really unfortunate that mileage is such a determining factor in the value of a car. Since looking at the speedometer is such an easy thing to do, most people seem to place more importance in "average" miles or "below average" miles than in the things that really make a car valuable or worthless. Which car would you prefer, one with twelve thousand miles of city driving in a year or one with thirty thousand miles of highway driving in a year? In all likelihood the thirty-thousand-mile car will have a much newer transmission, since highway driving requires little or no shifting, and a better engine since one cold crank causes as much wear as several hundred highway miles. That same car will probably have better brakes, too, and less wear and tear on its suspension system.

If you own a high-mileage car, you will have to expect it to be worth less. Don't run the speedometer back, though; leave that to the people who don't mind courting jail. Just tell people you drove only on straight roads and never used your brakes.

COMPUTING YOUR CAR'S DOLLAR VALUE

Whether you plan to trade your present car or sell it outright, *you will lose money* unless you really understand the term "wholesale" as it applies to the automobile business.

Automobile dealerships, all of them, know that the average customer has no earthly idea what his or her car is worth in actual whole-sale dollars, and they constantly use that ignorance to the customer's disadvantage. If you were to have your car appraised by Killer, for example, invariably the following would take place: Killer would drive your car up to the used-car manager's office and work him for the highest appraisal possible. Let's say the manager placed a true whole-sale value of $5000 on your trade. Your car is at the moment a hot number, one that has quickly climbed in wholesale value during the past weeks. When Killer returns to his office, you casually pull out a copy of some wholesale book that indicates the value of your car is $4500 and inform Killer in no uncertain terms you'll not take a penny less. Of course, you've already lost—your big mouth has already made Killer $500 richer. He takes the book from your hand and starts reading interesting footnotes to that particular edition: "Deduct for no power windows; deduct for body damage; deduct for cloth interior; deduct for non-factory equipment." Within five minutes Killer has used your own sword to slice your throat a little deeper, and you accept $4100 for your car.

Even if you are too smart to pull out some book figure or to show your hand, Killer will start by offering you much less than the ap-praised value of your car. This little exercise in self-destruction is called "underallowing" the sucker, uh, make that customer. It is *con-tinually practiced by every single salesman in the business,* and you have absolutely *no* defense unless you read on carefully and learn how to shop your car before you sell or trade.

Your car's *wholesale* value (what the car is worth to someone who plans to resell it) will seldom change during any transaction. For in-stance, when a salesman tells you he will allow you more in trade, it does not mean the value of your car has changed; he is simply taking some of the profit built into the price of the car you are trying to buy and adding that to the wholesale value of your trade. As an example, let's say you are looking at a new car with a mark-up, gross profit of $2500. You're trading a used car with a true wholesale value of $2000. If the salesman says, "Sir, I'll allow you $2400 in trade," he has "over-allowed" you $400, cutting his profit from $2500 to $2100. But the wholesale value of your car has never changed.

The wholesale value is the lowest dollar amount your car will be worth in any reasonable time period (two weeks or a month, usually). It is the amount you know you can get for your car at any time. The *retail* value of your used car is the wholesale value *plus* the profit a person hopefully will pay to buy the car. Remember, the retail value is what you *hope* to receive for the car. And you will never, never receive that figure unless you sell your car yourself.

DETERMINING WHOLESALE VALUE

All successful used-car operations, whether they are affiliated with a new-car store or not, are continuously looking for fresh meat, new pieces of merchandise for their lots. All of these operations purchase used cars outright from wholesalers, brokers—and individuals. *The only way you will know the value of your present car* is to take advantage of this continuing need for fresh meat. Jim Wright knows just how.

By two o'clock in the afternoon, Jim and Gloria were riding down the road in their shiny car. "Damn!" Jim's eyes took in the polished hood and spotless interior. "Honey, I don't even think we should trade it! The car looks better than the day we bought it." It was running nearly as well, too. Jim had put the car in the shop just a few days ago for some minor repairs. A couple of badly worn hoses had been replaced, the EGR system checked, and a new distributor cap put in —just about all the repairs needed, $200 in all. The expense was worth it, though, because the Wrights planned to spend the afternoon trying to sell the car. Or, rather, that's what they wanted the car people to think.

The first lot they pulled into was one of the oldest used-car operations in the city. The lot also specialized in cars that were just a few years old, like their car. The moment the engine stopped, Gloria started acting nervous. After all, this was the first time she had been on one of Jim's "fishing" trips.

"Gloria, for God's sake, they're not going to shoot us or anything; now just calm down and I'll do all the talking," Jim said, as a young salesman walked to their car. He looked at the car more than the people in it. Jim liked that. He also seemed like a nice enough guy. That made Jim feel better, too, since he was just a tad nervous himself. Even after all the years of buying cars, Jim Wright never had become really comfortable when it came to talking about selling his car.

Jim told the guy what salesmen call the "basic truth"—just enough of the story to accomplish their objective. "Hello. My wife and I have been thinking about selling our car, and I was wondering if you guys might be interested." Why was he nervous, damn it? The guy looked at the car again for a few seconds and said, "Well, we do sometimes, but that's usually handled by another man. Can you hold on a minute?" The guy headed inside, and both of the Wrights breathed out slowly and deeply.

"Jim, is this really necessary? I mean, after all, we are going to trade it in on the new car."

Jim looked at her and shook his head. "Honey, we're going to trade it *only* if we can get as much money as one of these places will give us. And, anyway"—he looked at the two men heading toward them—"these people *may* end up with our car anyway. The dealership may sell it to them. That's okay with me, as long as we get real wholesale dollar for it. I just don't want the dealership to steal our car, and this is the only way to know its real value, shopping it. Now relax, okay?"

Jim nodded at the two guys. The other man was really nice, too. "Howdy!" The older man was talking now. "I understand you folks want to sell your car."

"Well, we're thinking about selling it if we get enough money. It is a pretty nice car," Jim said in a slightly defensive tone.

The Wrights walked around the lot as the older man took their car on a spin. He was back in a few minutes and yelled, "I'll be with you folks in just a minute," as he walked into the office. Good. He must be going in to figure what it's worth, Jim thought.

Within five minutes the man was back with them. "Folks, you do have a nice car, and I can tell it's really been taken care of. Would you sell it to me if I paid you $4500?" Jim thought the figure sounded pretty good but didn't say so. "Well, I'll be honest with you, we were thinking about more like $5000 for it."

The guy's face bundled up in a few wrinkles, and he just stood there for a minute. "Well, I'll tell you what, we might could stretch it to $4700, but that would really be the limit. Would you take $4700 for it?"

"We might. But, as I told your salesman, we are going to visit a couple of other places before deciding. Will you hold to that figure for the next few days?" The guy really didn't want to hear that—he needed the Wrights' car on his lot; as a matter of fact, he needed all the nice cars he could find. "Yessir, I will hold to that price for a few days, maybe a week. As long as the car is in the same condition, you know."

They were on the road to a second dealership quickly, and now Jim's mood was just fine. "See! I told you this was worth doing! The guy at the bank told me it probably wasn't worth much over $4200! And did you hear me get that man to go up on his price? Now, let's see what the other places say."

The next used-car operation they visited wasn't quite as cooperative as the first one; they weren't buying cars from individuals right then and really didn't even seem to appreciate the question. The third place put the same figure of $4700 on the car. The fourth stop, at the used-car operation of one of the largest new-car stores in town, yielded a figure of $4300. And Jim couldn't raise them, either. On the whole, the fishing trip was definitely a success, though. The Wrights had learned the most important thing in any car transaction: what their car was actually worth in wholesale dollars, resale value. *You* must know the same thing.

Prepare your car for "showing." Clean it up and clean it out. Then drive it to three different car lots around the city. If you have a kid who drives, you can even let the kid go by himself, if you like. Just don't give him your power of attorney. Whoever is driving should go straight to the used-car department of a new-car store and also to a big independent used-car lot or two. Tell the boys you want to sell your car, that you are not interested in trading. Be firm with them; let them know that you really might sell if they give you enough money. Tell them you are going to decide where to sell it within a few days. Tell them you want a *definite, firm* offer.

Gather at least three bids in this way, and use the highest. Probably for the first time in your life, you will really know what your car is worth in *wholesale* dollars. It's probably worth even more than this, too. Car people always make conservative offers.

The vast majority of customers who receive bad deals in the automobile business do so because they don't know this simple figure. It doesn't matter whether you plan to trade your car for a new one or a used one; it doesn't matter if you plan to sell your car outright. You will never know how good or bad an offer is unless you have done your homework.

During times when new cars are selling slowly, all used-car operations are desperately in need of cars owned by individuals because of the simple mathematics of the used-car business in general. Normally, every new-car sale generates at least three trade-ins, and these trade-ins keep used lots in business. But when new cars aren't selling, there is a genuine shortage of nice used cars. Normally used-car operations grow in profitability during new-car recessions, for even though people may shrink from paying new-car prices, they continue to buy used cars.

But what if your car isn't a thing of beauty but a heap that has the ambiance of an abandoned tenement? You still need to shop it. Any car that runs is worth something. You'll find many used-car operations that specialize in cars worth hundreds instead of thousands, too.

WHAT ABOUT "BOOK VALUE"?

Believing in "black books," "blue books," or "yellow books" is another sign you're a sucker. A man drives into the lot with his own copy tucked away in his pocket and tells the salesman, "Now, son, when you have my car appraised, just be sure those fellows know I've got my *own* copy," patting his pocket in pride. Don't worry: The salesman will tell his appraiser, "Hey, Mac. We've got another sucker with a Bible."

These books are simply the average prices for which particular cars have been selling at various used-car sales around the country. The books are important to financing institutions because most of them lend money on this "book" value, usually eighty percent of the book value of any particular car. The problem with books is simple: *They can't write checks.* Just because a car is selling for $2000 in March at a sale in Lakeland, Florida, does not mean the same car is worth

$2000 at some sale in Michigan. It doesn't mean the car is worth $2000 *retail,* much less wholesale, at your local neighborhood lot.

The books also vary tremendously. They don't usually reflect the current "hot" cars. Do not believe books. Shop your car as we've discussed. Many times that's what car people are doing when they supposedly drive your car around the block.

SHOULD YOU SELL YOUR CAR YOURSELF?

Killer would say no, and his arguments are persuasive—at least to the innocent. Take the Grays, the couple who were with Killer yesterday. The Grays had an average car, one that seemed nearly invisible on the highway. The paint was a dull beige, with very little chrome or other dressing to add sex appeal to the exterior, and the interior was stark and a little soiled. It was also a four-door. Until yesterday the Grays had liked the car; it had been a good statement of their lifestyle. Mr. Gray works in the accounting department of a large electronics company, and Mrs. Gray is a housewife. The extent of this couple's involvement in the business of buying and selling anything has been limited. Mrs. Gray was in charge of the cake sale at the church, but even that little foray into the business world was embarrassing to her. She would blush when someone asked her the price "of that nice chocolate layer cake" and apologize profusely as she took their money.

Mr. Gray's expertise is at about the same level. He loves to visit garage sales but has yet to bargain for anything, including the magnificent moose head now sitting in his garage. Mr. Gray didn't want the thing in the first place, but an enthusiastic neighbor—Robert DeMarco—had convinced him: "At this price, Albert, you can't afford *not* to buy it. These things are going up in value every year. And look at the points on it! Why, people will think you are the great white hunter! Now, do you want to take it with you, or can I drop it by the house later today?"

Gray was bagged as quickly as the moose, asking only one last question before loading the thing in his car. "Well, uh, Bob, it was the price that bothered me. Is that a fair price?" What do you think Killer said?

The Grays were sitting in the office with Mr. DeMarco. They had finally decided to trade in their car after at least two months of discussion and probably wouldn't be buying then, ". . . but, Bob, we know you. It's so important to know someone when you buy a car, don't you agree?" Killer just loves people like this. He is quite comfortable with their style of speaking. Virtually every sentence ended in a question of confirmation—Little Red Riding Hoods seeking comfort from granny wolf—and Killer happily told them just what they wanted to hear.

"Albert, you are more right than you know. You just wouldn't believe the horror stories in this business." Killer neglected to tell them most of the stories were about him. "Now, have you folks decided on any particular type of car this year?"

"Well, no, we just felt the time had come to trade. Bob, there are just so many new cars, many of them so sporty, what do you think would be a nice car for us?"

At that moment, Killer was sure he'd died and gone to heaven. "I'd like to show you a couple of cars. But before we do that, why don't I run your car up the hill and have it appraised? It'll just take a minute or two."

The Grays rustled in their chairs, and Albert started to speak, a slight stutter betraying his nervousness. After all, they didn't want to hurt Killer's feelings. "Uh, Bob, we think we're going to sell our car ourselves this time. We don't want to have to worry you with it. And you know, Mr. Merit, my supervisor at work, says it's actually much more profitable to sell one's trade-in directly. Is that right?"

Killer chuckled, a chuckle meant to imply, "Boy, have you people been misled," leaned forward, shook his head slightly, and spoke in a hushed tone of confidentiality: "I *wish* that were true, Albert . . ." He paused, as if the words were just too horrifying to be spoken in polite company. "But *that*—selling your own car—takes you out on very, very thin ice." The Grays probably had visions of pulling up "Jaws" while fishing through the ice with a light line, and they sat there, stunned and immobile, as Killer continued. "The used-car business is a very complicated business, filled with people—individuals, even—who like nothing better than finding nice folks like yourself. Just the other day I read about a couple who sold their car to some stranger, only to find that the man's check was worthless; and then there were the Smiths, customers of mine who sold their old car to friends. The car broke down within a couple of weeks, and since there was no warranty on the vehicle, the Smiths' friends decided to *sue* them. What makes that story even sadder is the fact that the Smiths received only $100 more than I would have given them in trade."

Killer stopped just long enough for these heart-wrenching words to sink in, then continued: "And, of course, there are the practical problems. What price would you ask for your car? What if the person who wants to buy it has a payoff on his old car—how would you handle that? And who is going to make all those trips to the Department of Vehicle Registration and prepare the affidavits?" His description of the paperwork sounded more like a visit to the Gestapo than the title office.

"And, Albert, do you really want to put your phone number in the paper and have perfect *strangers* calling your home any time of night or day?"

Each of Killer's words chilled the Grays to the core. My God, how could they have been so stupid as to suggest this in the first place? Albert spoke with the conviction of the most rabid born-again type, fire and brimstone crackling in every word. "Bob, of course you are right. It was just a thought, anyway. And I'm sure you'll get us the maximum dollar in trade, won't you?" Uh-huh.

It would take one of the newest PCs to store all the lies and dealer-encouraged myths about selling your own car. Dealerships want you to think the process is difficult or dangerous to your health, the real cause of warts, the heartbreak of psoriasis, and stuttering, all wrapped into one. But why shouldn't they want that? The used-car business is more profitable than the new-car business. Many dealerships will sell you a new car at cost or below simply to own your trade. So, why give your car away? That's exactly what you do if you let them have your trade-in at wholesale: give them a car worth $2000 wholesale, and they will give you $2000—at most. Wouldn't it be nicer to make a profit, perhaps get $2800 for your car? And still buy their car at close to cost?

That's exactly what Merit, Albert Gray's supervisor, did—or nearly did. The man had done his homework. He had shopped his car at several lots, and one of them had been just a little higher than the others, offering $4000 in cash. It wasn't a nice car, either, but simply an adequate set of older wheels, a good second car for some family.

After leaving the last lot, Merit had stopped into a local market in his neighborhood and picked up a copy of the community "swap and shop" paper, along with copies of every other newspaper on the rack. Merit wasn't ready to place an ad just yet; he simply wanted to see the prices other people were asking for a four-year-old Chevy like his.

Arriving home, Merit grabbed his oldest son and headed to his low, comfortable front porch with all the papers tucked under his right arm. Within twenty minutes, the two of them had circled every similar Chevy ad in each of the papers and written each asking price on a separate piece of paper. "Hey, Dad, here's a dealer that's asking $3200 for one."

Merit looked at the ad. "Well, I'd say those people have the right idea for sure. They certainly aren't shy when it comes to asking for the moon." Most of the individual ads had asking prices below that figure, but the average price for all ten was right at $5000. "Okay, now; if most people are asking $5000, we'll just ask $5200 and write a better ad than theirs."

Merit just wanted to be in the ballpark—not too high or low, but in good dickering range. Since he knew the car could be sold to a used-car operation for $4000, he would have $1200 to play with. Even if he sold the car for $4400, he would be making money. Merit put that sheet of paper away and put the business of selling out of his mind for the day. Two answers were enough for the moment: He knew what his car was worth wholesale, and he knew the asking price he would build into his ad.

On Friday Merit placed several phone calls. The first one was to his bank. "Okay, you say the payoff on my car is $879.23?"

"Yessir, and that payoff is good for ten days. After that time it will go up slightly."

"Well, thanks very much. Now let me ask you something. I'm planning to sell the car to an individual. Just what do I have to do to get you people to release the title on the car?"

"Just come to the bank with that individual. Please have him bring a certified check made out to you for the total sales price. We'll cash that, pay off the car, and give you the difference and the title while you're here."

That sounded simple enough. "But what about the sales tax? Don't we have to pay sales tax on this?"

"You don't have to worry about that. The buyer pays the tax, not the seller. The person buying your car simply takes your bill of sale to the tag office. He pays the tax when he has the car registered in his name."

"Good. Well, thank you again. I hope I'll be down there to see you right shortly."

Merit then placed the same ad in three newspapers. "Chevy Cavalier. Low mileage. Clean, one-owner car. Serviced regularly. $5200, no trade. Call 9–5 weekdays, 10–6 weekends. Individual." The ad was simple, but it contained all the important information, including the fact that an individual was selling the car, not a dealer. Many people are convinced that cars can be bought less expensively from individuals, and Merit knew that.

Merit's first phone call came as he walked in the door Saturday afternoon. "Hello, I was calling about your ad in the paper—the Chevrolet."

"Yessir, what can I tell you about it?"

"Well, sir, my name is Robert DeMarco. I'm a salesman, a new-car salesman here in town. But I have a customer that's been looking for a car like the one you described in the paper."

"I'm sorry, I'm not interested in trading my car, thank you for calling, anyway."

"Sir, before you hang up, can I ask you what you'll be driving when you sell your car?"

"Well, I will be buying a new car."

"If I could give you more than $5200 in trade on a new car, would you consider talking to me? I really do have someone looking for a car like yours, and perhaps we could kill two birds with one stone, as they say." Smart car salesmen are always doing this. They simply sit down during slow times and call numbers listed in individual classified ads. And they invariably have some customer just panting to own your car. It's a very effective technique.

"I'm sorry, what did you say your name is?"

"DeMarco, Robert DeMarco."

"Well, Mr. DeMarco, I appreciate your call, but I'm really not interested right now. I will be happy to write your name down, though. Thanks very much for calling."

Scratch the first phone call. Hell, that call had really been more productive for Killer. He at least found out that the guy was going to buy a new car. Killer will call Merit back in a few days.

The next three phone calls were inconclusive. Each of the people asked guarded questions about the car and invariably asked, "Is that a firm price, or will you come down some?" Merit told them all he was a reasonable man. But none of the three made any attempt to set an appointment to look at the car. Maybe this car-selling idea wasn't so good an idea after all.

The fifth call—it didn't come until the next evening—sounded a little more promising. It was a lady. She asked a few questions, then made an appointment to see the car that night. She never showed up.

Finally, on the third day, a man actually appeared at the Merit residence. He was nice enough and didn't act nearly as nervous as Merit. After all, this was the first time Merit had ever done anything like this. Merit's hand would have passed for a cold fish as he grabbed the guy's palm. There was another man with him, too, or rather an eighteen- or nineteen-year-old kid, who walked around the car as Merit talked. The kid looked under the hood, opened the driver's door, and peered in without sitting.

"Why don't we take a drive?" Merit volunteered. He climbed in the back seat and sat there quietly as the older man pulled out of the driveway. Merit didn't even recognize the buying signals the two of them were giving out.

"Hey, Dad, it's got a stereo radio." His father didn't seem to hear that. He was busy spreading himself out in the front seat, right arm resting comfortably on the seat back, left hand lightly holding the wheel. The man had a slight smile on his face.

As the car pulled back in the drive, Merit searched for some appropriate words. Hell, he didn't have the slightest idea what should be done next. "Well, Mr. Johnson, how do you like the way she drives?"

"I like it. It really seems like a pretty nice car. But I just don't know about that price. We looked at another car yesterday that was several hundred dollars less than yours."

Merit didn't have the presence of mind at the moment to ask the man if the car was the same year and model, much less if the car was as nice as his. But the guy had given him a clue. "Well, Mr. Johnson, I honestly don't want to sell the car for much less than $5200." Merit made a good statement without knowing it. He didn't say he *wouldn't* take much less; he simply said he didn't want to. "But you said the other car you looked at was several hundred dollars less. Are you saying you would pay $4900 for this car?"

Johnson sat there behind the wheel for a few seconds and said, "Well, I might. But I would like to show it to my wife before saying yes. Would it be okay if my son and I drove it over to the house?"

Merit didn't like the sound of that. Regardless of how nice the people looked, he really didn't like the idea of strangers driving away in his $4000 piece of merchandise. "Mr. Johnson, I would be happy to do that, but my insurance company just won't let me. Why don't I follow the two of you home; I'll be glad to do that."

"That'll be fine." Johnson's reaction made him much more comfortable. Merit is a pretty good reader of people, and an indignant show of impugned honor would not have impressed him in this instance.

Mrs. Johnson liked the car and liked the price, too. They decided to buy it. "Okay, I guess we'll take it. Now what do we do?"

Merit had trouble thinking for a moment; all that he could visualize was the $900 he was earning for perhaps twelve hours' work. Even after the cost of the ads and the gas it took to shop his car, he'd be netting over $800. "Well, Mr. Johnson, if you could give me a deposit tonight, I won't show the car to anyone else. And then tomorrow, if it's convenient, we can go to my bank to get the title. If possible, you do need to be with me, since those people will notarize the title for us."

"And how much money will I owe you, $4900 even?"

"Yes, you'll have to pay the tax yourself. And you'll need to bring a certified check with you. My bank says that is necessary."

"Well, I'm planning to finance the car. Maybe I'd better get the serial number tonight, and I'll call the credit union in the morning. I think they will make the check out to me, but if there are any problems, we can talk on the phone during the day."

Merit said his good-byes and headed home. He was excited, but also concerned about one little problem: What was he going to drive until he bought a new car? Merit was on the phone to Mr. Johnson the moment he entered the house and breathed a little easier when Johnson agreed to pick up the car in two days, not tomorrow. If worse came to worse, he would hitch a ride to work with Albert Gray for a few days after that. After all, Gray did have a pretty nice new car.

Merit was at the bank when Johnson arrived. He had typed up a simple bill of sale at the office and was prepared to hand it to Johnson on the spot.

Merit's venture into the car-selling business raises and answers several important questions about selling a car. Since you'd like to do as well, let's review.

What Should You Sell Your Used Car For?

Remember, you are now a horse-trader. You have determined the wholesale value. If you can objectively say you have an appealing and popular car, don't be afraid to put an asking price of $1500 over the wholesale figure. The newspaper can give you a few guidelines for asking price: Look in the classified ads. What are other people pricing similar cars for? What are the dealerships' asking prices? If everyone in your town is advertising four-year-old Hirohito Fastbacks at $5500, you would do well not to price yours at $8500.

Regardless of the asking price, remember that you can always lower your price but never raise it. Dealerships are famous for putting comically high prices on some used cars, knowing that smart people will negotiate them down and dumb people will make them rich. Why not use the same technique?

What's the Best Way to Hawk a Hirohito?

Once you have determined your car's wholesale value and decided on an asking price, call up your local community newspaper and your bigger city newspaper. Find one of those "trading" rags that will run your ad for free if the car doesn't sell. Place an ad in each of these papers.

Don't try to be Shakespeare when you write the ad, either. Start with the year and model. Use few words, but use words with real meaning to potential buyers. "One owner, low mileage, excellent gas mileage, very clean, service record available"—these words carry much more weight than "breathtaking and magnificent." Put your price in there, too, and then get a beer from the fridge and wait on the phone calls. You will get them. That is, if you remember to put in the best times to reach you.

Are You Afraid of the Dickering?

Don't be—it's easy and fun. Let's say that several people have called you and want to see the car. You've invited them at different times to come by your house. The first guy wants to trade: Send him on his way and tell the fellow to sell his car and then come back. The second person wants to drive your car alone. Tell him your insurance is no good unless you are in the car. Ride with him.

This guy has good taste; he likes your car and offers you a $500 profit over the wholesale value. Good grief! Don't take his offer, though. Come on, P. T., negotiate. Tell him you need another $500, or even tell him you've been offered another $500 by someone who is coming back in the morning. (Isn't it nice doing this to other people for a change?) He will come up, believe it or not.

In all likelihood, you'll end up splitting the difference with him. But that's okay. Unless you are really enjoying the salesman bit, split the difference with him and be happy with that $750 *profit*. Remember, if you had traded your car, the dealer would have given you wholesale; *he* would make that $750.

Your Payoff and His Financing

If you are selling your car, you will be responsible for calling your financing institution and arranging a payoff once you have a buyer for the car. But call your financing institution for a payoff amount *before* you place your ad. Compare it to your selling price. If the payoff is higher than your final offer from an individual, you are in the bucket. Sorry. Read pages 148–49, "If You Are 'in the Bucket' or 'Upside Down.' "

You will also be responsible for providing the new buyer with a title and a few other papers. None of these procedures is complicated. They do vary from state to state. Call your state Department of Motor Vehicle Registration or your local tag office for specifics.

The buyer of your car must be responsible for his own financing. You don't really care where or how he gets the money, unless the fellow looks like the type who recently made an unauthorized withdrawal from a bank. You are simply interested in cash or a certified check. Even if you know the person well, don't accept a personal check. You should provide the buyer with a bill of sale, too. This does not normally have to be a formal document. If you're neat, a simple handwritten statement like this will do: "Sold to ＿＿ for $＿＿, a 19＿＿ (make and model), serial number ＿＿. Signed and Dated: ＿＿." If your calligraphy skills leave something to be desired, use a typewriter, computer, or buy a pad of standard bills of sale at your local business supply store.

4

Dollars and Sense:
Know Your Financing
(*Even If You Pay Cash*)

It had been an easy deal for Buzz. The Crenshaws had dickered a little on the trading difference, but not much. They had hesitated when Buzz had asked for their driver's licenses and social security numbers. And they had also wanted to know how much their payments would be on the balance. At this particular store, J. C.'s store, customers are seldom worked for finance money until they come to pick up their car. J. C. likes it that way: The customers are excited, jumping in and out of their fantasy machine, chomping at the bit to drive away. At a time like that, who wants to sit around and argue payments? Buzz knew that policy and had done it by the book. "Mr. and Mrs. Crenshaw," he'd said, "your payment is going to be in the $175 range, give or take a few dollars. How does that sound to you?"

Well, it had sounded just fine. The folks had left the dealership very satisfied customers, and Buzz had waved them away, walking straight from their car door to the finance office. Ronnie Cheatum was there as usual, busy as usual, calling in one of Killer's deals. Ronnie, of course, already knew the credit history of the couple and could guess how much money the finance company would approve on them—the dealership pulled credit reports on all their customers the minute they were corraled in a sales office. All they needed was a driver's license and a social security number.

Cheatum nodded quickly to Buzz and continued talking. "Yeah, they're in Killer's office, and the deal's so sweet we've got to roll them now, if that's okay, so what will you give me on them?"

He nodded again, said a quick thanks, and hung up, turning to Buzz.

"Hey, Buzz, what type of crap have you got this time?" Buzz didn't laugh. For the past week, every single one of his deals had been either conditioned or rejected. One of his customers had been a "skip" from another town, someone who thinks you can run from bad credit. Another guy was rejected for "overbuy"—he wanted to buy a car that would have given him a $300 payment, and the guy's income as a student waiter was barely $300 a month. His *last* guy could probably have bought the car, but he had spooked the source, applied for loans on four other cars that week. But the Crenshaws were different.

"Screw you, Ronnie. These people are open with us now—they only owe eight payments on a car *I* sold them three years ago. And they showed me their payment book. They've paid ahead ten payments."

"Well, damn, that's nice of them," Ronnie injected. "If they've only got eight payments left, we've damn well got our interest. Hell, yeah, let them trade again! Here, let me look at that deal." Ronnie looked at the buyer's order and quickly figured their equity. "You say the car is appraised at $4000 and they owe $1400? Okay, it looks like they're into the car for at least $2600. I'll call on them right now, so just sit here." It looked like a safe deal for the store since the new car cost around $10,500. As Cheatum said, the people had about $2600 in equity in their trade. The financing source would be loaning only about $7,900.

"Ronnie, I know the deal's okay. Now, just make me some money. I've got a hell of a deal on the front, $800, and I want to make as much on the back." Buzz didn't need to worry about that. Ronnie Cheatum was the best—"Magic," as the guys called him.

At four the next afternoon, Buzz brought the Crenshaws in. They had already seen their new car, loved it just as much as the day before, and had walked quickly to Cheatum's office, the bounce in their walk betraying both excitement and impatience. They were a nice couple, a bright couple who even knew their financing would be more at the store than at a bank or a credit union. Of course, they had justified that choice to themselves. "Well, we know we pay a little more here, but it's convenient to finance like this. Plus you people agreed to the payment we wanted anyway." Ronnie flinched at that. Buzz had quoted them a payment on the discount rate—what the store paid for money.

Ronnie nodded agreement. "Well, you know, our rates are regulated just like the banks. You really don't pay that much more here. And, as you said, a payment is a payment. Now, did Buzz tell you about the new services we have been offering since you financed your last car with us?"

"Oh, you mean the life insurance? Oh, yes, I want that. I mean, it's only a couple of dollars a month, right?"

Ronnie looked at them with his most effective expression and said, "Yes, of course, you want life insurance on you, Mr. Crenshaw. But we have two other services you might want to consider. We can put life insurance on your wife, first. When you think about it, insurance on her may be more important than insurance on you. For instance, Mrs. Crenshaw, you work, don't you? And I believe you folks also have a couple of teenage kids? God forbid, if something should happen to you"—he looked at Mrs. Crenshaw—"your family will need all the money they can get, like the rest of us." Both nodded agreement.

"Now, Mr. Crenshaw, I would also like to suggest that you let us place accident and health insurance on the loan. This will only cover you, but if, for any reason, you should become ill or disabled, this protection will automatically make each and every car payment for you." Ronnie was glossing over the details of the actual protection, but that didn't matter; he had touched the high points. Both of them nodded again.

"But, Mr. Cheatum, how much is all of this going to cost?" It was the question Ronnie was waiting for. Ronnie turned on his computer and began to punch in all the necessary information. The first factor was the interest rate. Buzz had quoted these people on the lowest interest rate, but that would be corrected right now—he entered the highest rate. Then he entered the total number of months, cash selling price, trade allowance, and payoff on their current car, and looked at the couple. "You're only going to be talking about $229 a month." They both looked a little pale, but Ronnie just kept talking. "Now, I know that sounds like a pretty high jump from $200, but think about this for a minute: If something should happen to either of you, if you, Mr. Crenshaw, should become ill, that $29 a month will pay for itself many times over. Don't you really think it's worth it? Is it honestly fair *not* to protect yourself?"

Mr. Crenshaw adjusted himself in the chair and thought for a minute. "Well, you know, I want the protection. But we honestly just did not want to spend over $200 a month, or $220 max, for a car. I think we'd better pass on that other coverage. We'll just take life insurance on me."

Damn. With just the life insurance, there wasn't a way in hell Cheatum could raise the interest rate—the higher payment would be too obvious. "Mr. Crenshaw, since you are telling me you would like the coverage but want to keep your payment down, let me see if I can do something to help you." Ronnie punched a few more buttons on the machine, lowering the interest one half of one percent. The payment was lowered to $226. But he didn't tell that to the people; he simply sat there randomly pushing buttons. After a few minutes, he leaned back in the chair and started thinking out loud. "Well, I know you want the coverage. And I know you are concerned about the payments. But I just don't know how to get them any lower. I'll tell you what we could do, though. If you could pay about $200 in cash, I think that would get your payment down to about $226 a month. How does that sound to you?"

When he said that, Buzz quickly looked at the couple. Would they really fall for *that?* Ronnie was telling these people he would lower their payments $3 a month for thirty-six months—a total of $108— and in the same breath telling them to pay him $200 for the favor.

Mrs. Crenshaw spoke first. "Well, honey, I think we can afford the $226. And I think the insurance is a good idea, all of it."

Cheatum had to fight from smiling. But his job wasn't over yet. "And folks, did Buzz here tell you about our special warranty package and alarm package and our sale on the 'total protection' package— rustproofing, undercoating *and* fabric conditioning? Rather than you paying cash, as a service we can let you finance those, too."

"Uh, won't that raise the payments again a lot?"

"Just dollars a day. But you know, your insurance rates will drop dramatically with the alarm system—and you know, I'm sure, what rust does to the value of a car. Drops it *thousands,* sometimes." Ronnie laughed. "You may not believe it, but some people just ignore these dangers."

"What will they cost?"

"Oh, all three will run about $3.25 per day, *but* I'm going to keep your payment *the same.*"

"How are you going to do that?"

Cheatum smiled. "The finance company allows us to go an extra year for those good folks who protect their car with these packages —and *that* alone should tell you it's worth it." Without another word, Cheatum pushed the "print" button on his keyboard and discussed everything but payments as the contract quickly jumped from the printer. Within five minutes the papers were signed, and Buzz led them away.

It had been a nice half-hour's work. By raising the interest rate from the lowest to the highest, Ronnie had increased the financing department's profit on this small loan by $285 to $1450. The double life insurance premium netted him $241. The accident and health premium on Mr. Crenshaw netted him $275. The "back end" profit just on these three items was $1966.

But the biggest smile came to Ronnie Cheatum's face when he looked at the profit on the three "services" now sold by all of the dealerships owned by Gary Oliver Davies. Regardless of the price of the car—a cheapo or the most expensive car on the lot—these profits always stayed the same. Ronnie typed all the profits on his computer spreadsheet like this:

CRENSHAW: #1921	
Finance and Insurance Profit:	$1996
Protection Package	1000
Warranty	1000
Alarm Package	750
TOTAL FINANCE PROFIT:	$4716

Cheatum smiled again. Not bad at all for a cheapo car. He placed his computer on standby and walked quickly to the break room. Ronnie Cheatum had twenty minutes before it would be time to help another customer.

WHY SHOP YOUR MONEY BEFORE YOU SHOP YOUR CAR?

Whether it's blind luck or astute thinking, many people do buy cars at very reasonable prices. Yet many of those same people just as quickly make very bad decisions on financing that car. Countless others include financing negotiations in their actual negotiations for the purchase of a car and quickly become lost in the murky valley of annual percentage rates versus difference in trade, allowance versus months financed, or life insurance versus payoff. If you are going to be a smart buyer, it's important to realize the two can't be mixed. First, negotiate the best possible deal on the car. And then apply the best method of financing.

So why read this section first? Even if you plan to pay cash, you have to know how much money you need to buy a car and to know the tactics dealerships will use to try to switch you to financing. Most important, if you plan to finance, *you must know how much cash you can afford to buy and for how long before you know how much car you can buy*. You must know the best source and method of financing *before* you shop. To buy a car properly, you must first negotiate the sale, then apply the best method of financing. How can you apply what you don't know?

This section will help you determine the best financing source for your particular needs. It will provide you with a method of shopping your financing that will enable you to determine how much you really can afford each month. Once you have determined what you can afford, this section will tell you how to determine the total "Available Cash" you will have to purchase a car. This section will recommend the number of months any car should be financed and give you the pros and cons of life and accident and health insurance. It will provide a little advice for those of you in the bucket. Finally, it will show you a simple method to determine payments for a particular amount of money.

An hour here will save you $1000 or so.

The finance business is one of the least understood businesses in America—up, or rather down, there with the car business—*particularly* when you deal with car dealerships. The greatest pressure, the greatest deception, the most uniform lies live right there in virtually every dealership's finance office.

Understanding financing has become much more important with the advent of so-called "low" dealer rates. As we'll see, these rates are seldom as they appear but are simply bait for the unwary.

So how do you know where to finance?

Just do your homework, starting with a look at your options.

FINANCING SOURCES

As you'll see, where you finance at times isn't as important as the integrity of the lending source. So before looking at your options, why not memorize the following ironclad rule:

If a financing source refuses to give you the complete, exact figures for a loan—refuses to let you "shop" their loan—don't finance with them. Isn't that sensible? If the source is really cheaper, wouldn't they gladly give you their figures?

Apply this rule to all sources you shop—from credit unions to, God forbid, small loan houses—and repeat it often. It's the most important guideline you'll find in this book, and if you follow it, it will prevent you from paying perhaps thousands more without realizing it.

Now, with that rule in mind, here's a look at sources.

Cash Value in Your Life Insurance

If you're one of the few remaining people with whole-life insurance, you can borrow that cash value for a charge generally less than half of that from any other source. Your insurance will stay in effect, too. Call your agent and ask for a statement of cash value. If you choose to finance by this method, you would be wise to make arrangements to pay monthly sums back into your policy.

A Home Equity Line of Credit

If you are a responsible borrower, a home equity loan may have certain advantages for you, particularly from a tax point of view. But don't use this method to finance a car into the next century—keep the loan as short as you can stand.

As with all your potential sources, compare the total cost of this loan to the cost of others. Then estimate how much you might save in tax breaks.

Credit Unions

NOTE: Because I have consulted extensively with credit unions around the country and have designed an educational program for the 17,000 credit unions that belong to the Credit Union National Association, please hold what I say about the value of credit unions to the highest scrutiny. If you do, I think you will find that most credit unions are your cheapest and certainly least deceptive source for a loan. And most of them give good consumer information, too.

But unfortunately, a number of larger credit unions are being more deceptive and less helpful to their members in ways you need to watch for.

These credit unions have "gone to bed," as we say, with the car dealers themselves. This alliance usually shows itself in a deceptively simple way: you don't have to go to the credit union to get your loan, you simply apply for it and even sign the paperwork for it at the dealership.

This "convenience" is called "indirect" lending, and dealerships are quick to tout its benefits to the buyer: "Oh, we're so close to your credit union, they let us do the paperwork for them," a salesperson will say. Instantly your defenses go down, and you begin to believe what your salesperson has been saying. Why not? How could this be a bad dealership if your good credit union trusts them like that? "And think of how convenient it is, folks." Another reason to handle the financing details at the dealership, right? Shoot, you finance at the dealership and thank your credit union for the convenience.

Trouble is, the dealership forgot to tell you one little thing. Your credit union—which is supposed to be saving you money—is paying the dealership a fat commission for processing your loan: sometimes up to a thousand dollars. Would you drive to the credit union to save a thousand? Or even a paltry two hundred?

So, what's the warning here? If a dealership offers to do your credit union paperwork, forget it. Go to the credit union directly. And while you're there, why not find your credit union manager and ask him or her why you weren't told about this little deceptive "convenience" that costs hundreds of dollars.

But even with these problems and a few others, credit unions have quite a few pluses going for most of them.

They're member owned, and employment there shouldn't rely on selling. Used to be, all credit unions cared more about protecting their members' financial resources than selling to them. That has unfortunately changed somewhat, too. Some big credit unions have put aside their responsibility to educate their members to the dangers at automobile dealerships and now sell as aggressively as banks and dealerships.

But don't let these few sad credit unions keep you from considering yours as a financing option. If yours still does the paperwork and tries its best to educate you, talk with them.

They have no selling bias. Credit unions couldn't care less if you buy a Ford or a Honda. Their advice, therefore, is generally much more impartial.

The cost for a loan there is generally less than at most banks and virtually all dealerships—even during dealership "rate sales." Boy, is this an important point. We'll show you how to make this comparison yourself, as I said, in your own area. But generally speaking, credit unions are a cheaper financing source.

Used-car loans are generally made at new-car rates. Compared to financing at a dealership, most credit unions will save you several percentage points in interest if you're planning on financing a used car.

Their charge for life or disability insurance is usually dramatically less than that at dealerships and banks. Seventy-two percent of all credit unions provide life insurance at no cost. On a $20,000 loan, that can save you *$800 on your life insurance alone* compared to the charges at the average car dealership.

But what about "4.9 percent" and the like? Credit unions generally beat that, too. Just take the rebate that's offered in lieu of a low rate at the dealership and use it as a down payment at the credit union. Though the dealership *rate* may be lower, the total *overall* cost of the loan is usually lower at the credit union. Look at this for a moment:

COMPARING A 4.9 APR DEALER LOAN
WITH A 10.0 APR CREDIT UNION LOAN

48-month Loan	Dealer's Loan	Credit Union Loan
Cost of car	$12,000	$12,000
Rebate	0	1500
Amount to finance	$12,000	$10,500
Finance charge @ 5		
percent* and 10%	1265	2283
Total Cost	13,265	12,783
Monthly Payment	276	266

Savings with rebate and credit union loan: $482

* Although we used 5 percent rather than 4.9 percent—because our tables have only .25 percent increments—the tenth of a percent difference is close enough for a fairly accurate reflection of savings.

Even though the dealer loan sounds cheaper because of the interest rate, you'll save $482 by financing at the credit union.

As we'll see, you can use the same technique—taking the rebate rather than the dealer rate—if you want to finance at a bank, too.

Credit unions lend money on a simple interest basis and determine interest by the declining balance method when a loan is prepaid. The vast majority of dealerships and many other financing sources charge interest by the "add-on" method and use the "Rule of 78s" method to determine how much interest you owe when you pay off a loan before its contracted term is over.

If a simple interest loan and an add-on loan have the same Annual Percentage Rate (APR) and you pay out the total term of the loan, you will pay the same amount of interest. In fact, these days, you won't hear anyone mention add-on rates—it's illegal to quote them. But what if you trade in your car before you have finished paying off the note on it? Then the Rule of 78s will cost you money because it loads more of the interest onto the front of the loan repayment.

For example, let's say you borrow $10,000 for 48 months at 10 percent APR. If you pay off the loan at the end of one year and the lender figures the interest due using the Rule of 78s method, you will pay interest equal to an APR of 10.41 percent, not 10 percent. Under the simple interest method you always pay 10 percent.

Okay, you say, but the dollar amounts can't be that great, can they?

After all, the greatest differential on that $10,000 loan would be about $42—so what's the big deal! First, the dealerships and other sources that use this method of figuring interest have no reason to use the method except that it makes more easy profit for them. Just multiply that $40 times 100 or 500 or 1000 loans and it adds up to a tidy piece of change: $4,000, $20,000, and $40,000. Second, the longer the loan term (have you noticed those seventy-two- and eighty-four-month contracts dealers are now offering), the greater the difference.

Doesn't all this make you want to open a loan company?

Financing sources that use this method, such as GMAC, Chrysler Credit, Ford Motor Credit, and a number of banks, try to justify this insanity by telling credit union customers, "You can borrow the money there, but if you do, you won't be building any credit. You know, credit unions do not report information to credit bureaus." Years ago that was a true statement. But today most established credit unions *do* use and report to credit bureaus. But even if yours doesn't report, are you concerned about building your credit badly enough to be a victim of the Rule of 78s?

Banks

Banks are generally cheaper than the "captive" houses used by dealerships (such as GMAC or Ford Motor Credit), and they're certainly cheaper when you take a manufacturer's rebate in lieu of the "low" rate and apply that rebate as a down payment.

Banks' particular lending rates for auto loans are usually determined by your credit rating and the number of months the car will be financed. Many banks also give lower rates to customers who already have checking or savings accounts with them. Many are also beginning to offer simple interest loans.

Bank employees are also "low pressure" salespeople, much like credit union employees. Their life and disability insurance is generally cheaper than that offered by dealerships and slightly more expensive than insurance that is purchased through credit unions.

A warning: If you plan to finance with a bank, do your paperwork at the bank, not at the dealership. You'll find that the dealership will be happy to "handle the paperwork for you as a service," as the dealership finance manager will tell you with a smile, but you'll pay a fat premium to the dealership for that convenience. How much could you pay extra? Try $400 to $2000.

Dealership Financing

The dealership sources themselves—GMAC, FMCC, Chrysler Credit and the like and usually a bank or two—are reputable though generally more expensive on the whole than credit unions or financing arranged independently through a bank. Even, as we mentioned, during rate sales. But the source is not the problem. We're going to show you how to always find the cheapest source.

The problem with dealership financing is the enormous amount of lying, deception, confusion, and pressure virtually all dealership finance managers use to try to force you to finance with them.

The reason is simple, too. Financing has become the most lucrative profit center for any dealership. It is the heart of the entire dealer selling process, and the salesperson there—known as a finance manager or "business" manager or, if the dealership has a sense of humor, "financial counselor"—is the highest paid *salesperson* at the dealership.

And do remember that job description: sales. The person in the finance office couldn't care less whether or not you can afford a particular car or really need their very expensive insurance or vastly overpriced warranties and protection packages. Job security comes only from selling.

And there are some very interesting people in the finance manager's job these days, too. Women are very popular ("not as threatening"); grandmotherly types are the most popular ("they 'look' trustworthy"). On the whole, the people in the job are nice and nonthreatening. As long as you do what they want.

But the moment you don't—for instance, the moment you say no to insurance, or want to go home and think about it, or (God forbid) ask for a copy of a dealership contract so that you can compare figures—the niceness is put away and the tough psychological warfare begins.

"I need to go home and think about it."

"Oh? Didn't you hear me say we're the cheapest? So what do you need to think about? Are you always afraid to make a decision?"

"Well, I don't want that insurance."

"Don't you care about the welfare of your family? Are you saying they're not worth a few pennies a day?"

"Well, I don't want the protection package then."

"Why not? *Everybody* that's sensible gets this protection. Now, sign right here."

"Well, can I have all the figures to take away and compare, you know?"

"Why would you want to do that? Figures get very confusing, so we can't give them out. But don't you believe me?"

"Well, uh . . ."

The badgering can become endless, if you let it. Try to leave, and they'll bring in another manager. Put cash on the table and they'll push it away. Present a check from your credit union, and they'll tell you there will be a special "processing fee" if you pay by credit union check.

And I'm only telling you how they do it at the nice dealerships.

HOW TO STOP THE PRESSURE

First, know that the pressure and double-talk is coming. Second, never agree to any purchase from a dealership for anything without comparing its cost and features. We'll show you how. Third, always insist on an *exact copy* of any finance contract, completely filled out, *before* you are to sign it. Use that contract to compare costs. And do you remember what to do if a dealership won't give you an exact copy? Don't under any circumstances finance with them. Shouldn't you have the right to compare?

BATTLE TIME! The second part of this book, will give you many more details on handling the finance salesperson's pressure at many points in the buying transaction. Cash buyers, don't forget to read that section.

WHEN DEALERSHIP FINANCING MAY BE USEFUL

First-Time Buyers/College Graduates

If you are new to major installment credit or are graduating from college with no credit but a job in hand and your credit union or bank doesn't have a first-time buyer plan (many credit unions and some banks do), several of the captive financing sources have designed financing plans for you. Some will even give you a down payment for starting your credit with them.

Unfortunately, you have to put up with special pressures from the sales force if you fit into these categories. But we can prepare you for that pressure. Read the section "Dealing with the Finance Manager" on page 261 very carefully.

Longer Months

Dealerships will generally arrange financing for longer periods of time than most banks or credit unions. While we don't recommend extended financing (you'll see why in a moment), dealerships will be happy to give you the tricentennial plan. All you have to do is ask.

Marginal Credit

If you know for a fact that your credit is minimal in quantity or marginal in quality, dealerships may finance you when others may not.

But don't forget that people who think they have credit problems are now the favorite target at most dealerships. And I said "think." Your credit probably isn't as bad as you fear, but the dealership will try to use that fear to milk every cent they can from your pockets.

Don't fall for that. First, try to get a loan at a bank or credit union before you automatically finance at a dealership. Second, if you actually finance at the dealership, don't be badgered. You generally have the right to the same interest rates as a person with blue-chip credit, and you certainly have the right to negotiate the best price possible on a vehicle.

WILL DEALERSHIPS NEGOTIATE ON THEIR RATES?

Yes, they will, if you're insistent and if you again insist on specific figures for comparison. But even at their lowest rates, the dealership will generally be more expensive and certainly more deceptive than just about any source you can imagine.

Finance Companies

If you must darken one of these doors, you would do better to walk rather than drive. Finance companies, "dip" houses, "small loan" companies—whatever the name, the result is always the same. You will be charged two or three times more for the same loan and normally will be required to place your household goods, furnishings, maybe even your soul on their contracts as collateral.

These companies just love to tell us what wonderful service they provide poor people with no credit or people with bad credit. Well, in my book their service ranks down there with your local loan shark.

Most of the people who do business with places like this have better credit than they think. The vast majority deal with these bloodsuckers because they are uncomfortable in more formal banking situations and prefer the down-home atmosphere of Friendly Fred and others of his ilk. As a matter of fact, testifying in an Illinois court case, an official of Citibank estimated that fifty percent of the customers of their subsidiary, Nationwide Finance, could qualify for bank loans. Other banking officials agree that this is the general case. If you are currently supporting your local dip shop, though, what can you do? Before submitting to another fleecing, apply for a loan at a dealership or bank. If you have paid your dip shop loans on time, you will most likely qualify for credit. And don't be self-conscious. Lots of folks have experienced credit problems and survived.

"Buy Here, Pay Here" Lots

These are expensive and probably the most dangerous place for anyone to finance a vehicle. Do your best to stay away.

WHAT TYPE OF BUYER DO THEY THINK YOU ARE?

Car people lump the millions of people who buy cars each year into four categories: difference buyers, allowance buyers, payment buyers, and cash buyers. Since all of us usually do fit into one or more of these categories, it's important that you understand each of these terms. If you are an allowance, difference, or payment buyer, you need to understand the terms in order to *avoid* that particular type of buying. Invariably it is when you see yourself as a type buyer that you will be taken most often.

Why? Any method of buying that confuses the total cash price of the car is dangerous. For instance, **difference buyers** are concerned only with the difference between the cost of their present car and the new car. This type of customer will say, "Son, your car lists for $12,000. And I'll be damned if I'll buy it for more than $5000 plus my car." This man's thinking is logical, but flawed.

"Well, sir, how did you arrive at that figure?"

"Well, my car is two years old, and I expect to spend $2500 a year for each year I drive. *That's* why I'll pay you $5000!" Or he'll say, "My car cost $10,000 new two years ago. I figure it depreciated thirty percent the first year and twenty percent the second. *That's* why I'll pay you $5000!"

The man will barely feel the shiv. Both of his arguments are based on his *own* definitions, and neither definition is based on such a minor fact as the current value of his car. A salesman working this guy can: (1) Ignore the value of the man's trade-in. In all likelihood, the trade may be worth more than $5000. (2) Tell the man that people are now trading for $2800 a year rather than $2500. After all, inflation takes its toll. If the man agrees, he's just raised himself $600. *Magic formulas and percentages just don't work.*

And then there's the **allowance buyer.** This customer isn't concerned with the *value* of his trade, but the amount of money he is *allowed in trade.* He will in all likelihood say, "Give me $4000 for my car, and you have a deal." A smart salesman can handle this type easily. He'll invariably say, "Well, folks, we can't give you $4000 on an Expenso Minutula. But let's take a look at these Expenso Gargantulas." And of course the Gargantulas have a larger margin of profit. Switching these people from a less expensive car to a more expensive one always increases profit to the dealer *if* the allowance stays the same. *Allowance buyers never know the real value of their trade or the actual discount on a new car.*

And **payment buyers**? You are the easiest prey. Invariably a payment buyer has only one simple request: "I don't care about anything else, as long as my payments are low."

"Well, what would be a satisfactory payment?"

"Just as low as you can get!"

Both the salesman and the customer laugh a little, and then the salesman goes to work. If you don't have a specific payment in mind, he will pick some impossibly high figure out of the air. The payment will be designed to shock you. The salesman will then lower the payment slowly until you're breathing again. If you have a payment in mind, the salesman will try to set you on a car that could be financed for lots less than your figure. The company of course will finance at your higher figure.

Where is the flaw in the payment approach? The entire negotiation never was based on the value of your trade or the cost of their car, but *on some figure pulled out of the air.*

The horror stories generated by these methods of buying are endless. One poor sap, an allowance buyer, argued for three hours and finally received his allowance. The moment it was agreed to, he slammed his fist on the desk and said, "Now about the financing! I won't pay you a dime over $400 a month for the car!" The idiot. At the allowance figure he spent hours negotiating, payments would not have run over $365 a month. But the man raised himself $35 a month for forty-eight months—he increased the store's profit by *$1680.*

And then there's the couple who insisted on receiving $2500 for their car. The salesman agreed to give them $2500 on a $9000 tin can, one of the small cars. He then switched them to a $17,000 mid-sized car, allowed them the same $2500 in trade, and increased his profit by $600.

Need I say more? Buying a car based on allowance, difference, or payments will only draw your attention from the questions that really matter: "What is my car worth in actual wholesale dollars? What is the total cash I can afford to spend? What is the cost of the car I'm buying?" If you know the answers to these questions, you will always be able to get maximum dollar for your trade, and you will always be able to buy their car for the least profit. If you have accomplished these three things, you will naturally have the lowest payment possible. *All car transactions are based on these questions.*

You've already learned how to shop your present car to determine its wholesale value, and you'll learn how to figure the cost of the car you're buying in chapter 8. For the rest of this chapter, we'll focus on how to shop for money, and how to determine the total "Available Cash" you will have to buy a car.

NEW OR USED, HOW MUCH CAR CAN I AFFORD?

Most finance buyers find a particular car, one that sets the pulse racing, and then breathlessly wait for a salesman or finance manager to tell them the damage: what the car will cost them each month. Invariably the customer is shocked at the payment. Invariably the payment is "justified"—a favorite sales term that simply means convincing the customer that castor oil really is a delightful and tasty thing.

There *is* a better way. It requires a restructuring of car-buying ground rules. But, if you follow this approach, you will probably really enjoy the entire car-buying process for the first time—because you will finally understand what you are doing. Here's the approach in capsule form.

First: Shop financing sources. Obviously a bank and credit union, for instance, will have different terms, but the cost of money can vary even between two different branches of the same bank. Some sources provide services free that cost hundreds of dollars at others.

Second: Decide how much money you can comfortably afford to pay each month for a car. Don't think about new or used or specific models; just think honestly about the payment check you will be writing each month. Deciding what payment is comfortable for you is your *most important decision*. It will determine how much car you can afford to buy regardless of the value of your trade-in. Once you've decided this figure, *stick to it*.

Third: Decide how many months you will make that payment. Don't automatically plan to stretch your payments over the longest period of time, either. "Easy-payment" plans that stretch your payments over five years or longer are dangerous; many times you will be paying for a car long after its usefulness has departed. Even worse, extended-payment plans buy you less car for each dollar of payment. For instance, if you buy a car and finance it at an average rate of interest for two years, eighty-six cents of each payment dollar will actually pay for the car; the rest is interest. If you finance the car at the same rate for forty-two months, seventy-eight cents of each payment dollar will be applied to the car; the rest is interest. If you finance the same car at the same interest rate for sixty months, only seventy-one cents of each payment dollar is applied to the car; the rest is interest.

Fourth: Determine your "Loan Cash." An installment loan simply *buys you a lump sum of cash*. Once you have decided on the monthly payment and the number of months, once you have found the best financing source, use this information to compute the total cash dollars your payment will generate. You will learn a simple three-step method shortly.

Fifth: Let your "Loan Cash" determine your purchase. You may want to purchase a new car but decide to purchase a used one, or vice versa. You may be able to buy more car than you thought, or you may need to buy less. This chapter will show you how to derive and use your total "Available Cash" from your "Loan Cash" and the value of your trade.

Now, before going on to the detailed discussion of these steps, read the capsule description again. Understand the approach. If you will become familiar with each step and apply that knowledge, you'll have no surprises once the actual buying process begins. Incidentally, all the information and decisions can be determined while you're relaxing at home.

Shopping for Rates and Terms

Is it really worth the time to shop for your money? After all, what's a couple of percent, here or there? Or twelve months or so longer? It's a lot of money, that's what. On an $11,000 loan for forty-eight months, the interest charge can vary more than $2000! At the same APR, financing that $11,000 for twelve more months can cost over $1000 more. Can you think of any good uses for that money? Shopping the money market will make you lots of money. It is also easier to shop for money and terms than it is to shop for your car. But you will need to understand a little of the industry jargon.

Annualized Percentage Rate

With the passage of the Truth-in-Lending Act in the mid-1970s, the government began to require lending institutions to quote installment-loan interest in a way that would actually tell borrowers the true cost of their loans. Since, as we mentioned a few pages ago, lenders may compute their interest charges on installment loans by various methods, such as simple interest and add-on interest, the feds require all lending institutions to quote interest as an annualized percentage of the monthly loan balance. Thus no matter the method used by a lender, the Annualized Percentage Rate, or APR, adjusts the actual rates to reflect the true cost of the money annually. As long as the APRs of two different loans are the same, you will pay the same amount of interest if you pay for the total contract term. But remember, if you pay off the loan before its term is complete, you will pay more interest if the loan is not a simple interest loan.

The real advantage of quoting interest as an annualized percentage rate is the convenience it provides you when comparing rates at different loan sources. The actual calculation of APRs is very complicated, but don't let that bother you. Use APRs to shop for money.

Finance Charge

The finance charge is the *total cost of the loan.* The charge includes the interest, any charges for insurance, state fees, credit checks, and the like. The finance charge tells you *how much more it costs you to finance rather than pay cash.*

Now, reread each of these definitions. Pay special attention to the preceding paragraph on finance charges. Many loan institutions will quote you a low annual percentage rate and then add charges for things you don't really need, such as the insurance we mentioned. That's how they stick you, folks. They will say, "Our loans have an APR of fourteen percent." They will then promptly stick you with other charges that make their loan vastly more expensive.

SIMPLE MONEY SHOPPING, STEP BY STEP

Don't assume that any one source will necessarily be your best bet. Some credit unions and banks won't give you extended terms, for example. Others may have reached their loan limits and may want to charge you more. You would be smart to call at least three different sources, gathering the same information from each. If you have a credit union, call them and two other sources. Call the bank you deal with most often. Perhaps call the dealership you are most likely to purchase a car from. Tell each source what you are doing, too; in all likelihood they will work a little harder to get your business. And, for Pete's sake, don't be shy. No lending source, including credit unions, is doing you a favor—you are the reason they exist.

GATHERING INFORMATION

Take a pad and put down a few basic assumptions. Are you going to buy a new car or a used car? Used cars are financed with rates that vary with the year of the car. For comparison purposes, the exact year is not too important; just if you plan to buy a one-year-old car or a five-year-old car.

Next, how many months do you plan to finance your car? Are you determined to hold the number of months down? If you are, you will save money. If you are buying a used car, the number of months will again be affected by the year of the car. But for comparison purposes, simply decide how many months you would *like* to be making payments, and write that number down.

Now, take your pad, and list each of the sources you plan to call by name across the top of the paper. Draw vertical columns under each source. Then, down the left margin, list the following questions:

1. What is your APR for new/used car loans for _____ months?
2. (If you plan to purchase credit life insurance) What is your charge per month for each thousand dollars (or each $100) in credit life insurance coverage? _____ per $1000 or _____ per $100.

     If the source cannot or will not give you the above, ask this alternate question: How much will the total charge for credit life insurance be on $10,000 at _____ APR for _____ months (the rate and term quoted in answer to question 1)?
3. (If you plan to purchase credit disability insurance) What is your charge per month for each thousand dollars (or each $100) in disability insurance? _____ per $1000 or _____ per $100.

     If the source cannot or will not give you the above, ask this alternate question: How much will the total charge for credit disability insurance be on $10,000 at _____ APR for _____ months (the rate and term quoted in answer to question 1)?
4. Do you have any other charges for making a loan, such as credit checks? (If so, write down the item and amount.)
5. (If you are calling a dealership) What is the amount of cash rebate offered on _____ (the car you're most likely interested in)?

Now give your loan prospects a call.

If you're calling your credit union or bank, simply ask for a loan officer. Generally speaking, these sources will be happy to give you specific information with no hassle.

If you're calling a dealership, ask for a finance manager. But expect a runaround here or, worse, lies. I know that's a terrible statement, but dealerships generally refuse to give out any information on the phone, and when you insist, they usually give you inaccurate information designed simply to "hook" you—to get you into the store. How do you handle that? Simply refuse to finance with the dealership under any circumstances.

Now, before picking out the best place to finance, take a look at how dealership rate sales and rebates affect the true cost of your loan.

Evaluating "Rate Sale" Gimmicks

Every day you see the ads, don't you? Zero percent or five percent rates that make you want to jump from your chair and rush to the nearest dealership without thinking and scoop up that wonderful money saver.

Well, as with most things in the car business, rate sales, as we've said before, aren't what they appear to be. First, they're always "qualified" in some way, usually with severely limited months. Want that zero percent? Great! But we can only give you 24 months, and your monthly payment now will be $600 rather than $250.

Rate sales usually have such stringent restrictions that few people finance with them at all. Not long ago, Ford Motor Credit admitted that only *eleven percent* of the people who financed with them actually used the low rates. Why didn't the other eighty-nine percent? They couldn't afford the payment. Well, why do Ford and the other manufacturers keep advertising these great-sounding rates if people can't use them?

Because the rate sales are simply a gimmick to get you in, so that the dealership can begin working you on their track system and eventually turn you over to their finance salesperson. Rate sales are the most deceptive and (probably for that reason) the most successful auto promotions in history. Many experts also argue that the rapid rise in new car prices has occurred in part to cover the cost of incentives such as rate sales. So you pay for these "bargains" anyway: Not only does your new car cost more, but because its price may be inflated over its true worth, your chance of owing more on that new toy than it's worth is much greater. That's bad for the vast majority of customers but oh-so-good for those nice dealers.

But even though the cheap rates won't do you any good, you can turn the industry's gimmick to your benefit. Just take the factory *rebate,* always offered if you don't want the cheap interest, and apply it as a down payment on your loan from another source. If you do that—and here's the important point—often the overall cost of your loan will be lower and you can finance for a reasonable number of months rather than the severely limited months offered in the rate sale deal.

Here's another example of how this works to your benefit—often even with the most enticing "sale offer."

A major warning: Many dealerships are going to try to steal your rebate. They will try to keep it as profit, rather than use it to reduce what you owe them. This theft is becoming a major concern in many state attorneys general and consumer affairs offices.

Shady dealerships who do this in effect say, "Okay, you owe us $20,000. Now, if you'll give us your rebate, you'll then owe us $20,000." Trouble is, they say this with confusing paperwork rather than words. And while dealerships simply call this "making more profit," I call it theft. Tens of thousands of consumers involved in class action lawsuits agree.

So how do you prevent that? Never let the dealership "apply" your rebate to what you owe them. The rebate check is a direct gift from the manufacturer to you. Don't mix it into the transaction. Tell the dealership to "forget the rebate—I want that check to come directly to my home." Negotiate as if there is no rebate. And then when your check comes, use it to make a down payment at some source other than the dealership.

So, Where's the Best Place to Finance?

Identifying the cheapest source overall for you will depend on your particular needs and the particular car you're interested in. By now, you've given your loan prospects a call and have the basic information you need to understand two more very important concepts— **Loan Cash** and **Available Cash.** After you learn how these concepts can help you buy a car right, we'll use what you've learned and the information you just gathered to help you compare all the variables and determine your best overall loan source.

An Aside on Applying for a Loan

Unless you plan to finance your car at a dealership, apply for your loan at least a week before you plan to purchase the car. Make an appointment with the source and go to that meeting well prepared. Take your social security number, credit cards, and the institution names and account numbers of both checking and savings accounts, plus any current installment loans you have paid off in the past two years. If you have already determined the exact car you are going to buy, take that information, too. If you have not decided on a specific car, be prepared to tell them the approximate price range of the car you intend to buy. Most lending institutions will be happy to approve your financing without knowing the specific car.

If you're financing at a dealership, you should not apply for your loan until after you and the dealership have agreed in writing on a vehicle price. If you apply before this point, dealerships may use your creditworthiness or lack of it to your disadvantage. Don't give them this chance.

How Much Can You Afford to Pay Each Month? How Long Will You Pay It?

As we have mentioned, payment buyers are the most easily taken customers in any dealership. The reason is twofold: Most customers do not know how to relate a payment to the cost of a particular car transaction, and they do not understand that a payment represents a *lump sum of money*. Now, please reread. Put another way, you will not know how much money you can *spend* on a car if you do not know how much money your payment will *buy*. You know, for instance, that you can buy more car if you can afford to spend $200 a month rather than $100 a month, but tell me the answer to this: If you have a trade-in worth $4000 but owe $3000 on that trade, how much car can you buy for $200 a month for thirty-six months?

Many sales managers have trouble figuring that one out easily— it's called "backing up" a deal—but it is very important to understand how to deal with all of these variables: How much money will a payment buy? How do you compute the effect of your trade on that money? How do you compute the effect of the payoff on your present car?

It's not really hard to do this. Grab your pad again and follow my thinking. If you will spend some time learning these few steps, you will know more about the mysteries of financing a car than your salesman. More than most dealers remember. More than many finance managers. Hell, you'll be the smartest kid on the block.

The Concept of Loan Cash— The Soul of This Book

You won't find the term **Loan Cash** in the dictionary, and you certainly won't hear the words used in a dealership; those guys want you to stay confused. But if you plan to finance a car, understanding Loan Cash is one of the most important things you must do.

The concept is simple: Cars aren't bought for "$199 per month," or for "only $500 down and $100 a month." All cars are bought for *cash.* Every time. *The payment you make simply buys you a lump sum of cash.* If you, for instance, tell me you can afford to pay $240 a month for 48 months, you're really saying "I can afford to buy about $9500 ($9463.72 to be exact)," if the APR on your loan is 10 percent.

When you know how to determine Loan Cash, you're on your way to becoming that smartest of buyers—a cash buyer. When you know your Loan Cash figure, you won't need to rely on a salesperson or finance salesperson to vaguely translate figures for you. So right now you need to learn how to develop Loan Cash figures.

Figuring Loan Cash from a Payment

In our example above, how did we know that $240 a month for 48 months at 10 percent APR would buy a lump of $9463? We used a handy chart and a little simple math—just like you're going to do. A calculator will save you some time and long division, but it isn't necessary. The complete chart is in the Appendix, but this sample will be enough for our lesson.

Now, let's see how we got the $9463 Loan Cash figure. First, look at the chart. You see that the monthly payment per $1000 borrowed at 10 percent for 4 years (our terms) is $25.36. To determine the amount a payment will buy, divide what you plan to pay—$240—by this payment-per-$1000-borrowed figure—$25.36. Your $240 payment will buy 9.46372-thousands or $9463.72 of Loan Cash. (To convert the answer into dollars, just multiply by $1000—i.e., move the decimal three places to the right.)

Okay, you try it with this example: If you can afford $210 a month

HOW 10% APR CAN BEAT 0% APR		
	0%	*10%*
Cost of new car	$15,000	$15,000
Less equity in trade	3000	3000
Less rebate	0	2000
Months finance	24	42
Amount to finance	12,000	10,000
Finance charge	0	1895
Monthly payment	500	283
Total Cost of financing	12,000	11,886
Savings at 10% APR	0	114

for 48 months at 10 percent APR, how much Loan Cash will you have? Remember, to get the answer, divide the payment you can afford by the chart's figure for the payment per $1000 borrowed at the right rate and term. Right. You have $8,280.76. The steps: $210 ÷ 25.36 = 8.2076 (× $1000) = $8280.76. Of course, you can round off the cents, but we wanted to be precise here.

Isn't that easy? Now, practice time: Take your pad and use the chart to develop Loan Cash figures for these examples:

1. You can pay $175 per month at 10.5% APR for 36 months.
2. You can pay $235 per month at 10% APR for 60 months.
3. You can pay $300 per month at 9.5% APR for 24 months.
4. You can pay $220 per month at 10.5% APR for 48 months.

The answers are below.

Putting the Loan Cash Concept to Work

Now that you're a financial wizard, take some time and think carefully about how much money you really would be comfortable spending

4. $220 ÷ 25.60 = 8.59375 = $8593.75
3. $300 ÷ 45.91 = 6.534524 = $6534.52
2. $235 ÷ 21.25 = 11.058823 = $11,058.82
ANSWERS: **1.** $175 ÷ 32.50 = 5.384615 = $5384.62

CHART OF MONTHLY PAYMENTS PER $1000 BORROWED*			
Length of Term	9.5%	10%	10.5%
1 yr	87.68	87.92	88.15
2 yr	45.91	46.14	46.38
3 yr	32.03	32.27	32.50
4 yr	25.12	25.36	25.60
5 yr	21.00	21.25	21.49

* A note about APRs used in examples. Since rates vary considerably over time, throughout the book's examples, we've used rates in the middle ground between lowest and highest rates.

each month on a car payment. How much should you spend? Many financial counselors recommend that you spend no more than twenty percent of the money you have left after paying your normal monthly bills. You may wish to check with your credit union for its guidelines, but don't pay any attention to what a dealership recommends (even if they use a fancy computer program to try to prove it to you). Remember the dealership has a vested interest in getting that payment and profit up, not in helping you control your budget.

Why not stop right now and work on this budget figure? Then write the amount you can honestly afford right here:

THE MAXIMUM PAYMENT I CAN AFFORD: _____

Now circle it, and commit it to memory. This figure is all the money you have in your "budget bank." Whatever you do, you can't buy a car with a payment larger than this or you'll be, in effect, bouncing a check—going over budget.

Now, decide how many months you want to make that payment. And remember that the longer you finance, the less car you can really buy—longer months simply mean more interest. Can you be happy with 48 months? Do you need a 54- or 60-month fix? Write the number of months here:

I WON'T PAY MORE THAN _____ MONTHS

Now, using the rates quoted to you, figure the Loan Cash for your specific payment and months for each of your loan prospects. When you have considered a few other factors, you'll use these figures to determine which option will be best over all for you.

> **LOAN CASH FOR PROSPECT 1 IS:**
> **LOAN CASH FOR PROSPECT 2 IS:**
> **LOAN CASH FOR PROSPECT 3 IS:**

The Concept of Available Cash

But you may have more cash available to you to buy a car than just your Loan Cash, right?

For instance, your old car may be worth some cash. If its wholesale value is higher than its payoff, your old car will contribute money to your cash pile. If it's worth $4000 wholesale and you owe $1000, your old car will contribute $3000 to your cash pile.

And what about rebates? If you're thinking about a car with a $1000 rebate, you can count that cash, too, can't you? Or maybe you would like to use some money from your savings?

Available Cash is simply all the money you have available right now to buy a car. So that I'll know you're not sleeping, why don't you tell me how much Available Cash you have in this situation:

> Your Loan Cash is $8000.
> Your old car is worth $5100 and you owe $3200 on it.
> You're looking at a new car with a rebate of $1000.
> You have an extra $500 in savings to put down.
>
> *Your Available Cash figure is:* _____

Did you get it? $11,400. Now, what is that figure? Available Cash is *all the money you have to spend if you plan to stay within your budget.* We're going to go over this again later, but please repeat that. In our example, go out and spend $11,400 on *anything,* and, for the first time in your life, you're going to have a payment that fits your budget.

How Much Money Should You Finance on a Particular Car?

A very good question which obviously affects your Available Cash. If you listen to lending institutions, down payments are an easy thing to compute. On new cars, they'll loan the actual cost of the car; on used cars, the loan value of that particular car, a fixed percentage of its wholesale value.

Well, thanks to this friendly advice, there are millions of folks out there who don't drive cars—they drive enormous metal hunks of liability. These people owe more on their cars than any reasonable person would be willing to pay them; they literally cannot sell or trade their cars without *paying* someone to take them. For many the down payment was a small amount of cash; for others, simply the equity in their trades. Some actually allowed the seller to arrange *two* loans— to "dip" them—to make even this minimum down payment.

Financing a car like this with a minimum down payment is dangerous. It means you will always owe more on your car than it's worth. Don't put yourself in that position. If you plan to buy a used car with a true wholesale value of $4000, for instance, don't finance $4000. If you plan to buy a new car, don't finance the cost of the car. If you use the following guidelines, your car will never be a true liability— it will almost always be worth more than you owe.

On a New Car

In Chapter 7, the section "What Do Those Pretty Cars Cost the Dealer?" shows you how to compute the cost of a new car. Be sure that the amount you plan to finance is twenty percent *below* the true cost figure.

On a Used Car

Be sure that the amount you plan to finance is twenty percent *below* the car's loan value.

If you plan to trade your car and have enough equity (the amount of its wholesale value over and above your payoff) you may not need cash. But if it still takes money from your pocket to be twenty percent below, *pay it.* It isn't easy to part with your hard-earned cash like this. But it is the only safe way to buy a car. If you will follow these suggestions, you'll normally be in a position to sell your car at any time and receive cash back.

If you simply cannot afford these suggestions, you will have to pay down a sum equal to the following: The sum of the profit you are paying on the new car plus the tax and miscellaneous charges. Since you don't know at this stage what the final profit figure or tax figure will be, be safe. Assume the profit will be $400 on any car you buy; assume that tax will be computed on your Loan Cash figure. For example, let's assume that your Loan Cash figure is $10,800 and that you live in a state with four percent tax. Your down payment would need to be:

Minimum Down Payments on a New Car

Tax on $10,800.00	$432.00
Profit of $400.00	400.00
Charges for titles and other fees	100.00
TOTAL DOWN PAYMENT	932.00

Minimum Down Payments on a Used Car

The difference in the actual loan value of the car and the total amount of money you will owe on the car, including taxes and other charges. Since you don't know any of these items yet, assume that tax will be paid on your total Loan Cash figure and that you will pay at least $500 over loan value for any car. For instance, if your Loan Cash figure is $4000, you would need to pay the following down:

Tax on $4000. (we assume four percent; use the rate for your state)	$160.00
Amount you are paying over loan value	500.00
Charges for title and other fees (to be safe, always assume $100.00)	100.00
TOTAL DOWN PAYMENT	760.00

Determining Available Cash for Different Buying Situations

Telling you how to put this step into action is the subject of chapters to come. But right now, you need to know how to arrive at an Available Cash figure for specific buyer situations. Perhaps you are merely thinking about buying a car now; in that case, just read through this information and go on. But if you are seriously planning to buy a car, read this section carefully, stop and think, then actually work out a tentative Available Cash figure for several situations that might fit you as a buyer. For instance, you might be considering buying a new car and trading or simply buying a used car straight out. You should work out an Available Cash figure for both situations. After you've done so, note these figures and save them. You'll need them later.

IF YOU PLAN TO BUY A NEW OR USED CAR AND HAVE NO TRADE

If you plan to buy a car without trading, the Loan Cash figure tells you how much your payment will buy. This figure plus your down payment is the total amount of car you can buy—your Available Cash. For example, if you wish to buy a car and have decided to spend $150 per month for 48 months at 13 percent APR, your Loan Cash would be $5591. If you plan to pay $1000 down, you'll have $6591 in Available Cash. Your Available Cash must pay for everything in the transaction: the car, tax, tag, and all other extras, such as credit insurance.

IF YOU PLAN TO BUY A NEW CAR OR USED CAR AND HAVE A DEBT-FREE TRADE

In this situation, your Loan Cash and the wholesale value of your trade will determine your Available Cash.

Once you have carefully decided how much you want to spend each month and for how many months, use the interest rate from your shopping list and develop your Loan Cash figure. Let's say you have decided to pay $350 a month for 36 months. The interest rate is 8 percent APR. Your Loan Cash figure will be $11,168.

You have also shopped your trade and know it has a true wholesale value of $4000. Since you own the car outright, the trade will contribute its full $4000 value to the transaction.

How much can you buy and still keep your payments at $350 for 36 months? Loan Cash of $11,168 plus wholesale value of $4000 equals $15,168, your Available Cash. You can buy $15,168 worth of car, including tax, tag, and other charges. In all likelihood, you will not have to make any other down payment than your trade, too. Just always be sure you are twenty percent under, as we mentioned.

IF YOU PLAN TO BUY A NEW OR USED CAR AND OWE MONEY ON YOUR TRADE

This section applies to most of us. Your Available Cash will be determined by the Loan Cash you can afford plus any equity you have in your trade. *Remember, equity equals wholesale value minus payoff.* Your car has more value to you than debt only if the wholesale value is higher than the payoff. For instance, if your car is worth $4000 and your payoff is $3000, your equity is $1000—its real value is $1000 more than you owe. If you owe more on your car than its wholesale value, you have no equity. You're in the bucket.

Since you owe money on your car, you need to know which situation applies to you. Call your financing institution and ask them for a "net payoff." The net payoff is simply the total amount you owe the lending institution minus any rebates for unused insurance and, at times, prepaid interest. Now compute your equity. Subtract your net payoff from your true wholesale value. If the answer is a "plus" figure, if your wholesale value is higher, breathe easier. If the payoff is higher, go buy a bottle of hundred proof before reading further. Then see the section below, *If You Are "In the Bucket" or "Upside Down."*

IF YOU HAVE EQUITY

Now, sit down and determine how much you want to spend on a car payment for each month and for how many months. Look at your financing shopping list, and choose the rate from the source you are most likely to finance with. Now, develop your Loan Cash figure for that payment and write the amount down by your equity figure. For instance, if you have decided to spend $220 per month for 48 months at 10 percent APR, you know your Loan Cash is $11,527. If your trade is worth $4000 and you owe $3000, you also have $1000 in equity. *Your equity and Loan Cash combined determine what you can buy: your Available Cash.*

In this instance, you can buy a car that has a total selling price of $12,527. But don't combine the figures together just yet. Remember that you will have $1000 in equity only *if* your car has a wholesale value of $4000. And since you are trading your car, the dealer is obviously going to try to give you *less* than $4000. For now, just be sure that you have four figures together somewhere on your pad: (1) The amount of your Loan Cash. (2) The wholesale value of your trade. (3) The amount of your equity. (4) Your Available Cash, the sum of one and three. Then skip to page 145, for the step-by-step process of using the charts to determine payments.

IF YOU ARE "IN THE BUCKET" OR "UPSIDE DOWN"

If you have a car that is worth $4000 but owe $5000 on it, you unfortunately don't have any equity. You have what is called negative equity, a nice way of saying that you are in the bucket. Negative equity simply means that you owe more on your car than it is worth. You probably will not be able to trade cars without paying cash down.

Now, before looking at an easy way to determine how much cash you will need to pay down in this situation, please listen to one piece of advice. If you are in the bucket and don't have the cash on hand necessary to trade cars, *don't* trade cars. Keep your car for a while. High-pressure dealerships and small loan companies—"dip houses" —survive on people who borrow money to bail themselves out of their present car. Each one of these people is simply digging a deeper financial grave in preparation for the inevitable. Thousands of people have had their cars repossessed each year because some nice salesman has told them "Don't worry about the money, sir. We can borrow that extra down payment for you." You don't need friends like that.

At times dealerships will bury you deeper in the bucket *without* dipping you. For instance, let's say that you are in the bucket, but still want to trade for a newer used car. You want to buy a Jetta for $4500. You have a car worth $2000 and owe $2500 on it. You're in the bucket for $500. And Killer is waiting on you.

"Mr. Jones," Killer explains carefully, "you have agreed to buy the

Jetta for $4500, and I am going to give you $2000 for your old car. If you don't mind, however, I'd like to write this sale up a little differently, so that we can have you riding tomorrow *without one penny down."* You quickly slip your tongue over your lips in anticipation. Sure he can do that. "What we are going to do is raise the price of the Jetta to *$5500,* and raise the amount I'm giving you for your old car to *$3000.* Now, it will look like your old car is worth more than the $2500 you owe on it. That's important to the bank, Mr. Jones— they just won't approve any deal if you owe more on your car than it's worth, unless you put some cash down, too."

Killer quickly begins to scribble down a small column of numbers. "This is how we'll write up the order. We will deduct the $3000 I'm allowing you from the $5500, and that leaves $2500. Since you owe $2500 on the old one, the amount remaining to be financed will then be $5000. And *that* just happens to be the loan value of that Jetta!"

It's one of the oldest tricks. If you'll think about it, you'll realize that Mr. Jones may be getting a car with no money down. But he is also getting himself even deeper in the bucket on the Jetta. Mr. Jones didn't really win any battle in this transaction; he simply postponed the time of his defeat. Every time that you buy a car, new or used, you are simply postponing the pain by not paying lots of money down—and that's why most people's cars are liabilities on their financial statements, not assets.

Depending upon the amount of your negative equity, you may be able to retail your car, sell it yourself, and at least come out even. For instance, if your car has a wholesale value of $3000 but your payoff is $3500, you are in the bucket only $500. If you'll read the section on selling your own car, you should be able to receive at least that for your car.

IF YOU STILL PLAN TO TRADE CARS, AND YOU ARE IN THE BUCKET

Here's a good way to know how much cash you will need to pay down. This is extra cash, cash from your pocket. It has nothing to do with Loan Cash.

IF YOU ARE BUYING A NEW CAR, the total amount of down payment that will normally be required will be the total of the following:

1. The amount of your negative equity
2. The amount of profit you plan to pay on the new car
3. The charges for taxes, tag, title, and other things such as rustproofing

IF YOU ARE BUYING A USED CAR, the total amount of down payment that will normally be required will be the total of the following:

1. The amount of your negative equity
2. The difference in the car's total price (excluding your trade) and that specific car's loan value (you can call your bank, and they will provide you the loan value figure)

If you find that you are only $500 in the bucket, don't think you will only need $500 in cash, either. Let's take an example. You are planning to buy a car that has a true cost of $6000. You have agreed to pay the dealer a profit of $400. And your payoff on your trade-in is $500 higher than its wholesale value. According to the formula above you will need:

1. $500 in cash (the amount of your negative equity)
2. $400 in cash (the profit you are paying the seller)
3. $240 in cash (tax, if you are paying four percent)
4. $100 in cash (your tax, title, and other fees)
   TOTAL: $1240

You will need at least $1240 in cash *from your pocket* to trade cars. And you won't be twenty percent under, as we recommend; you'll be financing the maximum amount. Do you know what that means? You will be in the bucket in this car, too, from Day One.

Do you still want to trade cars? Okay, dope. Sit down and determine how much you want to pay each month on your next "bucketmobile." Don't forget you will also be paying out lots of cash from your pocket when you determine that monthly payment. Then, look at your financing shopping list, and choose the APR from your lowest source. Now, develop your Loan Cash figure for that payment. Forget your trade—you would be much better off if you didn't have one.

If you are in the bucket, you will need to find a car that *fits your Loan Cash figure,* a car whose total price, including tax, tag, title, and other fees, is no higher than your Loan Cash figure. For instance, if you have decided to spend $150 per month for 48 months at 13 percent APR, you know your Loan Cash is $5591. That's all the car you can buy. But that's not all the money you are spending. Once you have decided on a specific car, determine how much actual cash from your pocket you'll need to pay down just to keep your payment at your desired level. But *don't* think that cash is buying you more car; it's not. It is simply bailing you out of the bucket enough to give some lending institution the privilege of putting you in the bucket again.

USING THE CHART TO DETERMINE PAYMENTS WHEN YOU KNOW THE LUMP SUM

We've been using the chart to determine Loan Cash, but it can also be used to tell you what the *payments* will be on a lump sum of money. This technique is a simple one and uses the information already at your fingertips: the number of months you plan to finance and the APR.

Why do you need to know this? If you are lucky, you may negotiate a final price on a car that is *less* than your Loan Cash. If you do, this technique will provide a quick way to compute your new payment. It will also allow you to check the other guy's figures—handy. The technique will also give you flexibility. If, for instance, you decided to spend $11,000 on a car but then find a red dream boat for $11,800, the chart will let you quickly determine your new payment. And finally, it can bring you to your senses should you accidentally fall in love with some beauty $3000 over budget. In Chapter 9, "Negotiating the Sale," we'll show you *when* to use this technique. Right now, let's learn how.

TO DETERMINE A PAYMENT FOR A LUMP SUM OF MONEY

1. Using the APR and months of your loan, locate the monthly payment per $1000 figure on the chart.

2. Divide your lump sum by 1000 (move the decimal three places to the left) to determine how many thousands you have in your sum.

EXAMPLE: $9736.42 = 9.73642

3. Multiply the thousands by the monthly payment per $1000 figure to determine the payment.

EXAMPLE: 9.73642 × $25.85 (payment per $1000 at 11 percent APR for 48 months) = $251.69

Note: If you are multiplying with a pencil, not a calculator, rounding your thousands off to the thousandth place (3 places to the right of the decimal) will still give you an accurate payment.

Now you try it, using the sample chart back on page 136. What would the payments be for these sums at these terms? (The answers are below.)

1. $4321 at 9.5% APR for 24 months?
2. $12,454 at 10.5% APR for 60 months?
3. $8688 at 10% APR for 36 months?
4. $10,503 at 10% APR for 48 months?
5. $5432 at 10.5% APR for 36 months?

SHOULD YOU BUY CREDIT LIFE OR DISABILITY INSURANCE?

Definitely yes—if your horoscope indicates imminent death or severe bodily injury within the very near future. (And if you believe in horoscopes.)

It's not that protection itself is a bad idea. Many of us do need to insure the payment of debt. But do you want to pay twice what that

ANSWERS: **(1)** $198.38; **(2)** $267.64; **(3)** $280.36; **(4)** $266.36; **(5)** $176.54.

insurance should cost you? You do that most times you buy credit life or disability insurance through a dealership.

The premium is the first rip-off at dealerships. It's very high because up to *sixty percent* of it, depending on the state and dealership, is pure profit to the dealer.

But that's not the only problem with insurance from your favorite car stores. Virtually all of them conveniently add the insurance premium to your loan, which obviously increases the amount you are financing and the total amount of interest on the loan. Then *they actually insure the insurance.* Nice. If you, for instance, decide to buy only life insurance on a $6000 loan for forty-eight months, look what happens:

Loan principal	$6000.00
Interest on the loan	1725.60
Credit life premium	241.08
Interest *on the premium*	69.33
TOTAL	$8036.01

The dealership is not going to insure this loan for $6000—they are going to insure it for *$8000.* At their very silly premium rates. On the loan we've just mentioned, you will pay $6.47 a month for forty-eight months. That doesn't sound like much money, does it? But look what the same amount of money would buy you from about any life-insurance man in town: if you are thirty-five years old, $6.47 per month would buy you almost $50,000 worth of *level* term insurance for *five* years—a lot more insurance for a year longer.

The key word here is *level:* The amount of insurance stays the same. If you die during the last month of the fifth year, you would still receive the full amount of the insurance. If you purchased your life insurance from a lending institution, only the *balance* of your loan would be covered. Die just before the forty-eighth payment, and your $8000 insurance policy will pay the last payment. Period.

What about Life Insurance from Credit Unions?

If you belong to the 70+ percent of credit unions that provide credit life insurance free, smile. If your credit union charges, you should already know how its costs compare with your other financing options (remember pages 121–29). If you're really smart, call your insurance agent and see what a five-year level-term insurance policy will cost you. If you're a little lazy, go with your cheapest source.

What about Credit Life Insurance from a Bank?

As we said earlier, it's cheaper than from a dealership but usually more expensive than that sold by credit unions. Banks do seem to have a habit of automatically adding a life insurance premium to their loans by "assuming" your consent. If you're not planning on credit life insurance, watch for this.

What about Credit Disability Insurance?

Credit disability insurance, also known as credit accident and health insurance, is theoretically designed to make your payments if you are disabled or ill. The concept is great, but the coverage is very expensive—even from a credit union—and always contains a number of exclusions.

For instance, your policy won't pay until you have been disabled and *under a doctor's care* for at least fourteen days (on some policies, at least *thirty* days). How many times in the past five years have you been totally disabled and under a doctor's care for at least fourteen days?

And pre-existing conditions are *not* covered. If you've had a little bout of something prior to buying your credit disability insurance, that illness won't be covered under the policy.

If you feel you must consider credit disability insurance, again, shop your sources carefully. Credit unions and banks will offer better rates than dealerships. In addition, some companies have much better ratios of benefits paid to premiums collected (one way consumer service is judged) than others. For example, CUNA Mutual, which provides credit disability insurance to a majority of credit unions, has paid out almost 79 percent in benefits. The average for the rest of the industry in the same year was just under 56 percent. Credit disability insurance provided by dealerships generally has the lowest payout ratio.

Can you buy credit disability insurance through an insurance agent? Not very easily, and usually with even more exclusions than through other sources.

Are either of these types of credit insurance ever a good buy? If you're in generally but not specifically poor health and cannot qualify for other types of insurance, yes. If you're older, yes. Since both credit life and disability insurance are essentially "group" plans, usually no physicals are required, and persons in their late sixties pay the same rate as twenty-five-year-olds.

But if you fit into any of the following categories, think before you spend extra money for any insurance. You might want to save that money for more car. Remember that insurance eats up your Loan Cash and therefore your Available Cash.

THINK TWICE ABOUT BUYING CREDIT INSURANCE IF . . .

. . . you are under forty and in good health. You can buy cheaper insurance from your insurance agent. Should you call?

. . . you are single. Insurance should protect survivors. If you die with no survivors, your insurance will be protecting the *lenders.* Let them worry about their own problems.

. . . you have enough existing insurance to cover your debts. If you're already *insurance poor,* why waste the money?

. . . you really want to beef up your insurance in general. See your insurance agent instead.

Can Finance Sources Make You Take Insurance?

An enormous amount of credit insurance is sold because customers feel they must take the insurance in order to receive the loan. But don't fall prey to this subtle blackmail. In most states it is against the law to approve credit on this basis.

DETERMINING YOUR BEST LOAN SOURCE OVERALL

At last. Did you think you'd never get through this chapter? Well, now that you understand the importance of knowing your Loan Cash and Available Cash and have considered the facts about down payments and credit insurance, you are ready to compare the loans offered by your various prospects and see which is best for you. So make sure that you have handy the answers you got from the lending sources and your budgeted payment and term, and turn to a fresh page on your pad. Sharpening your pencil wouldn't be a bad idea either.

We've prepared a chart for you that will allow you to fill in all the variables you've gathered and compare one loan to another. It may look a little complex, but it's not really.

Before we start, review these decisions:

1. I plan to pay _____ a month for _____ months.
2. I do _____ or do not _____ plan to buy credit life insurance.
3. I do _____ or do not _____ plan to buy credit disability insurance.

Comparing Loan Opportunities

On a piece of paper make two or three columns, one for each of your loan sources. This chart will enable you to check your best deal by figuring your best Available Cash figure. This will not give you a precise figure for a specific car, but because the variables are constant in the example, the process will allow you to determine which lender is your best overall source. Be sure to do the process again with your real figures after you have picked out and figured the cost of a new vehicle but before you negotiate.

If you do not plan to take any credit insurance, the largest figure represents your best overall loan opportunity. If you plan to take credit insurance (credit life and/or credit disability), complete the rest of the chart to take these costs into account.

The most accurate way to determine what credit insurance will cost is to call each source back and ask them what their charge for credit life is on your Loan Cash figure above. Ask for a separate quote on credit disability if you plan to take that. The second-best way is to ask for a quote on a $10,000 loan. This will allow you to compare which insurance is more expensive.

Now let's look at an example to illustrate the first part of the chart. I can afford to pay $210 a month for 48 months. But I'm also attracted to an offer on a car at the dealership that offers a finance rate of 4.9 percent for 24 months or a $750 rebate. Two other loan sources have quoted me interest rates of 10.5 percent APR and 13.5 percent APR. I owe $2100 on my present car, which has a value of $4250. Which is my best overall source? Also, I have plenty of insurance and don't plan to take credit life or disability on the loan.

What's my best loan source? Lender B. Now you try it.

COMPARISON OF LOAN OPPORTUNITIES			
	Source A	*Source B*	*Source C*
1. APR quoted			
2. Months to finance (your budget term or, if applicable, sale rate limit)			
3. Payment per month you can afford			
4. LOAN CASH (using nos. in 1,2,3)			
5. Equity (or neg. value in trade if applicable)			
6. Subtract payoff (5) from Loan Cash (6)			
7. Rebate if applicable (if in lieu of sale interest rate, don't enter under that source)			
8. Loan Cash + Rebate (Add lines 6 & 7)			

	Source A	*Source B*	*Source C*
9. Charge for credit life insurance on Loan Cash (or on $10,000 loan)			
10. Subtract 9 from 8; largest figure is your best loan opportunity			
11. Charge for credit disability			
12. Subtract from 10 (or 8 if not taking life insurance); largest figure is your best loan opportunity			

COMPARISON OF LOAN OPPORTUNITIES			
	Source A Dealership	*Source B Lender 2*	*Source C Lender 3*
1. APR quoted	4.9%	10.5%	13.5%
2. Months to finance (your budget term or, if applicable, sale rate limit)	24	48	48
3. Payment per month you can afford	$210	$210	$210
4. Loan Cash (using nos. in 1,2,3)	$4786*	$8200	$7755
5. Equity (or neg. value in trade if applicable)	$2150	$2150	$2150
6. Add equity or subtract payoff owed (5) from Loan Cash (4)	$6936	$10,350	$9905
7. Rebate if applicable (if in lieu of sale interest rate, don't enter under that source)	N/A	$750	$750
8. Loan Cash + rebate (add lines 6 & 7)	$6936	$11,100	$10,655

* If you could afford to pay $360 a month, you could get $8200 Loan Cash—your best figure—at this sale rate. The 13.5 percent APR, by the way, happens to be the dealership's rate for forty-eight months.

5

Big Town, Small Town: How the Boys Play the Game

If you live in a really small town—one of those places where everyone knows the dealer and his salesmen, along with the latest gossip about the young couple who just moved into the house with a bidet, for pity's sake—you're a very lucky person. You're probably not going to be the victim of "system selling." In all likelihood you'll deal with a single individual who may appraise your car, work you, and act as his own finance manager. Because of the "know-it-all" nature of small towns and their dealerships, you're just not as likely to be taken in some overly egregious manner.

Unfortunately small towns and true small-town dealerships are about as rare as a straight-talking car salesman, and *that* is rare. If you find one of these dealerships, trade there, and tell your friends to trade there too. How can you recognize the little gem?

FINDING ONE OF THE FEW GOOD DEALERS: WHAT TO LOOK FOR

Your salesman will negotiate with you entirely without asking *anyone's* opinion—either on the phone or by leaving the office.

He'll not ask for identification unless you are financing the car at the dealership or taking delivery that moment.

He'll not ask you to sign anything until you have a firm agreement on price.

He won't ask you for money until a manager has approved *in writing* your offer on a car.

He certainly won't force you to talk to a finance person unless you are financing the car at the dealership.

Watch out, however, for small-town dealerships that are actually part of chains—the norm now. These places, though deceptive in their small-town nature, work you just like the worst.

A LOOK AT SELLING SYSTEMS IN THE REAL WORLD

Killer and J. C. want to share a little about systems with you in a minute, but first, will you please go back to page 50 and reread "The Selling Systems." Right now. I think the words will mean a little more to you, now that you're a little more savvy.

Intermission

Pretty scary, isn't it? System selling, as it's performed by just about every dealership in the country now, just doesn't give the unwary or uneducated consumer a chance. But if what we've seen in this book gives you a chill, remember that there are *hundreds* of systems working on people in thousands of dealerships.

You will never, never come out the winner in this game if you don't accept the fact that systems are based on these two things: control and confusion. God help you if you forget. And God help you if you're a sales manager and you neglect to enforce your own particular store's selling system.

It was about six in the afternoon when J. C. walked into the control room, the sales manager's office overlooking most of the showroom and parts of the new-car lot. Without saying a word, he sat himself by the night manager, picked up the gross book, and stared silently at the rows of names and figures. Each line contained the history of each sale, detailing the customer's name, trade, new-car stock number, total gross on the new car, wholesale value of the used car, financing income, and financing source—the dealership's own finance company or one of the outside sources, such as a bank or credit union. The night manager just watched him. J. C. could be the friendliest boss in the world, but when he was this quiet, no one liked to be near him, much less sit by him. J. C. started talking, not to anyone in particular, but more a general venting of the things running through his mind. He always did this, talking around things out loud before drilling the matter dead center, and the night guy knew very quickly that the bit was going to come down on him.

"It's the damnedest thing. All day long our grosses are running odd—$1351, $1419, $1125, $1881. But then each night every single one of them runs even—$1400, $1200, $1600. Hell, you'd think the boys look at the invoices or something like that." He continued looking at the book, then finally turned to address Crowley Miller, the night man. "Crow, look here. Here's a God-damned deal for $100. And another one. And another one. What are you guys *doing* around here at night, son?" J. C. had a way of saying that last word as if he *were* your father, and very mad, at that.

"J. C."—Crow paused a second before continuing, some shoring up of nerves—"it's just been too busy around here at night for us to go in on every deal, and our grosses are good, anyway, so what does it matter if we're letting the guys work from tissue?" His words were definitely not what J. C. wanted to hear, but Crow was unprepared for the violence of J. C.'s reaction.

"Too busy! Why you little bastard, I don't pay you to sit here and be a God-damned secretary! I pay you to work deals for me, not put names in this book!" J. C.'s finger was now jabbing Crow's chest in cadence with every word. "Eve-ry-bo-dy-works-deals-from-list! The boys don't *need* to see an invoice! *You* are leaving money on the table and it's *my* money."

J. C. left the office as he had entered, without saying another word, and Crow quickly picked up the intercom, paging all the salesmen to his office. Leaving Killer and one of the other guys on the floor, he led the rest of them back to the conference room, closing the door behind him. Crow was really a good guy. All the salesmen liked him because he was real easy on them, seldom sending anyone back for a raise and never taking a turn with a customer himself. When a salesman would come into his office, and say, "Crow, I've got this guy settled on a car. What type of deal do you want me to work him on?" Crow would simply look up the cost on that particular car and give the salesman a figure: "Tell the guy he can buy the car for $8700 and his trade-in. And don't go below $8400 without coming back to me." Sometimes Crow would just tell the guys the cost on a particular unit. Sure he was well-liked. But the salesmen working under him each night were making consistently less gross per unit than the day guys. All the salesmen on day shifts were made to work the system, whether they liked it or not. "The system" was now the subject of Mr. Crowley's special sales meeting.

"Boys, as you can probably tell by the large hole chewed in my ass, J. C. isn't too happy with how we've been running things around here at night." Everybody grunted in frustration. "So from now on, this is the way we're going to work deals. And *everybody* is going to work this way, too. Now, when you get someone set on one particular car, get them settled in your office and take their driver's license and credit cards. Then get their car appraised. On the way back from the used-car lot, pick up the stock card from that particular car. If that card says a car lists for $16,000, you are to work your deal from $16,000, *no* discounts in the beginning." "Shits" and "damns" flew around the room quietly, seeming to pop from one mouth into another.

"If a customer has a trade that's worth $3500, you are to tell him, 'Sir, we've been *taking in* cars like yours for $2800'—*do not* tell them their car is *worth* $2800. You are then to take the $2800 from the $16,000. Now, I know everybody is going to jump, but that's the way we are going to do it. If your customer won't bite at that figure, you are to ask him, 'How much *will* I have to give you for your car?'" Whatever that figure is, I want you to write it, to fill out a completed buyer's order, and get lots of cash and bring it to me. Whatever the man says, even if he lets you write him on a list deal, I want you to tell the guy you will *try* to get his deal approved, but that only management can approve a sale.

"Once you have written up your customer at some figure, I want you to show me the deal, and then I want you to go back for more. Even if you have a list deal. Even if you lowballed the guy on his trade and have an overlist deal. And when you can't go back anymore, I'll go in there with you. I want every single cent of profit we can make. We are not going to leave a damned cent on the table. And one thing else—nobody is to walk. If your guy jerks on you, hold him by the arms until I can get to him. If I'm not around, grab another salesman and 'turn and burn' those suckers. And if *that* doesn't work, *rip their heads off*!"

It was a good way to end the meeting, and most of the guys filed out in pretty good humor. Of course, they didn't really like the system. But they all knew it *would* make them more money.

In most system stores, salesmen very seldom know much more about the individual transaction than customers do. From long experience, dealerships have learned that salesmen who know the cost of cars will always work from that figure rather than from the list price. And while most stores know that few people pay sticker price for new cars, *all* people bargain on a relative scale. For instance, if a car actually costs $17,000 and a salesman simply adds an additional $2000 to that figure, offering to sell you the car for $19,000, in all likelihood you will negotiate downward in even increments until you buy the car for $17,500 or $17,600. If the salesman had been working the system, he would have looked you straight in the eye and said, "The price on this car is $20,500." Sure, you would bring him down some, but probably not to $17,800, much less $17,500. Dealers who force their salesmen to use a high first-asking price always have higher average grosses than dealers who don't. System stores also know that there are still a few people out there who will pay list price for a car. And, as one of my favorite sales managers says, "If the sticker price says $30,000, then we are entitled to every single dime of that profit." And he was talking about the dealer sticker, of course.

That's why the "T.O." is an integral part of every selling system. Every dealer in America believes money is left on the table after the sale of each car. The amount left lying there may not be great by itself, but in the aggregate, it can be a really tidy sum. If J. C.'s store, for instance, could raise each of its customers just $25—not hundreds— Mr. Gary Oliver Davies's net profit for the year would increase by $100,000. If your salesman brings in some smiling face and says something like, "Folks, I'd like for you to meet my manager," don't think you're being accorded a great honor. You're just being T.O.'d for a little more profit.

Another version of the T.O. simply has the salesman constantly talking on the phone to the manager as he smiles at you. Many times, of course, there's no one on the other end.

You shouldn't put up with any type of T.O. Even Killer disdained them when he started in the business. He left the dealership that used them, but he does stay in contact with Lanny Maxwell, maybe the sharpest salesman at that store. You see, that store is just six miles from Killer's store—and the Dead End.

Lanny and Killer were sitting in their usual back booth, right by the ice machine and the entrance to the rest rooms—no one really liked to sit there, and the booth seemed to have some unhung "reserved" sign on the corner of the seat closest to the john. Lanny was expansive, legs sprawled far apart, his diamond tie tack hanging loosely, not at all connected to the mauve silk shirt with the shortcut collar. "One of these days I'm going to retire and work at a store like yours," Lanny said. A typical toot of the successful salesman's horn, Killer thought. Lanny must have had a really rich day.

"Bob, I want to tell you, it was madness! It was the last day of our 'Invoice Plus a Dollar' sale, and the damn people staked out the car they wanted like it was a great big pot of gold just waiting to be mined; hell, I wrote five deals before the second session." At many system stores sales meetings aren't held twice a week or once a day—they're held two or three times a day, and the hot car in the morning, the car with the bonus on it, is long forgotten by the two o'clock meeting. On this particular day, though, the hot cars were all "old maids," the Plain Janes that seem to adopt a dealership and spend months there collecting dust and rent.

"Perry [the sales manager or, rather, one of the nine sales managers who report to the new-car sales manager, who reports to the general sales manager, who reports to the general manager], Perry was frothing at the mouth to get all the old maids off the lot. Joey, the new-car sales manager, got the word from God himself that the cars were gone or he was gone—I'm telling you, we sold some cars!" "God" to people at this store is Anthony B. Scarri. His six stores sell more cars than thirty dealerships like Killer's. Mr. Scarri is one of the more than 200 megadealers in America. He has several large homes, a nine-passenger jet, and a sixty-seven-foot Burger yacht.

Lanny Maxwell's average commission per car sold is more than Killer's and the commissions of the boys who sell in the country. He, of course, doesn't say that to customers, though. Instead, he'll pull out a sales slip from some deal where his commission was the minimum $25 and show it to every customer who walks in. "Folks, see for yourself. I made $25 on that car, and the dealership made only $75. That's why I have to sell lots of cars just to make a living. And that's why you'll be glad you bought a car from me." The ploy works, naturally. Lanny may sell some cars for a low profit, but he sells a lot more for thousand-dollar profits—to all the suckers who automatically think big stores sell for less.

Lanny is a tall, slender man. He's a little flashy, too: thick, gray hair swept back, seemingly carved in rock, the result of five or six sprayings of VO5 each day; his shoes are patent leathers or genuine alligator, and his tie is always just a bit too busy. Lanny's selling techniques are just as flashy. He's one of the few salesmen at the megastore who greet their own customers—most of the other guys talk to ups after the "greeters," the full-time glad-handers, have led one and all to the welcome desk. Like at many stores, every up is entered directly into a computer, which makes unauthorized credit checks *so* easy.

But, as at Killer's store, new computer systems do more than tell a dealership about your credit. If you're unlucky enough to live in an area where many dealerships are part of the same chain, *everything* one dealership knows about you is shared with all the other dealerships: What is your old car worth? Which person is the real decision maker? Are you a payment buyer or a difference buyer? Are you a "Larry and Lois Laydown?"—rough dealership slang for people who will fall for any dealership ploy? Computers have added a new level of deception at many dealerships.

Lanny's way is a little more direct. "Howdy, folks! Are you going to buy a car today?" Before the ups can speak, he answers the question for them. "Of course you are, and what a stroke of luck that I'm your salesman!" Lanny turns his back on these people, his right hand swinging in the air in a pulling motion as if he's hauling some high-flying kite behind him, and utters his most famous line: "Come on! Follow me, and you'll die rich!" All the time he's walking away from the people without once looking back. Nine times out of ten, everyone follows him, as if drawn by that magical string. Who can resist the open con? The other boys at the store do get a laugh every few weeks when this line doesn't work. They'll see Lanny marching across the lot, mouth moving faster than any seasoned auctioneer's, hand waving in the air—as the customers who should be following him quietly open the door to their car and slink off the lot. Lanny always seems to look back just as they drive off. He quickly turns in a circle in mock bewilderment, lifts out his right lapel, peers into the pocket to make sure the ups haven't crawled in, and breaks out in a grin from ear to ear.

He's one of the few refreshing things in this particular store. A megastore is like those large, fast-moving assembly lines. Each employee has a specific task to perform over and over again; the line is always moving, and there's not a moment when the line workers can relax. First there's the greeter, who turns you over to some younger salesman. The young guy's chore is to qualify you—ask enough questions to know for sure that you have a reasonably good job and some type of credit experience. If you sound like the type of up that can buy, the young guy will normally turn you over to a lot walker, another nice young man who will help you find the car you like and then take you for a drive—usually in a demonstrator of the same make and model, not in the specific car you like. City people don't seem to want any miles on their "new" car, so the megastores use salesmen's demos for that first ride. Then when you return from your drive, the lot walker T.O.s you to a "closer," a man who does nothing but turn all the emotional screws, tightly. Closers are usually the best salesmen in the place next to the finance sales personnel, and their knowledge of the psychology of selling techniques is enormous. Several closers may work you, or one may work you, depending on the selling system.

It sounds like a lot of people to deal with, doesn't it? But as we know, you're not finished yet. Once you agree to buy, you've then got to see the "business manager" or "financial counselor."

What would be your answer to a conversation like this with that nice but nasty seller: "Mr. Speck, I know that you want to pay cash for that pretty new car. But look at these figures for just a moment. You owe us $8000, the balance due on the hardtop. If you leave that $8000 in your mutual fund account, you'll continue to earn close to eight percent per year. That's $660 a year. Now, let's assume that you finance the car with us for 60 months. As you know, we're offering 12.5 APR right now. Your interest each year on the loan will only be *$560.* And, since your savings is making you $660 per year, you're in essence financing the car for free. Plus, your $8000 in savings is there when you need it. And, Mr. Speck, let's say you get life insurance in your contract. If something unfortunate should happen to you the day you drive out in that car, your wife will owe nothing on it—it will be hers free and clear. *And* that $8000 in savings will still be working for her."

"Now, wait a minute," Speck says, "if my savings are earning eight percent, and if your loan is for 12.5 percent, how can the savings be earning $660 per year and the loan be costing only $560 per year?"

The guy laughs a lot—he thought Speck was more sophisticated. Obviously, he's not. "Mr. Speck, mutual fund earnings can compound daily. Installment-loan interest is computed on an annualized percentage basis. The effective annualized yields of your savings and the loan are, of course, different."

The finance salesman is garbling his facts on purpose; by this time, Speck has developed a mild headache and redirects his thinking to more familiar waters. "Well, if financing that car is going to make me so rich, I'll do it. But I'll do it through my credit union. I want them to check over the deal, anyway." And that's just what the finance man doesn't want anyone to do—credit unions are another pain in the neck for salesmen. They have an unfortunate habit of telling people, "Boy, that's a high price!" Credit unions, like banks or any other outside financing sources, also remove control of the sale from the dealership.

"Mr. Speck, if you need to check with the credit union before buying this car, why did you sign the buyer's order? Didn't you agree this was a fair price?"

Speck stutters; he's vaguely aware that logic seems to be defeating him again. "Well, yes, I think it's a fair price."

"And don't you agree with me that it makes sense to finance? After all, you *did* say you would finance with your credit union."

Poor Speck. He's going down for the third time, small bubbles of frustrated air rising to the surface. "Well, yes, I did say that, but won't your financing cost me a little more?" The man is pleading for an honest answer, and he'll get it. Of a sort.

"Yes, it will cost you a little more—maybe fifty cents a day, probably what you'd spend on a Coke. But why would you want to tie up that credit source for a car? What if you want to buy something else in a few months? If your credit is tied up at the credit union on this car, you'll probably go to some other financing source. Mr. Speck, we finance nothing but cars. That's definitely to your advantage."

"But I'll have to *buy* life insurance if I deal with you—the credit union puts it on loans for free."

"Mr. Speck"—the finance man's voice has that slight tone of contempt again—"you know as well as I do that nothing is free. The credit unions simply build the cost of life insurance into their loan rates. Now, when do you prefer your payments to begin, on the first or the fifteenth?"

Unless money is your profession, don't duel with finance men at any store until you have studied carefully the sections in this book on financing.

Okay, you're thinking, I'll just bypass the whole system, and get on the phone to some dealership, find some nice salesman who believes in phone selling, and do the whole thing by long distance.

No, you will really be in trouble if you do that. If you call a dealership and ask for a salesman, some nice voice will come on the phone and say something like, "Ma'am, you caught me in the break room. Give me your number and I'll call you right back from my office. That's where my stock cards are." Without thinking, you give him your number, at the same time giving away your anonymity. It's a great phone technique. Salesmen are instructed always to be in "the break room," or the shop, when they first talk to a phone up—this little white lie always works. When the guy calls back, you could ask him if he has a seven-door, five-wheeled, nuclear-powered tank in stock, and his answer would either be "yes, ma'am," or "no, but we've got one coming in sometime today. But lots of people have been waiting on that tank. If you think you might be interested in it, you should come down right away." Well, you don't want to go down there without agreeing firmly on some price on the phone. "Ma'am, I can't appraise your car over the phone, and I assure you our prices are as competitive as anyone's in town."

Regardless of the store size, all salesmen believe strongly in this wish-fulfillment—whatever you say you want, new or used, they will say they have it or can get it for you. Many people rushing down to a store supposedly to see some mythical car will be easily switched to something actually sitting on the lot. The telephone just isn't a friend of the car-buying public.

Is there any hope? Are you really brave enough to enter a dealership after all this? Absolutely. You can defeat system selling, and you can help stop the really bad dealerships from hurting people, too. Don't be afraid of the large stores, if that's all that's available to you, but don't be shy when you find a really bad dealership, either. Tell your friends what it's like there, and then *write me with your story*. We just might send a professional shopper to investigate your discovery.

And now back to the Dead End.

Lanny Maxwell and Killer had one last drink before leaving the Dead End, walked out the side door, and drove in one car to the lodge. It was a weekly ritual: seed-planting time. Within an hour each of them will have given out small packets of their business cards to eight or ten members of the noble order, asking the brothers to "put your name on the back of each one, give 'em to your friends, and tell them to bring the card in when they need a car. Every one I sell is worth twenty-five bucks to you." And many of these guys take their bird-dogging seriously, working just as hard on this part-time job as they do on their regular jobs.

Lanny and Killer were back in their booth at the Dead End by nine, and Killer ignored the barmaid's message from J. C. at the store. "Honey, tell him to go stick it in his ear. I've done my work for the night." His next drink was a double tequila, straight up. A good start for "cocktail hour."

The Dead End is located perhaps halfway down from either end of "automobile row," the twenty-mile stretch of new- and used-car dealerships that skirts the city. Or at least all the salesmen who frequent the place believe it's downhill, since their cars seem to roll in that direction automatically each night at closing. By the time Killer's tequila was rumbling around in his belly, the bar's parking lot had filled up with new cars of every description—demos—and used cars with dealer tags either stuck in the back window or fastened on the trunks with a magnet. Most of these guys didn't mix, except Killer, but hung out with their own, reviewing the day's war stories between sips of bourbon-and-Coke or Scotch-and-7-Up. And few of the new-car guys ever mixed with the "lot boys," those who worked at the anonymous little used-car operations that seem to sprout and die daily along the row. It's a matter of prestige: New-car salesmen consider themselves more "professional" than the strictly used-car boys. Salesmen from Cadillac stores are higher up the ladder than Chevy salesmen. And down there at the very bottom are the "paper" men, the guys who advertise: "Bankrupt? On the lam? Bouncing checks all over town? Nobody walks at Friendly Sam's."

"Hey, Sam, have you got that Chevy back on your lot? Damn, I bet you've popped that piece of junk six times this year." Killer smiled.

He was yelling to the best paper man in town—or the worst, if you will—and he waved the guy over to the booth. Sam didn't see that comment as anything bad, and he grabbed Killer's hand. "Well, hell, Killer, I thought it'd popped eight. I must be slipping."

The car in question was a ten-year-old Chevrolet. Killer had traded the thing in perhaps a year ago, a "giveaway" car. The damn thing was so bad the dealership had given its owner nothing for it. That hadn't bothered Killer; he simply raised the asking price on the car the guy was interested in by $300 and wrote another $300 on the "trade" line of the buyer's order. The junker had quickly been sold to Sam for a "buck fifty," $150. Sam had then put the car to work for him. When some poor sucker came in with the worst credit in the world, Sam would just tell him, "The Chevy's $800. You pay me $150 down, and $20 a week, and it's yours." There were no credit checks, either. Why should Sam go to the trouble, since he had every penny of his investment back from Day One? Invariably the customer would pay on the car for two or three months, then fall just a little behind on his weekly payments. Sam would repossess the car immediately and sell it to someone else for a buck fifty down and $20 a week. This particular car had made Sam over $1400 in the past seven months. But that was business, "and besides, who else is going to help these suckers if I don't?"

Convenient logic: Sam is helping people, that's why he's in this end of the business. Like most car people, he can make anything, any technique a just act. But compared to Killer, Sam is an amateur at the game of convenient logic. A little friendly one-upmanship is as much a part of an evening at the Dead End as the drinks.

Killer wet his throat with another swig, grinned at Lanny and Sam, and launched into the Merit saga. "Hey! Let me tell you about a switch!"

Merit, Albert Gray's boss, was the guy who did do something right—he sold his trade-in straight out. He was pretty cocky after that, especially after talking to the loan officer at the bank. The officer had given him real "inside" tips on buying a new car, and the man obviously knew what he was talking about. "Mr. Merit," he'd said, "the smartest thing you could have done is sell your car. You see, there really is no way any of those guys can take you since you don't have a trade. For, Mr. Merit, we *know* what those new cars cost. The simple work comes next!"

Merit liked the tone of the guy, for sure. How could he go wrong now? The bank would tell what any car cost; all he would have to do is add a little profit on top of that and drive out with the best buy of his life.

As these nice thoughts were floating through Merit's mind, Killer was dialing the number of the phone sitting on the table right by Merit's head. The first ring seemed to push itself into the center of his mind, and he picked up the receiver, speaking quickly, as if he wasn't quite composed in his thoughts. "Yes?"

"Mr. Merit, this is Robert DeMarco. I called you a few nights ago concerning the car you had for sale."

"Yes, I'm sorry, but the car is already sold."

"Really? Well, I hope you received a good price for it. I bet you did." Killer knows the value of a well-placed compliment.

"Well, yes, actually I came out pretty well on the car." Merit resisted the temptation to say how well he did but continued to talk, a small bell finally pulling from this memory the name DeMarco. "Aren't you the person who works at a dealership someplace?"

"Yes, sir, that's me. And if you don't mind me asking, have you had a chance to find yourself a new car yet?"

Merit thought fate was on his side again. Here was a man who not only sold cars but seemed to be nice, to boot. Probably not smart, though. "No, I haven't. I have been to the bank to arrange the financing and, incidentally, also arrange to learn the cost figures on the new ones. You know, I'm a pretty tight man when it comes to cars. They're really nothing but transportation to me." Merit started saying several more things like this. He was certain it was a good way to let Killer know he wasn't any pushover.

And Killer was loving every minute of it. This guy sounded real sure of himself, and, nine times out of ten, people this sure could be tripped with their eyes open on a well-lit parking lot. Killer responded in a tone of subdued respect. "Mr. Merit, I like the way you talk. What are the chances of setting an appointment to meet down here for a look at our cars? I'm certain there is a car that fits your particular needs. And I'm equally certain that you will buy that car at a very, very low price." Both of them laughed. Merit's laugh was one of satisfaction. Killer's laugh? He was feeling pretty satisfied, too.

Sitting on the back of Killer's lot was a two-door hardtop much like the one Merit had just sold. It was not a fancy car, and though it was new, it was old and wrecked. The guys referred to cars like these as lepers. Most of the salesmen walked around them daily, never acknowledging their dusty presence much less taking customers to them.

The car had been damaged the week it arrived while sitting on the lot. One of the lot boys had backed squarely into the left door and the rear quarter panel with the parts truck, hitting the car with such force the rear quarter panel had finally been replaced. The door had been "drilled" in the body shop; small holes were placed at strategic points to help the body men pop the metal to its original shape, and then both damaged sections were painted. The paint never really matched either—it was one of those metal fleck numbers that are a dream to look at but hell to repair. The car wasn't hot merchandise after this little episode, for sure, and it continued to gather dust for nine months, each month collecting a little of the salt spray that seemed to settle regularly on most of the cars there.

Killer walked back to the clean-up department and struck up a light conversation with Leon, the black man who had spent fifteen years at this one store making the cars shine, applying a little makeup when necessary. He was a good man, probably one of the hardest-working men at the store, and he liked Killer. After all, Killer was the only guy who would slip him a few extra dollars for doing a really bang-up job on special cars. "Hey, Leon, I've got an emergency job for you, major surgery! As a matter of fact, the damn thing may already be dead!"

Leon put down his buffer and smiled. "Bob, what are you talking about? I've got five cars sitting back here that the man says have got to be ready to roll tomorrow. How can I put one in front of that? Are you going to start a race riot or something?"

"Okay, smart-ass. If you'll put the little white palms of your hands to work on this one, I'll buy dinner for you and Lora at the pizza place this weekend. I'll even buy the beer."

"So, what's the car?" Killer just smiled. "Oh, damn it, you don't mean the tan one. You're the second guy today that has asked me to fix it. What have you got, a spiff riding on it?" Leon was right about that. J. C. had put a $200 cash bonus on the car that morning—a good enough reason for Killer to sell it to Merit.

By six that afternoon the car looked like a new one. Leon had buffed the repainted areas twice, and the slightly off-color paint appeared to match perfectly, until the light hit it at an angle. The small sores of rust that had slowly begun to push their way up through the metal had been sanded down carefully by hand and touched up lightly with a brush. Leon had even carefully used a razor blade to lift off the paint overspray that had been visible on several pieces of molding. The interior vinyl had been dressed, the tires coated with gloss, and each piece of rubber molding sprayed with silicone.

Killer was really satisfied. "Leon, I'm telling you, this is the best face-lift you've ever done! I mean to tell you, *I* would buy this car."

Leon looked pretty satisfied, too, making one last sweep with his cloth over the painted areas. "Yeah. But, let me tell you something, don't park the damn thing with the sun on this side. I did all I could, but the door really looks like it came off some other car."

"That's okay. The jerk that is going to buy it won't even notice. Now, do one final thing for me. Set the radio on a couple of those easy-listening stations and pull the car back where it was. I want the guy to discover it. And, Leon . . . can you smudge the bottom of the sticker just a little?"

Leon didn't really like the sound of that request. He'd heard it before. "Bob, I can't alter that sticker. I mean that's really against the law."

"Leon, I didn't say *alter* it. I just said scrape the bottom price a little, like you were cleaning the window."

"Well, I do need to clean inside again, I guess."

"Yeah, we want a clean deal," Killer said. He headed back to the showroom, stopping by the rest room as he entered. He looked in the mirror, pulled his tie a little askew, and tossed his hair just enough to give it the careless look. He wanted to appear appropriately humble when Mr. Merit arrived. After all, the guy was some big deal.

Merit drove up just on time and walked briskly from the car. Killer just grinned when he drove up—hell, the guy was driving the Grays' car. "Mr. Merit, I didn't know that you knew the Grays."

Merit looked surprised. "Albert works for me. Did you sell them this car?"

"I sure did. It's a small world, isn't it?" The two men shook hands, walking slowly from the parking lot toward the new cars.

"You know, Mr. DeMarco, I have very simply tastes when it comes to a car. I want something that is reasonably sporty-looking but isn't loaded down with a lot of crap. I don't want to spend money on things that are going to break down anyway, you know what I mean."

"I sure do. It's really ridiculous how much money people spend on useless options these days. I'm always telling the man who orders our cars to simplify! Simplify! But no, he won't order cars like that, because most people don't buy cars like that." Merit shook his head in agreement.

After a few minutes of casual talk, Killer decided to start sinking the man with his logic. "You know, Mr. Merit, you mentioned your bank when we talked the other night, the fact that those people would tell you how much any of our cars cost."

Merit liked the tone of Killer's voice. The man nearly sounded uneasy. "Yes, they will do that for me. Quite honestly, I think it's a much better way for a person to buy a car."

"Well, I just wanted to tell you that I agree. I would like to know just one thing. Assuming that we have a car here you like, what profit are you willing to pay? You see, Mr. Merit, I make a living by getting a percentage of that profit, and I don't mind telling you I would like to make at least $30 when I sell *you* a car."

Merit felt really smug when Killer said that. Hell, who would bust their collective ass like these guys for $30? "Mr. DeMarco, just what is your percentage of the profit, if you can tell me that?" Merit had always wanted to know how these guys got paid and his smugness grew as Killer appeared to agonize over the question.

"Mr. Merit, I would get fired if anyone ever knew I told you this. But I get twenty percent of our profit. Is that too much?"

"No, no, if you are saying you need to make a $150 profit, of course I'll pay that."

Killer looked grateful from head to toe. "Well then, I'll tell you what. And again, this must be private, you understand. Mr. Merit, I'll bring you the invoice on whatever car you select. You can study it all you want to. I want to sell you a car tonight, if I can, and if you need to see the invoice to buy, you'll see it. Just, for God's sake, don't tell *anyone,* including the Grays. I didn't let them see the invoice."

Merit was really beginning to enjoy this. In his entire car-buying life, he'd never seen that little secret piece of paper, and he enthusiastically said that of course, of course he could do business that way. Killer thanked him and directed their walk toward the back of the lot. He deliberately walked by two-door hardtops that were loaded to the hilt with options and carefully pointed those cars out to Merit. "My God, I didn't know there was this much money in the world!" was about the only comment Merit would make. Most of the cars were not only expensive but were coated in a thin coat of dust and looked nude without their hubcaps or wire wheels. All of the cars, that is, but the shiny hardtop sitting perhaps forty feet from the others. "Hey! What is that car? It looks like a nice one." The two of them walked toward it quickly, and Merit went straight to the sticker. "Damn! The bottom of this thing is smudged off. But the list of equipment is a lot less. I think we should take a drive in this one."

But DeMarco had a better idea. "Mr. Merit, why don't you drive me to the showroom, and I'll get you a tag. You can drive it by yourself while I get some information on the car." Of course, he didn't object, and the two of them drove to the showroom.

Killer jumped out of the car as it stopped and pulled a pad from his pocket. "Mr. Merit, since I don't see a stock number on this car, why don't you read me off each item on the sticker. I'll just copy it down and identify the car from that."

As Mr. Merit was driving the car, Killer walked to the manager's office and said, "Hey, Crow. You know that tan metallic coupé we've got in the get-ready, the one that came in yesterday? If you'll let me borrow the invoice on that car for a few minutes, I'll make you a good deal."

Crowley frowned. "Killer, you mean the one like the *other* one? Hell, man, why don't you sell the bonus car? I mean, we don't need two of those bastards, but at least sell the leper."

"Damn it, I'm *going* to sell that one. Now, just give me the tissue."

"Killer, you know that meeting yesterday? J. C. will kick my ass if I give you the invoice. He said sell from *list.*"

"Hey, Crow, I am going to make a hell of a gross and sell the leper. J. C. can't kick ass for that. Now give me the invoice for the leper's twin, okay?"

Crowley didn't even look up but reached into the drawer of his desk and pulled out one of the first invoices in the folder. He held it up in his hand and started talking again, without looking. "You know, Bob"—it was very unusual for anyone to call him Bob—"I hope you know what you are doing."

"Look. I'm going to sell the man a tan metallic car and give him every option he thinks he's getting. Is there anything wrong with that?" Crowley said nothing but started entering a deal in the gross book as Killer walked out of the office with the invoice. Merit was back from his solo drive in perhaps ten minutes.

"Hey, Bob"—hell, even the customer was doing it—"I really like that car. And I turned on the damn radio and heard one of my favorite stations." Merit realized that his enthusiasm was showing a little too much, and he pulled the giddiness back in. "Now, what did you find out about the car?"

"Mr. Merit, the car was prepared for delivery by one of the other salesmen. Some man said that he was taking it for sure but never came in to take delivery. That's why it's so clean, and that's why the stock number had been removed. The boss said that we should really hold the car, in case the man comes in, but I went ahead and just 'borrowed' the invoice anyway." There was lots of laughter from both men.

"Now, I want you to take a look. Here, let me explain all the different figures to you. Here are the costs on the base car and all the options. Let's check it with the list you read off to me." They read over each option carefully. "Now, this figure is the cost of dealer advertising that's built into every invoice. And this figure is the dealer holdback. I'm sure you're familiar with that." Merit didn't want to sound dumb at this point, and he was enjoying this tour through the invoice; his answer was a clipped "sure."

Within a few minutes Merit had agreed to buy the car. He even read the list of optional equipment off to Killer again, as each item was listed on the buyer's order. The order also listed the color of the car and its interior and the actual cost of the car. Plus $150. Killer neglected to place a stock number on the buyer's order, however. But that was of no consequence to Mr. Merit. The buyer's order was signed on the spot, and Merit also handed Killer a $200 cash deposit.

"Now, Mr. Merit, I can't promise you at all that the boss is going to take this deal. But I'll give it my best shot, okay?"

"Bob, you just tell your boss that he will take the deal or I won't buy."

Killer walked off, taking a slight detour by the small table that held the store's stock cards, the salesmen's records of cars actually on the premises. He didn't pull out the card for the newer tan metallic two-door, the one Merit had just seen the invoice for, but the card for the identical car in the back—the one Merit had driven. There were only a few differences in the cars really, so why should he worry? Merit had driven the car he would buy. Of course that car had the little bits of rust and the paint that didn't really match, but Merit didn't seem to care. The only substantial differences in the two cars were their age and price. Merit didn't know how to read the manufacturing date on a car—it's on a plate on every left front door—so it certainly wasn't Killer's fault he bought one that was ten months older. He hadn't checked the car's serial number either. And the price? The invoice Merit saw was for the newer car, the one with the three price increases. Killer would have no guilt pangs tonight. He would just pick up an extra $550 in profit. That was the difference in price in those "identical" cars.

As Killer finished his tale, appreciative laughter burst from Sam and Lanny. "Hey, Cherry, another round of the same for the man," Lanny volunteered.

By ten-thirty, Killer was alone in the booth in the Dead End, three empty glasses his only companions, or at least that's what he thought. "Hey, Mr. DeMarco, wanna buy me a drink?" Killer looked up, right into the face of J. C. It was the first time he'd even seen the boss at the Dead End—J. C. liked the fancier places—and Killer didn't really know whether to smile or run. He smiled, half-rising as he spoke. "J. C.! I'm sorry I didn't return your call, but I just got back from bird-dogging. Come on, sit down." J. C. didn't really look mad, Killer thought, he just looked real dry. J. C. sat down facing the men's john. "Boss, what are you doing here? I mean, you didn't come after me or anything, did you?"

J. C. grinned. He liked seeing Killer nervous for a change. "I'll tell you what. I'm going to come across the table real quick if you don't get me a drink." Killer didn't wait on Cherry but went to the bar himself, returning with a Scotch and soda.

J. C. drank it like cool water and started looking around the room and talking at once. "I wanna tell you, I hope Lake gets here pretty quickly," he said, pulling the glass to his mouth for one last taste. "That bastard said he'd be here at ten-thirty on the nose."

"Bobby Lake? I know that guy," Killer volunteered. "What are you doing with *him*?" For years, Bobby Lake had run the biggest buy-here-pay-here used-car operation in town. Most dealerships dumped their junker trade-ins there.

J. C. pushed himself back from the table, breaking into a smile. "Hell, Killer, I'm going to tell you a secret," J. C. said. "Let's see how long you can keep it."

Killer shifted his expression just enough to hide his curiosity. "Oh, you can trust me," he said quickly. The words and their practiced casualness caused them both to laugh.

"Uh huh. Well, anyway, people will know in a day or two. Davies and I are buying the Chevy store in Lomax and Lake is going to run the used-car department for us."

Killer looked at J. C. In the car business, the buying and selling of stores is the hottest gossip item, even more juicy than stories about who's making it with whom. But Killer's look wasn't about the gossip potential in these words. *He* should be a manager at Lomax, too, the new car manager. Who could tune up a new car sales department better? Killer started developing a plan right then, starting with another drink for J. C., a double. Killer knew that Lomax, a small, innocent town, really needed someone who was a pro in the car business. And he was tired of the rat race. Hell, Killer thought, I can do battle with tobacco chewers as well as city slickers. It was Killer's last thought as he headed home. But it was a pleasant one.

Do you live in the city? A rural community? Are you planning to buy on the Internet? Big town or small town, in person or by e-mail, there's a Killer waiting for you. He may be quiet or loud or invisible, he may belong to your church or coach your kid. But he or she is there, hand on your wallet. If you intend to control the amount of dollars that person will deftly lift from your pocket, you need a plan.

Something like the next part of this book—*Battle Time!*

PART II

Battle Time!

6

Some Preliminaries
to Shopping

DOWN THE ROAD OF GOOD INTENTIONS

During the last few years, a raft of well-intentioned publications have featured articles supposedly designed to clear up all the fog hanging over the car-buying process. Former used-car managers, salesmen, and even a couple of "serious" automobile traders have written books designed to accomplish the same thing. Unfortunately, most of these efforts have provided cheer and comfort to the wrong group of folks: the people who are selling cars.

For instance, one article entitled "How to Buy a Good Used Car" informs its readers that "a one-year-old car *can* cost twenty percent less than its initial purchase price." The article seems to imply that you'll be lucky to receive such a good deal. Well, anyone who swallows *that* little piece of advice will also be a candidate for your local Brooklyn Bridge sales contest. There is not a car made in America worth more than sixty percent of its original price at the end of the year. A popular consumer finance magazine once made even that advice relatively harmless. In authoritative style, the magazine suggested that you use one of the used-car books, such as the red book or the Kelly blue book, "before you make an offer" on a used car, adding proudly that "a few minutes of study will have you leafing through the book like a veteran." The article then concluded with a supposedly "good bargaining principle": "Offer $100 to $150 less than the asking price and stick close to it." If I were in the used-car business, that article would be the first thing given to every customer on my lot along with some copy of a blue book or red book. I would be a very rich man in a short time, too. Used-car "books" don't tell anyone, including wholesalers, the value of a specific used car; a $150 reduction in asking price is comical.

And then, there's another magazine's justification for buying one of those rental-company used jobs: "Before it's put on sale, it gets a more thorough going over: *The engine is steam cleaned,* fluid levels are checked, and all systems are tested." [Emphasis added.] How nice. What does a clean engine have to do with the value of a used car? Absolutely nothing. Under the cleanest engine in the world can lurk an equally prime piece of junk.

This same article informs the reader that "the prices posted by Hertz, Avis, and National for their used cars usually aren't negotiable—the figure on the windshield is what you pay . . . [and] checks with rental-company used-car lots in three cities indicate that prices are indeed lower than those of local used-car dealers." I'm sure that statement alone sent droves of eager bargain hunters to their graves, for what the article *didn't* say was the most important thing: Sure, Avis's "fixed price" of $5500 was lower than the $5900 "asking" price at the used-car lots. But the used-car lots would have most likely cut their price to $5200—if someone bargained a little.

Like these articles, most of the "how to" books on the market seem to be filled with nice logical statements, too. One former car salesman's book begins a discussion concerning "fair profits" for the seller by stating that "most dealerships will be happy if you offer them a ten to fifteen percent profit on a car." Happy? Every dealership in America would die of ecstasy if its profit on each car reached that level. This same salesman goes on to say, "For heaven's sake, don't be a 'be-back'—one of those people who tell salesmen they'll come back the next day, but never do." What does this man want you to do? Does he want you to say, "John, even if I find a car at a lower price than the figure you've given me, I promise to buy a car from you"? Customers have enough insecurities as it is without having spurious morality trips heaped on them.

As a customer, your chances for survival in the car-buying and -selling maelstrom are next to none if you depend on general answers, pat formulas, and simplistic logic in planning your attack. Your chances are good, though, if you'll learn the right questions, the specific questions that *you* can answer. For instance, there is certainly no value in knowing that your salesman will be happy with a fifteen percent profit; a more appropriate piece of information would be,

"What is the *least* profit a specific dealership will accept on that new Oldsmobile sitting there in the showroom?" Or, why depend on the information in some book to tell you what your car is worth? Wouldn't it be wiser to know exactly how much your specific car is worth in wholesale dollars in your community *today?*

The first part of this book addressed the questions you should have about yourself as a buyer, your present car, and your financing. The remaining portions of the book will help you use your answers, as you follow the correct procedures in shopping for and in negotiating the sale of your new or newer car.

These procedures are not hard to follow, but they will not exactly make you popular with salesmen—so what? As with any sale, the important thing to the seller is your money, not your friendship. Salesmen will be nice to you, laugh with you, support your ego to the fullest, as long as you are not threatening their opportunity to make the largest profit imaginable. But the moment you pull out a pad and attempt to discuss your purchase intelligently, most salesmen will be secretly cursing you under their breath. Why? Because they will have to work harder and longer with you than with most stiffs, and their profit will be less. Like most of us, car salesmen much prefer the path of least resistance when dealing with a customer. Accept that fact, and be prepared for at least small doses of contempt from that nice man. You will not only survive the transaction but you will always retain $2000 to $4000 of your money in the process.

SOME PRELIMINARIES ON ADVERTISING

J. C. flipped a cigarette in the puddle of water just by the front door to the showroom, opened the door, and headed to his office without once looking at any of the salesmen standing around in little clumps, each one of them quickly doing his best to look busy. Damn, things must be slow. It was a Saturday morning, usually one of the busiest days at the store, and J. C.'s lumbering body never made an appearance near the place on Saturdays. The showroom emptied as each one of the guys headed to his office and the phone. None of them really liked making cold calls, but it sure as hell beat a one-to-one session with the boss.

Killer had already been on the phone for an hour when J. C. settled behind his desk and opened his thermos bottle of Bloody Marys, at the same time turning his chair around to the sample and layouts on the chair just behind him. On that particular morning both men would be practicing their own particular version of the car-store lie. One thing was for sure: Business had stopped dead in its tracks, and everyone was going to "bust ass" for the next six days. J. C. tipped up the thermos and gulped. Gary Oliver Davies didn't care in the least that the first twenty-two days of the month had been record selling days. He didn't even care that Killer had nineteen cars out for the month.

"Damn it, J. C., we've written four deals a day for the past three days, and at least one per day couldn't be financed by the s.o.b.'s parents if their lives depended on it! Now, you find a way to get some people in this place, and you do it *today.*"

Davies didn't yell much, J. C. thought, just every hour on the hour. He took another swig and picked up the ad that was running in Sunday's paper. It was a full-page ad. The headline ran: 100 NEW CARS UNDER $100 PER MONTH. The small asterisk by the headline was barely noticeable.

Just below the main head were three other nice promises. The truck department's ad said: $3000 DISCOUNTS ON ALL TRUCKS IN STOCK. The new-car department's subhead showed a picture of a big "zero" and proclaimed ZERO PERCENT FINANCING AVAILABLE! Another asterisk closed that heading, too. The used-car department's head was just as enticing: ALL CARS FOR SALE AT PRICES BELOW NADA WHOLESALE. J. C. burped. "*Maybe this will bring the queers from the closet,*" he said out loud, taking one final nip from the thermos.

THE BIG LIE: DEALERSHIP ADVERTISING

It's time to have some fun, don't you think? As J. C. digests his Bloody Marys, why don't you laugh a little and learn a lot about the biggest joke in the business, dealer advertising? Start by digesting these spicy but very accurate tidbits of info:

All car and truck ads are part of a dealership's track system. Virtually all of them are designed to excite, confuse, mislead.

The main objective of dealer advertising is NEVER to do what it says. The objective is simply to say whatever it takes to deliver you, panting, to the dealership and the track system. This is true even of simple, words-only ads that say things like "Forget the hoopla and come to the friendly, low-key place."

You will be taken if you believe sales and "markdowns" automatically save you money. Deciding to buy a car on the basis of a dealer ad is as foolish as trusting a salesperson to define a "fair" profit.

But What about "Truth in Lending"? How Can They Print What's Not the Truth?

"If it weren't so we couldn't say it" has become a motto of many dealerships. "Why, truth-in-lending folks watch us like a hawk!" they say.

Yes, the law is there. After an enormous fight against the dealers, I might add. And yes, the law says the right things. It's there to "assure meaningful disclosure of consumer credit and lease terms so that consumers can compare those terms and shop wisely,"* but boy, have the car guys learned to get around those words.

What the law was intended to do: It was designed to prevent advertisers/lenders from advertising only the most attractive credit terms

---

* *How to Advertise Consumer Credit*, a Federal Trade Commission manual for businesses, p. 3.

in an ad. The law says that if you use certain "trigger" terms, you must then disclose enough facts to make that very attractive "trigger" term really understandable.

A FEW TRIGGER TERMS

➤ The amount of down payment ("10 percent down" "$150 down" "95 percent financing").

➤ The amount of any payment.

➤ The number of any payments.

➤ The period of repayment.

➤ The amount of any finance charge.

If advertisers use terms like these, they must also disclose:

➤ The amount or percentage of the down payment.

➤ The terms of repayment.

➤ The annual percentage rate (APR).

That's why you see all that ant-sized type on ads and on the TV. Now, I know you usually ignore the small type, since you probably don't keep a magnifying glass handy, but don't. The *small* type is where you'll find the *honest* information in ads.

Truth in lending doesn't prevent "Bait and Switch," either. The law says that if a dealer advertises certain items they must be for sale. The dealers get around that very easily by putting "qualifying terms" in their ads. One such "qualifying" tactic, for instance, is putting stock numbers by a really low price. Only one—or three or five—cars out of hundreds are available at that price. Go down to the dealership even before it opens, be the first one at the door, and nine times out of ten those advertised cars will be "sold."

Well, there's a little problem here. How do you really know if it's sold? You don't. Bait and switch works better for the dealers now than before the days of Truth in Lending.

Dealers' Favorite Advertising Gimmicks Used in Your Hometown

Do you have a newspaper handy? Especially one with a big fat automobile section? If not, hold this section until you find one, and then plunge into the thicket of dealer deception. See how many of these tricks you can find in your own area. You might want to make this a regular game with your spouse for a little cheap entertainment, and you certainly want to remember that new tricks come up every day. Take a look at the general layouts, too. How many are really designed to help you? To provide easily understandable information?

The universal lie of virtually all advertising is "Hey, we're the home of the Low Price and the Big Discount! Why, we fire people at sales meetings if they make money!" The tune is the same everywhere, but the lyrics vary a lot. *And here's the newest disgusting news:* In a second, we're going to check out some of the dealer's favorite advertising gimmicks, but first, guess who's now being asked to pay for them? You, of course. Now after you've negotiated for the car, many dealerships will tack $100 to $200 on the contract for their "Advertising Fund." Now, think about that. They want you to pay for deceptive advertising that hurts rather than helps? Why are you paying extra for the advertising, anyway? That's a cost of doing business.

This is all the more maddening when you realize that in buying any car you've *already paid* an advertising charge. It's built into the car's invoice—usually $100 to $350 depending on the cost of the car. When you buy a car, you pay the charge though you don't see it, and then the manufacturer sends a check to the dealer.

So what do you do when you see this? Refuse to pay it. Even if you have to break off negotiations, refuse. That's the only way to stop this fast-growing con.

Now, check out some of these popular advertising ploys.

The one dollar over (or under) invoice gimmick. Think "invoice" is what a dealer really pays for a car? Think again. Invoices for all domestic and most foreign vehicles are padded hundreds, and at times thousands, of dollars. Remember that "holdback?"

The Big Discount—$5000 or $6000. You'll see this on ads for trucks, full-size vans, and used vehicles. How can they give these great discounts? Easy. New trucks and full-size vans *don't have federally* *mandated Manufacturer's Suggested Retail Price Stickers.* Dealers make up their own. Want to discount a van $6000? Just mark it up $6000 first. The same gimmick is used on used vehicles.

"We'll pay you two thousand dollars if you can beat our deal!" Or "We guarantee to beat any deal in town!" Why, shoot, how can you go wrong here? Why, if they guarantee the lowest price, there's no reason for us to even *visit* another dealership!

That's certainly what these nice boys would like for you to think, but you'd be very wrong. First, you would need to find an "exact match" car at some other dealership—and that probably doesn't exist, since cars can vary in thousands of ways. And then you must present the dealership with a completely filled out, signed copy of a buyer's order from the competing dealership. And dealership managers never give out detailed buyer's orders with their signatures on them. So what's the outcome? Dealerships never have to acknowledge a cheaper price and certainly never pay off on these guarantees.

"Special purchase" vehicles at "thousands off Manufacturer's Suggested Retail Prices." One ad we collected showed a $6591 discount on a car with an MSRP of $17,588. Boy, had you better rush down and get one of these! There's only one minor problem, however. The ad is for *used* cars. Using a new-car asking price for a year-old used car is a little misleading, wouldn't you say? But that little bit of fraud is nothing compared to what many dealerships do to you on "Program" or "Executive" cars. More on that later.

"New Minutulas for only $4500!" Why, this must be the cheapest dealership in the world! Nope. If you read the fine print on ads like this, you'll always find some word telling you this is the *balance due* —after paying thousands down, and/or giving them a trade worth $5000, and after giving them your rebate. Real straightforward.

"This once-in-a-lifetime price applies to every single car on our lot." As long as it's stock number 3221. Legal bait and switch, as we said.

"Double rebates on every new car in stock!" These ads offer to match dealer rebates. How do they do that? Real simple. Take a car with a manufacturer's sticker that says $15,000, put up a dealer's sticker beside it that raises the asking price to $19,000 without adding any value, and then knock off a thousand of that inflated price as a "dealer rebate." Is there anything deceptive there?

"Brand-new Mosquitoes for $99 per month!" Payment ads are the dealer's favorite because so many people are suckered by them. But look at some of the wording in your own paper and you'll see—in ant print—a request for thousands down in cash or trade. Forget payment ads—they're for fools and mental lightweights.

Imply a low payment at a low rate. This approach is very popular at rate sale time. It promises low payments on the same page with cheapo interest rates. But if you look closely, you'll see that you can't have both: If you want the low payment, you have to pay lots of money down and pay a high interest rate. If you want the low interest rate, you can't have the low payment without a much bigger down payment.

"One-half" payment plans. Unfortunately, lots of us fall for this. For the first year your payment is easy—a couple of hundred for a very expensive car, for instance. But for the next *four* or *five* years, it's really high. Like $500. You pay hundreds more in interest for this little "favor," and, if you're like lots of folks, you end up having your car repossessed at the end of the first year. But does the dealership care? Nope. They've already gotten the majority of their profits.

"$229 a month for a Gargantula! This is not a lease!" Before you rush down to this fine establishment, do read the fine print however: "59 payments of $229 and one final payment of $21,000." We refer to this as the "Grim Reaper" financing plan.

"Free trip to Mars with every car sold!" If you can afford it, that is. This gimmick works one of two ways. Either the seller increases the minimum price he'll accept on a car to cover the cost of the gift (which means it isn't "free," doesn't it?), or the salesperson looks you in the eye and says "Folks, you're such hard bargainers, we just can't afford to sell you this car *and* give you our gift." And what does the customer do? Take the car without the gift, of course.

"Credit problems? No problem! No Credit? No Problem!" Now, think about it. Why would a dealership try to attract people with credit problems? As we said earlier, they do it because nervous people are so easy to make money on—thousands of dollars. Dealerships that prominently advertise like this are usually the toughest, meanest guys in town. They'll find a way to take people with marginal credit or even truly bad credit and finance them to the hilt.

Promotions mailed to your home: "Congratulations!" one mailer says, **"We've enclosed a *thousand dollar check* and selected you for a special *private sale! No negotiations necessary!"*** How can you be so blessed?

Of course, it's all a gimmick. Salespeople laugh at these "sales." They know the price of every car has been raised by a thousand to cover the phony "check." They also know anyone who falls for "private" sales is prime sucker bait, and target these suckers for extra-special sales pressure.

Throw direct-mail dealership promotions in the garbage, where they belong.

The ever-present use of weasel words. And how many times in your own local ads have you seen wording like this:

> ➤ "With approved credit" or "for qualified buyers"—who determines the criteria for approval?
>
> ➤ "All units subject to prior sale," and boy, are these cars sold before you can get there!
>
> ➤ "Dealer participation/contribution may affect consumer cost." The dealer was required to give up some of his normal profit to offer this, and you can bet he's going to get it back from you in spades.
>
> ➤ "Invoice may not reflect true final cost to the dealer." You remember that one, don't you?
>
> ➤ "No reasonable offer refused." Who determines "reasonable"?
>
> ➤ "Savings *up to . . .*" What does that mean? On which cars?
>
> ➤ "Starting at . . ." Of course, there's only one car starting at that price.
>
> ➤ "On selected models." And do you really think the model you want is one of them?

Whew! How Can You Find a Rose in All That Garbage?

It's really easy. Forget dealer advertising. Never rush down to sales. Laugh at their funny promises. The only sensible way to buy a car cheaply is to negotiate *up* from what a dealer paid for the one car you like. Do that, and you'll buy a car cheaper than any sale price any day you want.

What About Ads from Individuals Selling Their Cars?

If you are planning to buy a used car, classified newspaper ads can be a very productive source for locating a car, but not a price. Many classified ads are also placed by salesmen, not individuals. Smart salesmen will drive a nice used car from their lot home on the weekend to try to sell it.

Incidentally, Killer had a copy of Sunday's ad in front of him, too. He had asked for it the night before, and his request had brought a smile to J. C.'s face. Mr. DeMarco might not have the boss's personal esteem, but he knew how to work him. The ad was on Killer's desk, by an open phone book turned to the name "Smith," and Killer cleared his throat as the phone rang. "Hello, Mrs. Smith, this is Robert DeMarco. I just wanted to tell you that your new car arrived yesterday and will be ready for delivery on Monday morning. Would ten o'clock be a good time for the two of you to come down?"

Killer had never talked to these people before, and certainly there was no car waiting for them, either. The voice on the other end of the phone confirmed this. "I'm sorry, but you must have the wrong Smith. Were you calling Allen C. Smith?" The voice was a little surprised but friendly, so Killer continued.

"Oh, ma'am, I'm sorry. I was trying to reach Allen *D.* Smith. I sure hope I didn't bother you."

"Oh, no," she volunteered, "I wish we *were* getting a new car, our old one is honestly on its last legs."

Killer liked the sound of that. "I'm sorry to hear that. What type of car do you have?" His tone was that used more frequently by morticians.

"Oh, it's a three-year-old Sable, a blue one."

"Mrs. Smith! I think someone up there is really watching after us today! I have a customer looking for a used Sable right now. Even though you may not be interested in trading right now, I might be able to *sell* your car for you at a retail price. And then you *could* afford to buy a new one, especially on Monday. You know, we're having this special sale then; after you buy a car, we give you back $300 in cash and a color TV!"

Not all of the "wrong numbers" proved so productive as this one.

But the Smiths did come in on Monday, and Killer immediately gave them a demo to drive for the morning while he "showed" their car to his imaginary prospect. They spent three hours driving the demo and didn't even seem upset by the fact that Killer's "prospect" had already purchased some other car. That, too, was an old trick in the business. After spending several hours in a shiny new car, most prospects' sense of good judgment seems to pale. The Smiths would just trade their old tub, anyway. Killer made a really nice deal. And just think how many Smiths are left in the phone book.

DO CAR PEOPLE EVER—EVER— HAVE REAL SALES?

In an odd way, they never do and they always do. If "sale" means a low price, you can have that any time if you've done your homework. If "being taken" means paying more than you have to for a specific car, people are taken at every single sale in this country. Car people, regardless of the circumstances, are going to attempt to make a *maximum* profit on you, even if the car you're looking at is marked down to dead cost. To do this, they may give you less than your trade's worth, sell you add-ons, or simply raise their financing rates. By some method, they'll try to make more money.

Sales *may* be a fun time to shop, as we discuss in the next section. But you would do well to forget about sales. Forget about easy-payment plans and low-down-payment plans. Definitely forget about consumer lease come-ons. Your objective should be to get the lowest price on the car you are buying, the highest dollar for your car if you trade, and the most advantageous financing.

Do it like we tell you, and you'll always be purchasing a car at a *true* sale price.

IS THEIR AN EASIER TIME TO BUY?

It was two days before "show time," the intro date for the store's new cars, and J. C. was chairing the sales meeting again. Or, at least, he was chairing this special meeting at closing time on Saturday, and every damned salesman had been told to be there *or else.* J. C. had also passed the word that all the service mechanics and writers—even the parts men—had to be there and every single one of these people was nervous, especially after catching one quick glance at the boss. He was nearly frothing at the mouth, standing up in the front of the room by one of the store's videotape machines.

No one needed to call the meeting to order that day. Everyone was dead still and silent as J. C. began to speak—or, rather, to thunder. "Sloppy! This place is the damnedest bunch of pigs I've ever seen in my life, and I'll be damned if we're going to Intro Day without being a tight place. Every single one of you is going to know what's new and saleable about every single car. Now, I'm going to show you a tape. And if there is anyone in this room who doesn't watch every second of it, memorize every technique, I'll be damned if that person will be here long. Killer, pass out these pads."

Killer took the yellow legal-sized pads and started passing them down each row as J. C. continued. "And one other thing. Starting tomorrow morning, *no one* is to put a date on any of their deals. And *everyone* is to tell their customers all new cars will take three days to get ready for delivery. I'm talking about all the deals on current cars, not the show cars." No one said a word, though few knew the significance of J. C.'s request. The front row of lights was turned off, and as J. C. pushed the start button on the machine, he repeated himself. "Now damn it, *learn these techniques!*" He said that just as the first picture came on the screen. It took about three seconds for most of the guys to figure out what was going on. They were watching *Taboo II.* J. C. liked a good joke every now and then.

In the midst of J. C.'s joke, though, one important piece of information was passed out in that meeting—the matter of the dating of buyer's orders at show time. When the next year's cars are introduced, the vast majority of manufacturers give their dealers an extra three or four percent profit on all leftover new cars in stock from the previous year. Called a carryover allowance, it is important to the dealers, to put it mildly. But many dealerships like to cheat just a little bit. Why should they sell a car a few days before showdate, before it earns that extra percent profit? So what do these dealers do? They fudge the paperwork. If a deal is written on a car four or five days before showdate, the paperwork on that deal, including the buyer's order, isn't processed until showdate. The computer cards that are supposedly sent to the manufacturers the day a car is sold are held to showdate, too. Yum. Dealers just love this little sleight-of-hand.

Though this carryover allowance is meant to be an incentive for dealers to stock more cars at the end of the model year and then sell them for less money, don't expect to see any of this money in your pocket. Dealers are very jealous of both this end-of-the-year "holdback" and their normal holdback, and they seldom share this profit with their salesmen, much less their customers. If you are aware of the largess, however, you will be in a stronger position to negotiate your deal.

But is it a good idea to wait until year-end to buy a car in the first place? As with most things in the business, the answer is yes and no. During the course of a year, all manufacturers raise their prices on every car line by hundreds of dollars, price increases usually much larger than any savings you may earn by waiting. But if the year-end is the time you plan to buy anyway, you can certainly buy a leftover for less money than the models just appearing. And *if* you trade cars again two or three years down the road, and are trading for another leftover, you won't be hurting yourself. Many people will make the mistake of trading cars during the last month of a model year, then trading cars again in thirteen months. On the used-car market, that thirteen-month-old car is *two* years old. If the same car had been traded during the twelfth month, it would have remained a one-year-old car and been appraised as that.

So are there any "best times" to buy a car? If you remember that car people will always make more if you let them, and if you guard against that, timing can be important.

Every Day Sales

The prices are not really lower at sales, but the pressure to sell is greater. For instance, advertising and promotional expenses need to be recouped, and sales managers are continually under the gun of gaining "extra deals"—more sales than usual for the time period to pay for the added expense. At sale times a good bargainer may not get a better deal but may have an easier time negotiating that deal.

Before Christmas

Most people's minds are on other things at Christmas time, and many dealerships' sales drop dramatically. Managers are more inclined to take small profits during this time.

When Car Sales in General Are Low

When the economy and other factors depress the car business as a whole, competition is at its fiercest for those few customers who do buy *new* cars. As we've discussed, used-car sales are usually highest at times like this.

At Monthly Pressure Times

Car salesmen are under two great pressures. One is the pressure of the dealer, who expects his salesmen and managers to sell every day. When business is slow—when it's pouring down rain, for instance—the sales manager's neck is under the guillotine, and you would be surprised how much money some people save. Salesmen refer to rainy-day buyers as "fairies"—weird folk who only come out in the rain, invariably with a pad in hand. That's okay, though. You can afford to put up with this contemptuous attitude for enough bucks, right?

Another good time to buy a car can be the last of the month. Dealerships keep profit-and-loss statements on a monthly basis, and sales people can get a little desperate toward the last of the month if forecasts aren't being met. Even if the month has been a successful one, you will probably come out better—any deals made then are pure gravy.

If you really want to be mean, go down to a dealership thirty minutes before closing time on a rainy night on the last day of the month. You'll either get a really great deal or a really black eye.

REMEMBER: A really smart car buyer can usually get the same deal any day of the month. It's just easier to negotiate during pressure times.

7

Jumping into the Fray: Shopping the Right Way

"Damn it!" The bright blotch of blue ink had spread over six inches of Killer's shirt before he noticed it. "Why in God's name is it always a new shirt?" He said it out loud. Not that anyone was listening—saying it out loud just seemed to let out more anger. Killer pulled his car off the first exit and headed back home. Maybe he should have stayed there, too, but he didn't. After all, he was supposed to meet some lady and her husband, a lady who was definitely going to buy a car—or at least that's what she said. Gloria Wright had called him the night before and set an appointment for ten this morning.

"Hell, I'll sell them a car and buy *two* new shirts," he thought, as he headed once again to the store, speeding just a little bit more than usual. About a mile from the store, Killer flipped open the glove box and grabbed one of those small liquor bottles airlines dispense regularly. The tasty juice was down his throat in a swallow. Killer didn't know it, but even three of those liquid tranquilizers would not make this day any better.

He didn't really like the couple from the beginning, from the moment Jim Wright pulled out his pad. Hell, the guy was probably a pipe smoker, too. Everyone in the business knows that pipe smokers, those thoughtful, nonemotional s.o.b.s., are some of the hardest people to make money on. And every single one of them seems to have a pad glued to his palm. Killer also didn't like their attitude. These people didn't want to be led the least little bit but knew exactly which cars interested them. As a matter of fact, they knew the *one* car that interested them, and the damn thing didn't even have a bonus on it.

"Folks, I know you like that car, but you know, we've been having a little trouble with the transmission on that model. Let me show you something that could be a lot better value for the money," Killer said.

Like a car with a "spiff," a cash bonus: *That* was Killer's idea of value.

But Wright answered just as quickly. "Thanks, Mr. DeMarco, but we've done enough reading and riding to be satisfied with our choice. Now, why don't we go to your office and get to business. We have an appointment with another salesman at noon."

Oh, God, this guy was going to be a pain. He probably *did* have an appointment with someone else.

Killer grabbed a buyer's order as soon as the Wrights were seated and began to fill out each line. This normally was a good tactic. Before talking price, he liked to have the entire order completed except for the trade allowance. Then, after discussing price for a few moments, Killer would fill in the allowance "offer" acceptable to his customers, turn the pad around, and simply say, "Why don't you okay these figures for me?" Most people would sign without thinking, very easy. But hell, the Wrights didn't let him write one line.

Gloria made the point. "Mr. DeMarco, it isn't necessary to fill that out just yet. Why don't you take our car and have it appraised? We may be just wasting your time until we know that figure, don't you agree?" She smiled, a friendly smile. Killer smiled back as he took the keys, a very plastic smile, and headed out the door.

"Jim?"

"Yeah, honey?"

"Should we have told the man our highest wholesale offer on the car is $4700?" Forty-seven was the figure put on the car by a used-car lot not too far from the dealership.

"No. Maybe they will put even more on the car—you never really know. And anyway, I want to see if the guy lowballs us!" Jim Wright was beginning to enjoy this; he was the driver, rather than an unwilling passenger, for a change. They both were luckier than they knew, too. Killer's office wasn't bugged, unlike many offices in other car stores.

Killer returned within ten minutes, sat down, and began to write figures on a blank sheet of paper on the desk, seemingly preoccupied with the magical figures. Then he looked up, smiling again, and spoke. "Mr. and Mrs. Wright, I've got an excellent appraisal on your car! We have normally been taking in cars like yours for $4200, but let me ask you this: If I could allow you $5000 on the new car, really $1000 more than usual, would you buy that car? Of course, the boss will have to approve something like this, it's so much higher, but would you buy the car today?"

Killer had spoken the words in the one continuous stream, and the Wrights nearly fell for it. But as the word "allow" exited his mouth, alarm bells began to ring in the Wrights' ears. Gloria turned to Jim, and both of them began to speak at once, the echoes of a miniature Tower of Babel filling the room. All three laughed, but Killer's laughter didn't really match the slightly quizzical look on his face. Why had they reacted so quickly?

"Mr. DeMarco," Jim said firmly, "thank you for the generous offer. But we are not really interested in allowance—we asked you to have our car appraised. Now, what was the appraisal on the car, if you don't mind telling us? We'll talk about the discount on your car after we discuss our car, if that's okay."

Killer froze for a second, all the little cubbyholes up there in his mind opening wide, ready to throw out answers that worked every time. The real big cubbyhole, the one containing sarcasm, was trying to open, too, but Killer mentally pushed the door shut and locked it. So what if these people were know-it-alls? So what if they didn't want to do it the right way, or rather the dealership's way? Killer's mouth opened, and he hesitated perhaps another second. "Jim and Gloria— I hope it's okay if I call you that—let me tell you something. I can see that you are very intelligent car buyers, and *that's* refreshing. So many people don't know the first thing about buying cars." The line always worked. Get their attention with a compliment, and then do a number on them. Killer continued: "And of course we can discuss the value of your car first, the real value. As you probably know, our buyer's orders aren't designed to show discount on a new car and then actual wholesale value on your car—Mr. Davies, our owner, doesn't want to make it too easy on customers, you know—but I'll handle that." Another good line. The owner was the enemy, and Killer was the good guy, a lamb in wolf's clothing, of sorts. Right. *All* selling systems use some line like this.

"Now, about the wholesale value of your trade," he continued, "our used-car manager personally drove the car and placed a wholesale value of $4400 on it." Killer continued talking before anyone could speak, confident he was heading in for the kill. In truth, he was heading fast to the ground, tail high in the sky. The car had really been appraised for $4600; he was just lowballing them a little. Everyone could be taken just a bit; he was sure of that. Killer didn't know about the Wrights' $4700 offer. "And, Jim and Gloria, let me tell you: That's really more than the car is worth. The used-car man put such a high figure because he has a customer for the car." Killer smiled.

But the Wrights weren't smiling at all. "You know, Mr. DeMarco, maybe we are just wasting your time. You see, we already have a much higher offer than $4400 on the car. If you don't think your people can do $300 or $400 better, we'll just sell the car ourselves; I've done that many times before."

Gloria agreed with that sentiment, adding, "Jim, why don't we do that? And anyway, I want to look at the other new car; we could do that on the way. And, Mr. DeMarco, we can always buy a car from you without trading."

Gloria Wright's words pulled Killer back from the fog, and he spoke. To the experienced ear, his voice now betrayed just a little impatience, too. Customers weren't supposed to be talking like this. "Ma'am, before you do that, let me go back up to the used-car lot. Maybe they can do a little better. Now you folks just make yourselves at home."

At home? Hell, they were more comfortable than Killer at the moment. He headed back to the used-car lot and grabbed Timothy Raxalt. "Rax, I need another $100 at least on this car. The people say they have got it sold to someone for $4700 or $4800. What do you think?"

Rax didn't look at the car but at Killer. He had heard that line so, so many times. "Killer, I'm going to rename you Chicken Little. It's a damn nice car but I am not going to put another dime in it just to make *you* a higher gross. Now, go trade the thing at $4600."

"Damn it, I'm telling you the straight. Now, do you want me to send them on their way, or do you want the car at $4700?"

"What's got into you, man? Can't you allow them a little more?"

"Hell, no—the damn people won't talk allowance. I'll tell you what, though. Let me try one more thing. But then if they don't agree, can I go ahead and figure the deal from $4700?"

I don't really think the Wrights had noticed the tone in Killer's voice or knew how much their approach to buying a car was messing up the mind of our number-one salesman. But they might have had some hint when Killer returned. His shirt pocket was again stained in that same blue ink, and not once did Killer notice it. He was talking as he entered the door.

"Folks, the used-car department is going to call me in a minute— they are trying to do a little better—but do you really want to sell

your car to someone else? After all, the paperwork can be pretty
tricky, and—"

"Mr. DeMarco," Wright interrupted in mid-sentence, "we've handled the paperwork before, as I said. You don't need to worry about
that. Plus we will be selling the car to a dealer just down the road.
They'll be doing the paperwork this time."

Killer was hanging from the cliff of calm with one hand, and even
those five fingers were beginning to slip. He agreed to give them $4700
for their car. And then he started to discuss the new car. *That's* where
he would stick them.

"Now folks, on the hardtop . . ." Killer laid the stock card for the
particular car on the desk, pushing it around with his finger until it
faced the Wrights. It was a loaded car: power windows, cruise control,
the works. As they looked at the car, Killer caught one last glance at
the coded cost figure in the corner. Or rather, the packed figure. Killer
knew it contained a $500 profit. "Now, as you can see, this car lists
for $19,600. But let me show you something. See this figure in the
corner? It's the coded cost of the car. We are *never* supposed to show
that figure to customers but, since you are knowledgeable people,
why don't we simply add a profit to that figure?"

It always worked before; Killer was sure the Wrights would say yes,
add a small profit to that figure, and—zap—pay that profit plus the
$500 pack.

Wright nodded his head yes, and, for the first time, Killer smiled a
real smile. "Mr. DeMarco, that certainly sounds fair to us. Would a
$200 profit be acceptable?"

God, he had them! "Well, I can't say for sure what my boss will
accept, but why don't we write it up, and I'll go argue with them a
little. After all, I won't make any money if you don't buy at some figure,
isn't that right?" Another standard, logical question. Wright shook his
head again, and Killer started to write.

"Oh, Mr. DeMarco . . ." Killer looked up just in time to see Wright
reopen his pad. "If you don't mind, we've calculated the true cost of
the car ourselves. I'd like to check our figure against the card's figure."
Wright's words were as calm and self-assured as Killer's usually
sounded. Killer ran his right hand through his hair and pulled his tie
loose. His other hand? It was in the cookie jar, so to speak. Wright
compared the two figures, looked off into space, and then began to
talk. "You know, Mr. DeMarco, I'm afraid your bosses are pulling the
wool over your eyes. If my figures are correct, and I'm sure they are,

your card 'cost' is about $500 or so higher than the actual invoice."
Wright looked at Killer without blinking and just sat there. "But I'm
sure your bosses just made a mistake, don't you think?" Killer lifted
his eyebrows and shrugged, doing his best to look surprised, nod
agreement, and disavow any guilt with his movements. He instead
looked like the smoking gun itself.

Wright continued: "But since we seem to have agreed on a $200
profit, why don't we just take *my* figure and add $200 to that? As you
can see, we have the cost of every single item on the car, and our list
figures for those items match your list figures." Wright laid his pad in
front of Killer and turned the stock card back around.

Killer didn't touch them but looked down for a moment and began
to speak. He really didn't sound too enthusiastic, however. "Mr. and
Mrs. Wright"—he dropped the first-name bit—"my company will look
at any offer. If you are saying you *will* buy a car at that figure, I believe
the total would be $17,835, let's do write it up and I'll take it to the
manager. But Mr. and Mrs. Wright"—he looked at Gloria, hoping to
find a little moral support there, instead finding a nice frozen smile—
"the manager will not even consider an offer this low without a deposit. It's a policy, and I can't do a thing about it. If you will give me
a deposit, I'll go in there and fight for us."

Mrs. Wright's expression didn't change, but Jim's face dropped any
pretense of a smile. "No, Mr. DeMarco, I'm sorry, that won't do. We
didn't come to this dealership to waste your time or ours. And, quite
honestly, I am not interested in an hour of offers and counteroffers.
I'll be happy to sign the buyer's order, but there will be no check until
your man has approved the price."

As soon as Killer left the office, Gloria turned to Jim, a look of
concern on her face, and said, "Jim, what if they won't approve it
without money? You know, I really do like the car, and even if we did
have to pay a little more, we could afford it." These two never had
an argument, but her words nearly started one. "Look, we have gone
this far. Now let's be patient. Let's keep emotion out of it!" His words
made sense. After all, Killer had enough emotions right then for all
three of them.

He sat down in the manager's office, looking like some forlorn
puppy. Don had seldom seen him like this. "Killer, what is wrong with
you? I mean, did they bite you or something?"

"Screw you! I'm telling you, I haven't seen anyone like these people
in six months. Here, here's what the guy will do. And he says he'll

walk if I try to bump him. He won't give me a deposit, either, until you sign the damn thing." Killer threw the buyer's order across the desk and sat there, immobilized.

"Killer, I know why you're giving this car away," Don said. "You're worried about your shirt."

Killer looked down and saw the patch of blue ink, and started laughing. "Oh, man, I just *knew* this wasn't going to be my day. Hell, I'm going home as soon as these jerks leave. Well, come on, tell me what you want to do."

"What's their trade like, can we make any money on it?"

"Hell, yes, it's a cherry from the word go."

"Well, will Rax put any more money in it?"

"No, I already got him up a hundred, and he is strong in the car."

"Well, are you going to get any financing? Have you tried to sell them glazing or a warranty? Killer, you know you can knock them dead on something."

"Don, I'm telling you, the people won't discuss financing or anything until you sign the order. Now, what do you want me to do, put their asses on the road, or sell them the car? Hell, *you* come on in with me if you want."

During his four years at the dealership, Don Burns had never been asked to go in on one of Killer's deals. There had really been no need to go in, either; Killer didn't leave money on the table. Burns would have normally taken the deal just to get the trade. But this was a good chance to show the master a few tricks. Burns picked up the buyer's order, looked at the $200 profit figure, and headed out the door with Killer in lukewarm pursuit. Gloria was flipping through one of those car brochures as they entered, and Jim Wright stood up, shaking Burn's hand, returning his smile, too. "Folks, Don just wanted to have a chance to meet you—why don't we all sit down?" Killer said, with about as much enthusiasm as someone meeting his in-laws for the first time.

Don began to speak, the words a replay of countless other T.O. situations. This time he was using the "logical and fair" approach, which seemed to work best on people like this. "You know, Mr. and Mrs. Wright, I believe you are fair people, am I correct?" Both nodded their heads slightly, and Burns continued. "Let me tell you a little about what it costs to run a dealership this size. We have a hundred and twenty employees here. All of them receive benefits over and beyond their earnings. We also have nearly $3,000,000 worth of cars sitting here, and as I'm sure you know, we pay interest on every one of them. For instance, the car you folks like so much costs, as you said, $17,635. Our interest on that car runs just about one percent over prime, or about one point five percent of its cost per month. That particular car started costing the dealership interest payments about two and a half months ago—as you can see on the stock card, the car has been here about three months, but we receive a two-week grace period on each car before the interest starts. But during the past two and a half months, we have paid on this specific car approximately $421 in interest.

"Now, you have offered to pay us a profit of $200. If we sell you the car for that profit, we're really losing money on this transaction from the beginning. But there's more. I have to be paid something. Bob here has to be paid something. The title clerks in the office have to be paid for doing your paperwork. My point is simple. Your offer isn't really a fair one, is it?"

The expression on Don's face would have reminded you of Saint Peter's face as he sat there at the pearly gates, gently asking each petitioner, "Now are you *really* a nice man?" Killer looked equally sincere. During this entire sermon the Wrights simply sat there, good members of the flock listening patiently to the shepherd.

Jim Wright cleared his throat and responded, "Mr. Burns, you are a convincing man." Don had him, Killer thought. "But even at that figure, you know you are making money." Don's mouth couldn't move fast enough to keep Wright from continuing. "Now, before you interrupt, let me tell you what I mean. I know the 'cost' figure, the real invoice figure, has at least $450 extra profit built into it. I also know you are going to sell my trade and make at least $1000 profit on it. I am willing to let you have my trade, even though it would be easy for me to retail it. Mr. Burns, I'm also willing to pay you the $55 'title and documentary fee,' even though that little bit of work certainly doesn't cost $55. Now, if you don't think I am paying a fair profit, that is certainly your right. We have an appointment down the road, as I mentioned to Mr. DeMarco, so perhaps those people will think my offer is fair."

Burns had only four more bullets in his gun, but they were wasted before the trigger was pulled. "Mr. Wright, what you say may be true. I don't really know. The dealer doesn't tell us those things. And I'm not saying we won't sell you the car at your figure, either. But before I check, has Mr. DeMarco told you about the other services we can offer you?"

"Oh, you mean the protection package? And the special service agreement?" Wright said noncommittally.

"Yes. And our special alarm system package, too." Burns started figuring on a pad. "Let's see, all three items are on sale now for just $1895 total, and . . ."

"Sir, don't waste your time on discussing that junk," Wright interrupted. "Now, about our offer on the car."

"Oh, yes," Burns said, "and how many months were you planning to finance with us?"

"None, thank you," Gloria answered, even though Burns was looking at Jim. "We've already checked the various sources, and our credit union will be handling the transaction. As a matter of fact, the money is already in our checkbook, right here." Gloria laid the checkbook on the table. It was the stripper's last garment. Killer's tongue slipped by reflex over his lips as Don continued.

"Well, what I will do is talk to J. C. Hollins, our general manager." Don paused. "But there is probably one thing you can do to assure Mr. Hollins will accept your offer. You see, he really does want to know that offers like this are serious. I believe what we should do is this: Let me figure up the total cost of the car, including tax. If you will give me a check for the entire amount, I'm sure the sight of that check will convince my boss to approve your offer. I know it sounds silly, but money does talk in this business." Don was determined to do at least one thing right. If he could get the couple's money to keep them from running out, maybe J. C. would actually come in and argue with these flakes himself. People seldom go running out of stores if their checks are still in the manager's office.

Wright shook his head firmly. "Mr. Burns, I not only won't give you a check for the full amount now, I won't give you more than a $100 deposit, at most. *If* our offer is approved, I prefer to give you all the money only *after* I check out the car before we pick it up. I like to know the car is completely ready before taking delivery. And, quite honestly, I'm not interested in talking to anyone else, though your boss may be a nice man. That would be a waste of his time and ours."

Killer and Don Burns were probably thinking the same thing, slowly savoring how nice it would be to choke these people, to pull their fingernails out one by one. The two of them left the office with the buyer's order showing the same $200 profit—supposedly to visit J. C. They didn't have any deposit, either, much less a check for the full amount. "Well, Don, what do you think?" Actually Killer wasn't feeling all that bad at the moment. At least Burns hadn't sweetened the deal either.

But Burns was feeling lousy. He really did need the deal even though the gross was nothing. Business was slow. And the used-car boys needed the trade, too. He signed the order quickly and said, "Here, take the damn thing back in there and get me their deposit," pushing the paper into Killer's hand.

Killer returned to the office, another one of those plastic smiles glued to his face, and concluded his little visit with the Wrights, shaking both their hands and finally saying, "Now folks, we'll have the car ready for you by six tomorrow afternoon. And I look forward to seeing you then."

God, was that a lie.

Wouldn't you like to do it like that? You will. These people succeeded in beating the system because they did their homework: They took the time to shop their own car and learned its true value—using the steps outlined in Chapter 3; they shopped their financing sources, too—just as we outlined in Chapter 4.

The Wrights also spent a good deal of time finding a couple of specific cars that fitted their needs, and then computed the cost of those cars carefully. That's why Killer couldn't fool them with artificial cost figures. And that's what we are going to look at now: where to shop and how to compute cost.

SHOPPING: IF YOU PLAN TO BUY A NEW CAR

If you plan to buy a new car, you will have an easier time of it because the variables are fewer than when shopping the used-car market. First, consider dealerships close to your home or work. Some people purchase a new car sixty miles from home and then spend much more in gas having the car serviced under warranty than they saved in the actual purchase—if they saved anything. And don't think you can automatically buy a car far from home and then have it serviced at the dealership next door. Most cars are sold with two separate warranties. The "adjustment" warranty is usually for ninety days or so and includes problems such as squeaks and rattles, air leaks, and alignment. Since all adjustment warranties are the responsibility of the *selling* dealer, the expense is paid by the selling dealer. Obviously other dealers will not incur expenses for your selling dealer.

Your car's regular warranty has some restrictions, too. Normally, other dealerships are not required to honor regular warranty work if your selling dealer is located closer than fifty miles from the dealership at which you wish to have the work done. Some service departments will honor anyone's warranty work, but don't count on it. Warranty work, even regular warranty work, is relatively unprofitable for the dealer.

Once you have determined the make or makes of cars that interest you, locate two dealerships for each make. Car stores have personalities, just like the rest of us. Usually a new-car store's personality is determined by the dealer, and since many dealers are s.o.b.s, you need the option of comparing similar stores' attitudes and tactics. One store may have a friendly, laid-back way of taking you, and a similar store six miles away may emulate the tactics of Vlad the Terrible, the true-life model for Dracula. Good old Vlad was famous for having troublesome villagers boiled alive at his dinner table.

Different stores will usually have different inventories of cars, too. Some stores are "color queer": The person who does their ordering may be partial to blues and light colors, and fill their lot with nothing else. Others stock mainly dark colors.

If you are buying new, it is not important to worry about a specific store's profit policies or its trade-in policies at this stage. For shopping purposes assume that you will get the best deal from any store.

What About Service Departments? Obviously, you would do well to buy from a store with an honest and efficient service department. Equally obviously, service departments are hard things to evaluate. They are like restaurants: great food one night and slop the next. But it's easy to check out a particular dealership's service department. Drive down there at their busiest time and talk to some of their customers in the service line. Does the service department listen? How long do they keep you waiting? Do they take appointments and, most important, do they fix what's wrong? In fifteen minutes, you'll know plenty about the place. And don't be shy. People just love to talk about service departments, and don't forget how much time you'll probably be spending there yourself.

What Do Those Pretty Cars Cost the Dealer?

We're going to show you two ways to figure that:

➤ What do Firebirds in general cost?
➤ What does that red Firebird I just drove at Friendly Pontiac cost?

If you're thorough, you'll use the second method when you get around to serious buying: What did that one specific car I like cost the dealer? That's really the important question, isn't it?

Understanding "Cost," MSRP, and Dealer Stickers

But before we get into costs, you need to understand a few things about those fun terms "Dealer Invoice," "Manufacturer's Suggested Retail Price" (also known as MSRP or Manufacturer's Sticker), and "Dealer's Sticker."

Dealer Invoice is the amount of money a dealer *pays the factory* for a vehicle. The invoice figure isn't really what a vehicle *costs*, however. It includes kickbacks to the dealer, which add up to hundreds of dollars on every car sold. Every three months, these kickbacks are sent back to the dealer in a separate check—a nice bonus account filled with your money.

Kickbacks include 2 to 4 percent in extra profit (*the "holdback"*), a charge for putting gas in the car, a charge for servicing the car (though many dealers try to charge you again for this), and an advertising charge. On a car with an invoice cost of $10,000 the kickback to the dealer might look like this:

Actual cost of car	$9300
Holdback (extra profit)	400
Gasoline	35
Make ready (servicing)	85
Advertising fund	135
INVOICE COST	$9955

The dealer can now look a customer for this car in the eye and say, "Hey, this car cost me $9955, so you've got to pay me a profit over that," and most customers will pay. Then in ninety days the dealer will receive $655 *back* from the manufacturer. He's happy, too. Because that's *your* money.

Even though you'll seldom negotiate a dealer out of his kickback on any car, you can negotiate harder simply knowing it's there, can't you?

Manufacturer's Suggested Retail Price (also known as MSRP and the Manufacturer's Sticker) You'll find this sticker on the window of every new car sold in America. Or at least you'd better find it, particularly if the car is sitting in a showroom. Federal law says it has to be there.

MSRP is the "suggested" retail price for a particular car. It includes a profit for the dealer, but dealers are free to raise the price (and profit) as much as they want, as we'll see. But for the purposes of determining what a specific car *cost a dealer*, this sticker is what you need to find on the specific car you like.

Dealer's Sticker The *dealer's sticker* is usually taped right beside the manufacturer's sticker, and it's real easy to identify, since its total is so much higher than the manufacturer's sticker.

The philosophy behind the dealer's sticker is simple: Take an already handsome profit and bloat it as much as you can. What the dealer's sticker does is raise the *asking price* of a vehicle without raising the *value* of the vehicle a comparable amount.

For instance, do you remember the dealer's sticker we showed you earlier? Here's another one. And you could actually find all of these items on the windows of cars around the country.

Manufacturer's Suggested Retail Price	$15,000
Special Value Package	1800
Protection Package	1200
Striping and Special Tires	795
ADP	1000
DVF	1500
TOTAL PRICE	$22,295

The dealer, in this instance, has raised his asking price by $7295. And how much has he increased the value? The $1800 special value package cost nothing—it's simply extra profit. The $1200 protection package (rustproofing, undercoating, glazing, fabric conditioning) cost $150. The $795 striping and special tires cost $150.

ADP simply stands for "additional dealer profit." Nice of them. And the $1500 charge for "DVF"? I had to go to a local salesmen's bar that night to find out what that stood for. "Hey, don't tell anyone, okay?" said the salesman finally, after a few drinks. "But that stands for Dealer Vacation Fund."

So what has this dealer done with the sticker? *He's raised his asking price by $7295 but only raised the value of the car $300.*

How would you like to make money like that? And oh, did you catch the little mistake in addition on this dealer's sticker? Like every car on the lot of this particular dealership, the dealer's sticker has a *thousand dollar error in the dealer's favor.*

How would you like to be dealing with that dealership?

Recently, dealers have begun adding several hundred dollars to the dealer's sticker or sometimes the buyer's order for "National Advertising Fee." It's another way to try to boost profit at the customer's expense. Don't pay it.

The moral of this story: Forget the dealer's sticker. For our purposes of negotiating, pay attention only to the manufacturer's sticker.

And what if a dealership says they can't remove their dealer "add-ons"? Tell them to give them to you or find you a car without them. What if they say "Oh, we have to write this up from the dealer's asking price"? Tell them that won't do. The only way to negotiate for a new car is to negotiate *up* from what a dealer paid—never down from what he is asking.

Okay, So What Do Those Pretty Cars Cost, Then?

One other general warning before I tell you that: *Though dealers will still try to tell you to the contrary,* the profit margin on smaller and/or less expensive cars is now very close to that on larger and/or more expensive ones. For instance, a Cadillac might have an 8.5 percent markup, while a Chevy Cavalier might have a 7.5 percent markup or a Toyota Corolla an 8.0 percent markup. Salespeople will try to tell you smaller cars just don't have any markup at all. They say that to increase their bargaining power. Now you know better.

So, What Do They Cost?

Here are two ways to figure that. Use the first answer, What Cars Cost by Car Line, to help you determine the range of cars you might be interested in buying. If you are thorough, use the second answer, What a Specific Car Costs, to determine *exactly* what a specific car cost a dealer. Chapter 9, "Negotiating the Sale," was designed for either method of calculating cost.

What Cars Cost by Car Line

A section in the Appendix provides formulas for quickly determining, within one or two percent, the invoice price, or "cost," of most American and foreign cars. These formulas will require your help; you will need to copy the model number, the base list price, and the name and price of every item from the manufacturer's sticker on the window of the car you like. Then look up the make (like Pontiac) and model (like Firebird) in the Appendix. Multiply the sticker price by the number listed by that car. This figure will be the amount of profit in that particular car. Some cars have *two* numbers by them. These cars have different margins of profit for the base car and options. Simply use the two numbers to develop the profit in the base car and options, and then add your answers for the total.

EXAMPLE

1. A basic Pontiac Firebird has a sticker price of
   $17,250 $17,250
2. The number by Firebird in the table is .085. Multiply the list price by .085 and you have the "margin," or profit—$1466
3. Subtract that figure ($1466) from the sticker price   −1466

4. What remains is the "invoice" price. $15,784

Remember: The formulas will provide you with a good guide, but they will not give you the exact cost of a particular car.

What a Specific Car Costs

"Very specific" describes the method the Wrights used for arriving at the cost of the new car they wished to buy. Gloria was mainly responsible for this step. The family had all decided that a two-door sedan was their most practical choice, and two particular cars seemed to fit their needs. After the family conference Gloria visited two dealerships for each car, telling each of the salesmen the same thing, which happened to be the truth: "Hello, I hate to tell you, but I'm not buying a car today at any price! We *are* going to buy a car within the next few days, though. Now, could you let me drive one of those sedans sitting over there?"

At the end of each test drive, she copied down *all* the information from the sticker of each car, the stock number of the car, the salesman's name, and the name of the dealership. Then she headed home.

"Gloria, are you sure you copied off the total figure from the *manufacturer's* sticker, not the dealer's sticker?"

"Yes, I copied down the right price. Now, it's your turn to get to work." Jim was sitting at the kitchen table studying a small paperback book that listed the cost of every single car and option sold in America. He also had a piece of paper for the two cars now under consideration. Listed on each sheet were the options on each car and their list prices, the figures from the window sticker. Jim first checked these list figures with the figures listed in his book. They matched. "Hey, honey, you *did* buy the right book, after all. You bought the one with all the latest price increases. But I like the old prices better! Why don't we use that book?"

Gloria looked at him. "Jim, that's crazy. How are we going to know the real cost if we use an old book?"

"But the older prices are *so* much lower. Think of all the money we'll save!" Jim loved the look on her face—Gloria really looked ready to kill now. But he was just playing with her; it was one of the stupid things that drove her crazy and made her laugh at the same time.

Jim turned back to the book. Within an hour, he had figured the exact factory cost of each car to the penny. He checked the book's list prices against the list prices from the window of the cars once more, pushed his chair back, and sighed. "Hey! Gloria! I've done it again. I've figured the cost right!"

"Great! But let's see if these latest figures I just found on one of the online services agree." Gloria proudly waved her notes under Jim's nose before beginning to compare her figures to those on his pad. "Yep, you did do it again."

The Wrights now possessed the three most important pieces of information in any car transaction: what their used car was really worth, where the best financing was available, and what each new car cost. No question was hard to answer, either. Especially the cost of the new cars.

Like Jim and Gloria, if you really want the nitty-gritty, you're going to have to make a visit to your local drug or book store and spend five bucks, to boot. Hidden away there on the shelves is a book called *Edmund's New Car Prices*. This little book is a gold mine for the curious car buyer—it shows you nice fuzzy pictures of every car sold in America and tells you what each car and its options list for and cost. There are "New Cars, American and Imports," and "Van-Pickup-Sport Utility" editions. It is an automobile fancier's delight, a straightforward, meaty compendium of raw facts. It is, unfortunately, also the home to several ads for computer buying services and "price quotation" companies. Edmund's and other organizations also offer pricing information over the Internet; the basic data can be excellent, but as with the books, you need to be cautious about ads and links to buying services. Buy the book or consult the online information, follow the steps outlined in the following list, and you will determine the exact cost of just about any car. But don't pay any attention to the ads unless you've read the section on car-buying services beginning on page 217 of this book.

HOW TO USE *EDMUND'S*

1. First, find a few cars in the book that appeal to you by flipping through the picture section. Use these cars for practice only— once you actually begin to shop, you will be figuring the cost of a specific car and options, but for now, find something that appeals to you and turn to the pricing section for that particular car. All cars are listed alphabetically by make—Buick before Cadillac, Lincoln before Mercury.

2. Take a sheet of paper and "create" your ideal car. List the make and model of the car at the top of the paper. We'll assume for practical purposes you are going to create a Dodge Caravan.

3. Now make two columns on your paper. In the first column, put the "list" or retail price of the base car and write under that the name and list price of all options you would like on your ideal car. It's important to write down these list prices, even though you will be dealing with cost figures. The list prices will enable you to compare the list price of the same options with those from an actual car. If they don't match, you have a book with old prices.

EXAMPLE		
DODGE CARAVAN		
Item	*List Price*	*Base Cost*
Base Car with standard equipment	$17,235	$15,687
Climate Group I (air conditioning)	860	731
4-speed automatic transmission	250	213
7-passenger seating	350	298
TOTAL	$18,695	$16,929

Now, you have the list price and base cost for the Caravan. But at least two things need to be added to the base cost to determine the true "cost" of the car. The first is a charge for dealer advertising. Yes, you are charged for all those nice commercials. This figure varies, but averages about $100 per car. The second charge is for "oil and gas" —the manufacturers, those chintzy folks, aren't satisfied merely charging you thousands for a car; they want you to pay for the gas and oil necessary to drive it from the plant onto a truck. Most manufacturers charge under $50 for this privilege, but let's assume $50. By adding these two items to your total basic cost, you have the real cost of the vehicle.

Total basic cost	$16,929
Advertising	100
Gas and oil	50
COST OF CAR	$17,079

There's one more thing to add, though: transportation. You'll find that figure on the manufacturer's window sticker. Though every dealer certainly expects you to pay freight since he has to pay it— and that's okay if the charge is legitimate. We're now finding out *some manufacturers pad their freight charges hundreds of dollars,* fleecing consumers and dealers of billions of dollars in the process. Watch the news for stories on this sad development.

The Wrights' experience has shown you how to compute the cost of specific cars that interest you. After you have visited the dealerships and taken down the specific information for the cars that interest you, you can, by using *Edmund's* or other pricing guides, actually determine exact figures for those cars, with these exceptions:

➤ Manufacturers include in the base cost of their cars a charge for dealer preparation and handling. Many dealers will try to charge you for preparation again and will insist on adding an additional $100 or $200 to the list price of their vehicles. Don't fall for this.

➤ Because manufacturers change prices several times during the year, it will be important for you to have the newest copy of *Edmund's.* You can verify the validity of your book by comparing the "base list price" for a specific car, the top figure on the window, with the base list price of the same car in *Edmund's.* If your book is outdated, simply note the difference in the base prices and add that to your total cost figure.

➤ If you are considering a "leftover" new car, a new car left over from the previous model year, the dealer's profit margin will usually be *three to five percent more* than the margin listed in *Edmund's.* This is simply an incentive for the dealer to stock more new cars at the end of the model year. To adjust your cost figure down, simply multiply the *list* price by five percent and deduct that figure from your "total cost of the car."

➤ Automotive manufacturers periodically give their dealers other "incentives" on slower-moving cars. These are usually unadvertised bonuses to encourage dealers to lower their prices. Of course, they don't, preferring to retain these bonuses as additional honey for the pot. You and I don't know which cars may have these incentives either, but we can assume slow-moving, unpopular cars may have them. How do you know a slow-moving car? They usually receive the most sale advertising.

➤ Don't forget the normal dealer "holdback." All new cars have an extra two to four percent profit built into their invoices. Neither you nor the salesman ever sees this money—another spiff for the boss—but remember it's there when you begin to bargain.

Does all this sound too complicated? It isn't. If you will take your time, remain patient, and *think,* you will easily determine the true cost of a new car. But even if you miss the mark slightly, you'll still be ahead of the game. Our approach to buying, Negotiating the Sale (Chapter 9), provides you with the best way to deal close to any car's cost. By giving you specific tactics for specific situations—for example, if you are trading in your old car and financing a new car—we will show you how to use and modify the information in this chapter for your needs.

Other Nice Ways to Be Taken: Car-Buying Services

Most car-buying services provide you a printout of car cost, and most will also buy you a car at a price less than sticker price. Services also remove much of the confusion and pressure from the buying or leasing transaction. Those appeals are alluring, and have made buying services very popular.

But services in general won't save you money if you're a good bargainer. For instance, they can't buy you very popular cars cheaply—

dealerships have a right to hold out for big profits on those models, and certainly aren't going to cut their profits for buying services.

If you have a trade-in, services can't help you much, either. Most of the dealerships involved with these services will be happy to take your trade-in as an "accommodation"—they are just providing you a service, you understand. They're happy, however, because they're probably giving you much less for your trade-in than it's really worth. Dealerships which work with services invariably will still try to sell you unwanted add-ons, and will work hard to switch you to their financing plans.

If you're really watching your pocketbook, don't waste your time with buying services.

I still want to use a service. How do I protect myself? If you just can't stand the thought of negotiating, use a service, but use it with your eyes wide open. Know the value of your trade before you give it to a dealership. Don't be switched to dealership financing without carefully comparing it to other financing sources, as we show you in this book. And don't be pushed into useless add-ons.

Ordering a Car

If you are buying straight out, not trading your car, it makes sense to order. First, you'll have the exact car you like. But, more important, you will probably pay less; dealers don't pay floor-plan interest on ordered cars. Because of that, most sellers will accept smaller profits.

If you are planning to trade your car, ordering can be a little more complicated. The seller will appraise your trade at the time your new car is ordered but will insist it be reappraised when your new car arrives.

Many dealerships will write "subject to reappraisal" on their contracts and tell you, "Hey, your trade could drop in value before your new car comes in." That's true. But, as with most things at the dealership, these guys have found a way to make a little extra money. When your trade is appraised again—*even if it's gone up in value* (and that happens quite a lot), some dealerships will tell you, "Sorry folks, but that car of yours has become so unpopular we can't even give them away." And you lose hundreds of dollars unnecessarily without knowing.

How to protect yourself: If a seller wants the right to have your trade reappraised when your new car comes in, make a manager write this on your contract: "Customer has the right to have car appraised by another source." Make the manager sign the statement. If the dealership's figure doesn't suit your fancy when the new car comes in, shop it at other dealerships or used-car lots.

"Demos," Demonstrators, "Executive" or Program Cars

Demos are new cars driven by salesmen, managers, and other employees of a dealership. All of these cars are "new" in the legal sense only—they have not been registered to an individual but are still the property of the dealership or floor-planning institution.

Many customers actively seek out demos, believing these cars are less expensive than new ones. Nine times out of ten that belief is false, too. The average dealership's profit on demos is just as high as its profit on new cars. Other folks seem to prefer demos because they believe the "kinks" have been removed. These people assume dealership employees spend large amounts of time caressing and caring for their wheels—another dangerous assumption. Most dealership employees are careless with these cars because they don't own them and will be driving them for only a few months.

So, what's the advantage of buying a demo? There is none.

Fraud at the factories and dealerships: the selling of rental cars as special vehicles. Are you driving one of those "Program," "Executive," or "Brass Hat" vehicles the dealers were pushing for years? Would it bother you to know that your "special" vehicle was simply a rental car from Hertz, Avis, and other rental agencies rather than a car maintained by some fancy executive? Or bother you that you paid $1,000 to $3,000 too much for that rental car, folks?

It bothered lots of state attorneys general, who successfully brought suit against the perpetrators of this formerly favorite selling ploy. That's why the vast majority of dealerships have stopped their "special vehicle" sales. If you're unlucky enough to be at one that hasn't, walk out the door and call your attorney general's office.

SHOPPING: IF YOU PLAN TO BUY A NEW TRUCK OR FULL-SIZED VAN

Manufacturers are not required to place suggested retail price stickers on any new trucks or full-sized vans, thanks to a nice loophole in federal pricing regulations. Dealers, therefore, get to make up their *own* stickers, adding thousands of dollars to a vehicle's asking price and then slashing some of those thousands of dollars supposedly to give you a deal. Unh-uh.

If you plan to buy a truck or full-sized van, simply ignore the prices on the dealer's sticker. To determine what the dealer paid for the particular vehicle you are interested in, copy down the *items* on the dealer's sticker such as model number and options and then go home and reread "What a Specific Car Costs" on page 213. Follow the steps outlined there, substituting *Edmund's* truck and van book for determining cost. Then you'll know what the vehicle cost the dealer. Or use the truck tables in the Appendix.

Determine your offer for one of these vehicles as you would for a car: negotiating up from cost, *never* negotiating down from list price.

What's the most important thing to remember about advertising as it relates to trucks and full-sized vans? *IGNORE THE ADVERTISING.*

PUTTING THE INTERNET TO WORK FOR YOU

Why can't I use the Internet to find out the prices? And while I'm at it, why not just buy my new wheels over the Internet? I'm always seeing those ads. A very good question! The Internet is a terrific place to rummage around for information, and it may be a good place to find a good deal, too, if you understand the auto scams peculiar to the Net and if you understand how some online providers are in cahoots with your local dealers. But the dangers here are great and your legal rights if you do it wrong are virtually nonexistent. Here's a look at doing it right.

If you're up and running on the Internet, even if you're still a browsing novice, the Net offers you a fine way to do much of your homework when it comes to finding out about the vehicles you like, gathering price information, and gathering good safety information. *Shopping* online (as opposed to actually buying) is fun—a word I never thought described any part of the car buying process.

The Net also offers you dozens of ways to buy, finance, or lease vehicles—all of them promising no hassle and low prices. Unfortunately, many of these commercial services simply add another layer of profit to your transaction rather than lower prices. They also haven't exactly practiced restraint or (in some cases) ethics in developing their sales pitches, either. There are no legal guidelines for honest advertising on the Internet, and more important, no clearly defined legal remedies or penalties for false advertising. Finally, very few companies offer you any protection if your dealings through their online services go wrong.

That's why, if you've been thinking about letting a few clicks around the many offerings on the Net replace reading this book, hold that thought for sixty-four bauds and read here first. If you're not using the Internet, skip to the next section.

Just Who's Providing the Auto Information on the Net and World Wide Web?

Everybody with a dollar to make or an ax to grind has a site. There are *thousands* of sites out there and the players are always changing. But you can expect to find these broad categories:

Auto Manufacturers

Auto manufacturers have homepages for their parent company and generally for each model car. General Motors, for instance, has a page, as do Chevrolet, Oldsmobile, and Cadillac. Though pure hype, the pages are a great place to look at each vehicle and gather basic information on price range, passenger capacity, and the like. Think of these pages as slick brochures you can browse without going to a dozen dealerships. All these sites are free.

Manufacturer's Financing Companies

Manufacturer's financing companies also have slick but relatively useless pages. GMAC, FMCC and the like give you lots of reasons their companies are the best. And since the pages are free, why not flip through them? Just don't be a sucker and automatically finance with any of these folks without following our easy cost comparison methods right here in the book.

Car Pricing Services

Car pricing services, including Edmund's (http://www.edmunds.com) are here, too. These services tell you what specific vehicles cost the dealer and are generally very accurate. Some, including Edmund's, provide a variety of information for free; most charge for some or all of their information. Most of the commercial online buying and leasing services also provide reviews and pricing information free as part of their package. Do remember, however, that all these information and buying services have links, just a click away, to various "recommended services" for which there is a charge and which you must scrutinize as you would any offering.

Individual Dealerships

Individual dealerships have very fancy pages, too. Trouble is, the dealership pages just serve to lure you down to the dealership or at the least get your name, number and (at times) social security number. Presto, the dealership has a hot prospect for the dealership's normal fast-track selling system. Dealership pages are generally worthless except for one area: many list their new and used car inventory, which can make it easier for you to find the particular new car you might like.

Commercial Buying/Leasing/Financing Services

Here's the hot action, and here also is some powerful information. The major commercial services such as Microsoft's CarPoint (http://www.carpoint.msn.com), Auto Vantage (do a search using name) or Auto-by-Tel (http://www.autobytel.com) provide comprehensive, helpful, and objective information (and/or links to information) on specific car lines, dealer costs, insurance, and reliability issues. Many of their evaluations of individual vehicles are tough. Their prices for "shopping" their services are generally reasonable and identified up-front. (In addition, most offer an appetizer for free before you tackle their smorgasbord.) As a shopping aid, the services also provide very simple ways to see what vehicles compete directly with the one vehicle you like. Rather than driving to a dozen dealerships to gather information, look up Jeep Cherokee, for instance, and these services automatically list all the vehicles (like the Toyota Forerunner) which are comparable. And a detailed site on each car is just a click away. This feature alone makes these services worth using for gathering your information.

The big problem with commercial services. They all want you to buy or lease a vehicle from them on blind faith. They want you to believe their deal is the cheapest, their financing rates are the lowest, and their particular selling system is the fairest. *All* of these things *may* be true—but I wouldn't hold my breath. Most of these systems, including the very best, still require you at some point to interact with dealership personnel. Perhaps a "special representative" will even call you directly. You are in a trusting mood when that phone call comes—or when you visit the dealership. After all, getting info to date has been so hassle-free and low-key. So you fall for the sales spiels for everything from add-ons to hidden rebate stealing, lousy finance rates, and stealing your trade-in.

The solution to the big problem: use these commercial services to gather information, but *never automatically buy, lease, or finance with an online service without comparing each part of the transaction to other sources.* It's the broken record of this book, isn't it? Take your time, have two sources, and then make a choice.

Other Consumer Sources

Each week dozens of new consumer sites jump on the Internet, and many of them offer excellent, unbiased material. For instance, you can receive information about vehicle safety tests and recalls (and report your own safety problems) on the Auto Safety Hotline of the National Highway Traffic Safety Administration. Their homepage also has other information services (http://www.nhtsa.dot.gov). Check out the homepage of the Center for Auto Safety, established by Ralph Nader (http://essential.org/cas). You can get an online copy of the "Reality Checklist for Vehicle Leasing" we talked about earlier, too (gopher:// gopher.essential.org). The automotive articles of a number of useful periodicals such as *Consumer Reports* or the various automotive magazines are available online through your online service provider or services such as AutoSite (http://www.autosite.com); there is a charge for some of these.

Finding Information on the Net

As new automotive sites spring up almost daily on the Internet, you'll need to do your own exploring. Some good keywords for browsing include: Auto Safety Literature, Automotive Safety Tests, Automotive Buyers' Guides, Automotive Buying Services, Automotive Leasing Services. There are lots of other possibilities but these will give you a starting place. Just remember, apply the same criteria and cautions to information and services you get online as you would to those you get in person down at the dealership or from your financing source, and you can make the Internet work to your advantage.

SHOPPING: IF YOU PLAN TO BUY A USED CAR OR USED TRUCK

Buying a used vehicle can be one of the smartest moves you can make. It is also, unfortunately, one of the dumbest moves many people make. Because those people don't accept the fact that shopping for a used vehicle is *not* like shopping for a new one. Yes, used-vehicle buyers will need to bargain for a good price, and yes, they will have to choose the seller with care—just like new-vehicle buyers. But price and seller are not the most important factors in the used-vehicle process. What have you gained if the price on a specific vehicle is low and the seller is President of the Better Business Bureau, but the internal organs of your bargain—the things you cannot see and cannot judge easily—are junk?

The paramount factor in choosing a used vehicle is the condition of that particular vehicle. If it is sound mechanically, it's worth more money than a bargain vehicle; if it really checks out thoroughly, *who* sells it to you isn't important—a good used vehicle from your neighbor or even the local fly-by-night lot is better than an average vehicle from your Cadillac dealer.

It sounds easy enough: Just buy a good one. The process of finding that vehicle will probably be long and frustrating, much more so than finding a new one. Unless you are a gambler at heart, stop reading about used vehicles *unless* you are willing to follow a few suggestions that will probably be unpleasant to implement. Go buy a new vehicle, spend that extra money, and be happy. The used-vehicle field isn't a ballgame for flighty folks at all; it's for thorough ones.

We are going to be discussing the used-vehicle hunt and purchase in detail, but first, think carefully about these few "givens"—suggestions that all smart used-vehicle buyers have accepted since the first used vehicle sat on anyone's lot.

1. You must put away your shyness. If you are the type of person who feels that asking things of sellers, making notes, and

generally taking time to know a particular purchase is an imposition, change that feeling right now. You are getting ready to spend thousands of dollars, and it is not only silly, it's poor, poor business to spend money without really knowing what your money is buying. The only safe approach to buying a used vehicle assumes that you have a *right* to know everything about that vehicle before signing anything. If the seller doesn't agree with this approach, go somewhere else. Say good-bye, leave, and don't be embarrassed, either. Many sellers will imply that only *amateurs* check out a vehicle; they will tell you, "Of course, this isn't perfect, that's why it costs less," giving you a look normally reserved for the town moron. Bull hockey. Shopping for a used vehicle never should include too much concern for the seller's feelings. Invariably he will have absolutely none for yours. Remember that used-vehicle people are concerned only with your money, not your friendship.

2. You will need a pencil and a checklist. Two checklists are provided in the Appendix. The first list, the one you will be using, will help you take the emotion out of the buying process. It provides you with sixteen easy things to check on any used vehicle which will help you determine if it is as beautiful under the skin as it may be on the surface. Because all used vehicle operations make the exterior of their vehicles as beautiful as possible in order to take your mind off interior sicknesses, this checklist will be your first protection from the thousands of junkers sitting proudly on lots across the country.

3. You will need to wear old clothes. Don't laugh—if you are really going to check out a used vehicle, you will definitely get dirty and probably greasy. But so what? So what if the guys on the lot laugh a little when you crawl under the vehicle a foot or two? Would you get a little dirty to save $300 or $500 or $800 in repairs the moment you buy a used vehicle? Let them laugh. *You* can laugh all the way to the bank.

4. You will need a mechanic. Your checklist will tell you many things about a vehicle, but unless you have a shop in your backyard, you really can't check most of the important and less obvious problem centers in a vehicle. The second checklist in the Appendix provides your mechanic with a short list

of must things you will need to have checked before you buy any vehicle.

Choose your mechanic before you begin to shop. Car-care centers and tire shops usually have them. Your neighbor may know a good one.

Who should check out your potential new wheels? Diagnostic centers can do a fine job. And if you're lucky enough to live in a place which has a service such as Auto Critic, you're in luck. Auto Critic and its competitors aren't in the business of selling or fixing cars—they simply give used cars physicals. Auto Critic, for instance, checks ninety separate things on most vehicles. And these folks, like most of these services, *come to the car.* Simply tell the service where the car is located, and they'll go there, inspect it, and give you a written report on the car's health.

Whomever you use, find an inspection service and *use it!* You should pay no more than $95.00, and that money will be the smartest money you'll spend in your used car lifetime. *Having a mechanic is the most important thing you can do as a used-vehicle buyer.* Though the seller may not admit it, the mere fact you plan to take a vehicle to a mechanic will lessen his natural desire to stick you with a piece of junk. You will also be in a much better position to negotiate price once a specific vehicle has been checked. And you, you smart thing, will know what repairs will be needed on any vehicle, and how much those repairs will cost, before you buy. Which brings us to the final given.

5. Expect things to be wrong with every vehicle. As they say, wear and tear *is* the reason used vehicles cost less. But, if you know that a really nice one needs a complete brake job for $300, the vehicle might still be the best buy *if* you plan that expenditure as part of your purchase price. If a specific one you like needs a dozen things fixed at a cost of $1700, that vehicle might be a good purchase, too, *if* you plan that expenditure as part of the purchase price.

If you will accept these five points as a given, you will be a smart used-vehicle buyer and will in all likelihood outsmart the foxiest seller in the world. Most sellers will accept this approach to buying, too. Just remember: Those who won't do it your way, who refuse to have their vehicle checked by a mechanic "for insurance reasons" or other easy cop-outs, are not people you will do business with. Regardless of their smile, okay?

Why All This Work Is Worth It

You've been warned about the hard work. If you're still game, let's consider more specifically why this drudgery may be worth it. The only logical reasons to buy a used vehicle are price and depreciation—or the lack of it. Unless you plan, and I mean are sure, to keep a vehicle for a long time, a *new* car is probably one of the worst investments in the world. As a matter of fact, as noted earlier, 99 out of 100 new ones will drop *forty percent* in value the day they're driven home.

If you purchase a used vehicle wisely, you won't face such drastic losses. The only "depreciation" you'll face the moment you drive off the lot will be the amount of profit you've paid. For instance, if you pay $6500 for a used vehicle with a wholesale value of $6000, your vehicle will be worth $6000 the moment you own it, a depreciation of less than ten percent. If you maintain it well and drive it for a year, it will probably depreciate another ten percent. But, even at the end of those twelve months, you'll still be far ahead of the new-vehicle game.

Why It's Harder

In the first place, the vast majority of used-vehicle buyers must function in a less-than-pleasant environment. From road hogs to small independent lots to new-vehicle dealerships to the new mega-used car operations owned by blue-chip companies, the used-vehicle business is still tainted with questionable tactics from top to bottom. The road hogs are as disreputable as ever; new car dealerships still rip you off in financing; even the mega-dealers—who like to claim they're new from top to bottom—are run on a day-to-day basis by recruits from some of the toughest, meanest dealership chains in the country.

With all that said and done, you can surmount all these problems, and if you're triply cautious, you can make an excellent deal at virtually any used car operation. But, as a used car buyer, you are going to face five other discomfiting variables:

1. Each used vehicle is an original. Don't think you'll find an identical one down the road. Yes, you may find the same year and make and model, maybe even the same color, but it can be as different as the Gabor sisters. Used-vehicle dealers use similarity to their advantage continually. They may, for instance, advertise a nice low-mileage vehicle for $7000, and then sell you a virtually identical one with high mileage and hidden body damage.

2. Used vehicles don't have fixed wholesale values or asking prices. You will have a very difficult time "shopping" the price on any used vehicle. Asking prices change with the wind. They invariably go up if you plan to trade. They invariably go down if you look like you are going to walk.

3. A great vehicle may be at a rotten lot. And vice versa. You can't automatically assume that the fly-by-nighters sell only junkers, and you certainly can't assume new-vehicle operations will always have the most dependable vehicles.

4. It takes time to check out a used vehicle. Most of us evaluate a used vehicle on the basis of its looks. We make decisions involving thousands of dollars based on cursory evaluation rather than careful examination. Or worse, we let our emotions rule the decision-making process. Choosing a used vehicle will involve lots of time and a small amount of money, but it's worth it.

5. Financing rates vary tremendously on used vehicles. In automobile lingo, the "spread" is much greater. On new vehicles, for instance, the percentage spread between the cost of money and the highest legal rate that can be charged for money is usually two percent. But the spread on a two-year-old vehicle can be *twenty* percent. If you plan to finance a used vehicle, you must shop for the lowest rate for that particular *year* vehicle. Do not agree to finance from the seller, even if the seller

plans to use your own bank as the source; you *will* pay more for the money.

The Importance of Loan Value

Used cars obviously don't have set "invoice" prices. Vehicles of the same year and roughly equal condition can vary in value hundreds of dollars, depending on mileage and color—even on the time they were traded in. For instance, used station wagons are normally at a premium before the summer begins. Many folks trade for wagons then, planning on a nice family vacation in their newer tub. But in the fall buyers seem to look for smaller vehicles, hardtops and four-cylinder jobs to use for work and short trips. Station-wagon wholesale values drop dramatically at that time.

This variation in wholesale value poses a problem for lending institutions: What would be a generally safe amount of money to loan on a used vehicle? Lending institutions have historically wanted to loan less than the true wholesale value—a nice way to protect their loans—but haven't had the manpower to actually determine the wholesale value of particular models.

Over the years, lending institutions developed a "loan value" formula as a safe compromise for setting loan limits. They began to loan eighty percent of the "average clean wholesale" price for all vehicles of a particular make sold at auctions. For instance, if the average clean wholesale figure for all three-year-old Expenso Compactas last month at sales around the country was $5000, lending institutions would loan $4000 on those cars. Loan value is affected by a vehicle's general condition, mileage, and options such as air-conditioning, power steering, and power windows.

Since it may be impossible for you to know the true wholesale value of a particular used vehicle sitting on someone's lot, the loan value figure can at least give you a good indication of its worth. We will be using loan value as our benchmark in the examples in the next chapter. However, because some vehicles are actually worth *less* than their loan value, we'll always be offering *less* than loan value, raising our offer slowly from that figure. Your financing source will determine the particular loan value of specific vehicles for you.

Used-Vehicle Sources

If you are lucky, you will find a car that suits your needs without once visiting a lot. Dealers will, of course, tell you just the opposite: Never buy a vehicle from a friend or neighbor—it won't have a warranty, you will lose a friendship, and in all likelihood you will be "cheated" by your erstwhile buddy. Chicken feathers. No warranty from an acquaintance is better than most warranties provided by your neighborhood lot. Review these sources and consider giving the first few a try before walking on that lot.

1. **People you know.** Do you have neighbors who trade regularly? All of us have friends who trade every two or three years. Wouldn't it be better to consider offering that person more money for his vehicle than any dealership will give him? If you can find a friend or neighbor who is planning to trade, shop his vehicle with him as we have indicated and then offer him a profit. Both of you will be better off—your friend will be receiving more than wholesale and will be able to buy a new one with less hassle. And you will have a nice used vehicle with absolutely no hassle. Some smart used-vehicle buyers regularly buy the same person's trade year after year. Could that make sense for you? The paperwork involved in person-to-person dealing is less involved than at your friendly used-car lot, even if the seller owes money and you prefer to finance.

2. **Bulletin boards at work.** Your chances of finding a nice car by reading those little notices are just as good or better than your chances of finding a nice vehicle on some lot. Unfortunately many people who attempt to sell their vehicles like this are in the bucket—they owe more on them than their actual value. But that's the seller's problem, not yours. Once you have agreed on the wholesale figure plus a fair profit, the seller is obligated to pay off his vehicle.

3. **Classified ads and "shoppers."** Sure, it will take a little time to call those ads and personally inspect each vehicle. But hidden away in those funny little messages are some good vehicles that can be bought at very reasonable prices.

A warning: don't for a minute think that all classified ads are placed by *individuals* selling their own vehicles. Many used-car operations pay individuals a fee to act as "curbstones" for a particular vehicle, instructing them to tell potential buyers, "Of course, I put every mile on this beauty." Don't be shy if you plan to search the classifieds. Ask the party specifically, "Is the vehicle titled in your name?" Ask to see the title if you are uncomfortable with the person's answer. *A good rule:* don't buy if the vehicle isn't in the seller's name. "Curbed" cars are usually problem cars.

FAIR WARNING: Ignore any friend, bulletin board notice, or ad that says "assume payments" or "$500 down and assume payments." These people are obviously *deep* in the bucket. They can't sell to some used-car operation because they would have to *pay* an operator to take their vehicle. They can't sell to an individual for a lump sum for the same reason. Don't fall for this line, or you will automatically leap into the bucket yourself.

4. **Mega used car dealers such as "Car Max" and "Auto Nation."** Though these national chains will happily let you spend more money than you need to—and though, contrary to their advertising, you must use real diligence in dealing with these chains—mega used car dealers may still be your best source of late model, generally very clean and dependable used cars. Most of them also have a service department, which can come in handy.

But ponder these points before pulling out your checkbook:

➤ Most of their cars are rental or lease cars. This makes it practically impossible for you to talk with previous owners—which means taking one of these cars to your mechanic (or having a mechanic come to the car) is more important than ever.

➤ All of these chains say they won't negotiate. They will, if you're serious about buying.

➤ Though you'll experience very little pressure at their fancy places, you will still be subject to subtle pressures to both finance with them and buy extra options from them. Don't fall for those spiels. Follow all the normal steps we give you in this book when buying and/or financing a used car.

➤ Most offer "money back" warranties for a very limited period of time. But these warranties are not offered on all cars, and the "money back" guarantee *does not normally include add-ons* such as what you may have paid for extra warranties or for insurance. If you're looking at a car with a money-back guarantee, carefully review what parts of the transaction are really 100 percent "money back."

➤ Unfortunately, some of the worst mega new-car dealers are now entering the mega *used*-car business. You can expect these bad guys to use all their bad techniques, regardless of their fancy new facelifts. *How do you know if you're at a bad-guys lot?* You won't. That's why you must always follow the steps we outline here. For instance, *never buy a used car from even the fanciest mega-used car dealer on your first visit.*

5. **New-vehicle dealers.** Most of the used cars on their lots were trade-ins, an important fact in itself.

New-vehicle dealers can also be held more accountable than many used ones. Their operations are more visible in the community, and the caliber of their salesmen may be just a shade above the strictly used boys. As with all used-car operations, it will be important for you to select the vehicles that interest you. Don't be led by the nose. Salesmen are not interested in selling you one particular model that might fit your needs; they are interested in selling the vehicle with the highest likely profit or bonus for *them*.

New-car dealers also offer you the advantage of their own service departments. You certainly won't receive any price breaks on service, but you might have a better chance of buying a vehicle with fewer problems if you are dealing with a lot that has an in-house service operation.

6. **Used-car dealers.** Look for large lots that have been in business for years. Once you've found a few with nice selections, call your local Better Business Bureau. The Bureau will tell you if complaints have been lodged against those particular lots. If the complaints have been numerous, either forget that lot or plan to have your mechanic check their vehicles twice. Many independent lots purchase virtually all of their vehicles from new-car dealers and "road hogs," wholesalers who travel

from city to city peddling individual vehicles. A "bought" vehicle may be a fine piece of merchandise, but shy away from it unless you can locate the previous owner. Road hogs make their living by taking questionable vehicles to new market areas.

7. **Rental agencies.** These people must have good public relations organizations working for them. Countless articles have praised them as the used-vehicle-buyer's salvation. These articles enthusiastically tell you how helpful their selling procedures are. For instance, rental agency used-vehicle operations just love to brag about their "one price" method of selling. They tell you how much nicer it is to forgo dickering. And they are right—it is nice for them.

But not for you. You are paying a nice hefty profit, probably more than for a reasonably comparable vehicle on some other lot. They tell you, "Our vehicles are cheaper because there are no middle-men." Incorrect. Rental agencies determine the true wholesale value and then add their profit to that figure, as all used-car boys do. So who's getting the good deal? The seller, of course. Rental agencies also tout their "twelve-month warranties." It's the same warranty offered at most used-car lots these days.

Rental agencies are no better or no worse than many other sources. Shop them carefully. Decide if you really want a vehicle that's been driven by several dozen people, too.

8. **Red lights.** Do you remember the last vehicle you saw with a "for sale" sign and a price sticking in the back window? Don't try too hard, but do notice these rolling advertisements. If you see a pretty nice looking one, it might be worth a call, or at least a yell across lanes.

9. **A source to ignore: used-car auctions.** No matter how fancy the auction locale, you have no time or opportunity to check these cars out mechanically. Also you have no time to consider and negotiate price. Do you really want to buy a car in the heat of a bidding battle? Stay with the other eight sources.

10. **Another source to ignore: "Buy here, pay here" type dealerships.** You'll pay thousands more for a car at these places than it's worth.

Locating a Specific Used Car

Are you interested in a two-year-old candy-apple red Mercedes coupé? Or a three-year-old two-wheel drive Jeep? A service called AutoSearch can help you. The service knows the locations of hundreds of thousands of used cars at most of the nation's big dealerships. AutoSearch can send you the location of almost every red Mercedes coupé in the country, for instance, along with the phone number of a contact person. They can also give you a "take" price—probably not the cheapest price, but a good place to start bargaining.

AutoSearch can also tell you whether or not a specific used car has been in a wreck. A very nice service.

How much does it cost? This may change, but right now you can have them locate one car for $29.95, or for $49.95 you can have an unlimited search for ninety days, plus a "VIN guard" search to check for wrecks.

What's the best way to use this service? Remember that Auto-Search can't control the integrity of the dealers they deal with. If you use this service, use it with all the normal guidelines in this book. For instance, don't automatically trade in your old car at one of their dealerships and certainly don't automatically finance at any of their dealerships without comparing financing costs.

How do I call them? Try 800-633-7834.

Checking Out a Used Vehicle

Most people's idea of checking out a used vehicle is simply to walk around it slowly, kicking each tire vigorously in the process—an evaluation that usually results in nothing more than a sore foot. Some people are a little more thorough in their inspection—they will blow the horn, turn on the radio, or lift the hood.

Professional appraisers at most dealerships are never quite this casual when putting a figure on a vehicle; their job is the real essence of the automobile business. And Rax, Killer's favorite man on the used-car lot, knows that, too. His ritual is always the same. "First, I determine if anything needs to be spent on the car's drive train—the engine, transmission, and so forth. I crank it up, and let the engine idle for a few minutes, listening for clatter or other unusual noises in the engine. Then I slip the transmission into neutral, then reverse, then neutral, then reverse. If there's any motion there, clanking, you've got transmission problems, at least in that gear. Then I do the same thing, from neutral to drive.

"I've also got a road that serves as my 'drag strip.' After the vehicle is warm, I bring it to dead still, kick the accelerator to the floor, and look out the rear window. If there's smoke back there, she's burning oil. And valve jobs are expensive. An easier way to check for that, especially if it's dark, or on a busy road, is to simply rub your fingers inside the exhaust pipe. If there's oil there, you know the same thing. If I find anything mechanically wrong with the car, I make a little note on how much it'll cost to fix it. I make the same type of notes about the *outside,* too. If the paint's dull, will it buff out or will it need a new coat? If there's body damage, can it be hammered out or will the piece need to be replaced? I also look very carefully for rust. Usually the best places to look are leading edges under the hood and around the doors, really any place where water or salt can accumulate. Then I add up all the money it'll take to put the vehicle in shape and deduct that from the fair wholesale value when it's ready to go on the front line."

Anyone who plans to trade an old vehicle should be familiar with at least some of the factors Rax has been talking about. If you plan to trade for a new vehicle, you'll need the information to prepare for the battle surrounding the value of your trade.

If you are a used-vehicle buyer, you are a fool if you don't know the inside of a used vehicle. In all likelihood, most will appear very healthy on the outside. But you must know about all the hidden things that are more important than looks. So use the two checklists—one for you and one for your mechanic—provided in the Appendix.

The final mantra for all used-car buyers: Never buy a used vehicle from ANY source without doing these things.

➤ Always get the name and phone number of the previous owner. If a seller won't give you that information, don't buy the vehicle. If a seller says the vehicle was a lease car, the seller should still be able to give you the name of the person who actually leased the car. If the seller says a vehicle was a rental car, ask for a copy of the title to the rental company.

➤ If at all possible, always talk to the previous owner. For instance, if you're buying a leased car, the actual driver of that leased car will know as much about the car as if he or she owned it. And leased cars can have as many problems as bought cars.

➤ If you talk to the previous owner, ask for the vehicle's miles when it was turned in, and ask for a list of problems with the car.

➤ And then, as we've said, always have that car checked out by a mechanic.

8

Leasing a Car the Right Way

If you read the last edition of this book, you know that I have been one of the leasing industry's biggest critics in this country. You may not know that I, along with Ralph Nader, founded the Consumer Task Force for Automotive Issues to attack leasing industry problems head-on. About twenty-three states' attorneys general, hundreds of consumer groups, and many plaintiff law firms joined us in that attack. We continue to monitor leasing, and continue to bring national consumer class actions as we discover serious lease abuses. Even with the new federal regulations, leasing a car is still a minefield for your pocketbook.

There's a great irony here: *leasing, done right, is an excellent way to drive a new vehicle and save your hard-earned money.* The key, of course, is "done right." This chapter will show you how to do it right. Heed the warnings, take your time, and you'll be one of the (unfortunately) few persons who really benefit from this financing tool.

HOW LEASES WORK

In principle, leasing is a lot like renting a car from Hertz or Avis, but for a longer time. You are simply paying for the *use* of someone else's vehicle. You own nothing.

Although elements that make up a lease transaction are very much like those of your last purchase transaction, there is one important difference. In a purchase transaction, you pay for the *full cost of the car* with your payments and down payment. For instance, if you buy a car for $20,000, including tax and title, and finance that car for thirty-six months, you will make payments that total $20,000 plus interest, say $25,400. At the end of thirty-six months, you will have no payments and you will own the car. Let's assume the car will be worth $10,000.

If you were to lease the same car, the transaction would be the same for the lease car except for the fact that the $10,000 value of your car would be subtracted *in advance* from the amount the leasing company will charge you each month. In this instance, you would make payments based on $25,400 minus $10,000—*plus* a profit for the leasing company. At the end of the lease, the leasing company would then own the asset.

That's the theory: If you can lease a vehicle for a monthly payment *based on the same profit margin you would pay to buy that same vehicle,* and if other leasing terms are fair, leasing would be a wonderful thing for many of you. Why? You would be receiving the full benefit of the car's value at the end of the lease at the *beginning* of the lease.

In the real world, it doesn't work the right way very often. And though I seldom understate matters in this book, *that* is a real understatement. Dealerships and leasing companies have flocked to leasing because unwary consumers traditionally have paid *thousands of dollars more to lease rather than buy the very same vehicle.* In a nutshell, this happens because leases—even with the new disclosure requirements—still don't require leasing companies and dealerships to tell you what you need to know to compare the cost of leasing to the cost of buying the very same vehicle. As a matter of fact, the leasing industry has fought tooth and nail all attempts at meaningful disclosure.

But that's okay. You can still lease smartly, as we'll see.

Who Should Consider Leasing?

If you listen to the leasing industry, anyone that's breathing or at least still warm. But in the real world, see where you fit in here and then objectively decide whether leasing makes sense for you.

Will you be happy with payments for the foreseeable future or is your objective to own a vehicle debt-free? If you are the type who has built a car payment into your life just like you've built a housing payment, you are a potential candidate for leasing. If you're the type, however, who wants to spend some years *without* payments, stay away from leasing. Though all leases give you the chance to buy your car at the end of a lease, you will *invariably pay more* to buy a car this way. Usually a lot more. If your objective is "no payments in the near future," don't be switched to leasing.

Are you financially stable and stable in your job? Even the very best lease, as we'll see, is very, very expensive to break early. Don't lease if you're already having trouble paying your bills and are worried about your job. Leasing companies are, unfortunately, pushing leases as a way to solve financial problems. Leases *cause* financial problems, if you're not careful. Do not lease if you are in the least bit troubled about your financial future.

Before Choosing a Lease, Understand the Consequences of Doing It Wrong

If you think leasing might be right for you, you first need to thoroughly understand the consequences of leasing without doing your homework. Here's a quick rundown on a few of the realities you'll face:

Do it wrong, and you'll pay five to fifteen times as much profit to lease a car compared with buying the very same car. And that's if you lease from a really nice leasing company. Since federal regulations still don't require leasing companies to tell you clearly what you're paying for a lease vehicle, leasing companies can easily mislead you.

Do it wrong and you may be given absolutely *nothing* for your trade-in, even if it's worth thousands of dollars. Right now, dozens of class-action lawsuits and several government investigations center on this neat trick. The abuse occurs because regulations still allow leasing companies and automobile dealerships to hide the value of your old car: they don't list its value as a separate item on a lease. And if those guys can hide it, they can pocket its value as profit to them. How would you like to give away a ten-thousand-dollar asset?

Do it wrong and you may pay an extra 20 percent in finance charges versus financing the same vehicle conventionally. And it's so easy to do this part wrong because leases generally don't give you a way to compare leasing charges to financing charges. This book gives you a good way, however.

Terminate your lease early and lose thousands. Don't ever think about leasing if you're thinking about turning in your lease car early. Leasing is *not* like renting. You, for instance, are used to renting a car at the airport for a week and bringing it back in five days. Usually, there's no penalty. But if you bring a leased vehicle back early—for instance, within the first year of a forty-eight-month lease, you *may still be forced to pay all forty-eight payments.* And *that* would probably put a crimp in your lifestyle for a few months, wouldn't it?

Lease a lemon and you're stuck. Remember, you don't own the vehicle when you lease. If you end up with a real lemon, the leasing company has to do the complaining. If your car is out of commission, you're still making the payments, too. That's why finding the right vehicle—dependable and safe—is even more important in leasing than in buying.

"Nickel and dime" clauses can cost you thousands. You make your thirty-six lease payments, and you're happy. At the end of your lease, you zoom into the dealership to turn in your car, and find out that you owe the dealerships $3500 for "excess wear and tear." Trouble is, you kept the car like new. Trouble is, some leases seem to define *anything* as excess wear and tear.

Are There Different Types of Leases?

Historically, two types have been available. A closed-end lease, called a "walkaway," simply means that you have no further financial obligation other than making your lease payments—as long as you follow the terms of the lease contract. You are not responsible for the value of the car at the end of the lease—unless, as we've mentioned, you terminate your lease early for any reason whatsoever. "Walkaways" are usually the norm for all consumer leasing companies, both the good and bad ones.

"Open-ended" leases mean the consumer is responsible for the value of the car at the end of the lease. Leasing companies will happily tell you they never use open-ended leases because they place all the risk on the back of the consumer. But guess what? Almost all leasing companies turn your lease into an open-ended lease if you try to break your lease early.

Who Are the Parties in a Lease?

The companies involved in a lease differ slightly from those in a buying situation. Though you may contract for a lease at a dealership, that dealer is usually not the actual leasing company. You need to understand who the players are:

LESSOR: The company that funds the lease. For instance, a GMAC lease is funded by *GMAC.* This is the company that actually owns the leased vehicle.

LESSEE: That's you.

AGENTS: A general term for companies that represent the lessor. For instance, a Cadillac dealer would be an agent for GMAC leases. (Other terms for agents include "sales outlets," "leasing representatives," and "originators.") This is the company with whom you actually negotiate, come to terms and sign the paperwork/contract for a lease.

Who's Making the Big Profits Here? The Leasing Companies or the Dealerships?

Both. And how the two companies work together is a nice, scary lesson in free enterprise gone a bit amuck.

Leasing companies and automobile dealerships: hands in each other's pockets, shovels in yours. Because of the literally thousands of lawsuits now rumbling around out there against dealerships and/or leasing companies, neither really likes to talk about their relationship, except under court order. But if you are a student of business you might enjoy this peek.

Dealerships are the most interesting place to peek first. A dealership, as we now know, is interested in only one thing: how much money it can generate from the sale of a car. As we also know, that money includes profit from the sale of the car itself, from the trade-in, from financing, and from dealer add-ons and extras. When a dealership thinks of leasing a car rather than selling it, the same juicy thought is on its mind: how much profit?

That profit will be determined by how easy the customer is to "work," and in leasing, customers are easy to work. But profit will also be determined by how much money the dealership can get *financed* on that customer. It won't do any good if a dealership "writes someone up" on a $5000 profit, for instance, if they can't get some company to finance that much profit.

And that's where the leasing companies come in. Dealerships have dozens of leasing companies to choose from, and guess what criterion they use to choose their favorite? Do you think they look for the one that gives the best terms to the consumer? Of course not! Time and again, dealerships choose the leasing company that will lend the most money on every part of every transaction. Let's say Loving Leasing, Inc. has been writing leases for Happy's Expenso dealership. They've been loaning 100 percent of manufacturer's sticker plus tax and title and a little extra profit, and up until now Happy's Expenso has been happy.

But then the field representative for another leasing company stops by for a visit. His company, he cheerfully announces, will go *110 percent* of the manufacturer's sticker. Ten percent more of the sticker price. On a $20,000 car, that raises the dealership's profit by $2000 in one stroke. Which leasing company do you think Happy will use now? And who is hurt by that little competition? You.

The competition goes beyond percentages of list price, too. Leasing companies compete to offer dealers the highest "participation"—a cut on the financing charge. Some of them still compete to offer the most generous "add-on" guidelines. Until recently, most leasing companies would allow a dealership to charge whatever they liked for rustproofing, striping, warranties, and the like. The leasing companies would then gladly finance that charge. Why not? More finance income.

But in a little poetic irony, the leasing companies themselves started being victimized by the dealerships' enthusiasm in this area. Dealerships would charge unsuspecting customers $2995 for rustproofing and undercoating. The customers wouldn't yell because the salesman had simply said, "Oh, we've added our special environmental packages: it's only twenty-nine ninety-five," implying $29.95. Since such add-on charges don't have to be shown separately on a leasing form, the customer never knew the true price.

That $3000 charge didn't add any value to the lease car, but it did raise the lease loan by $3000. And if a lease customer defaulted on his lease, that $3000 would, as likely as not, be eaten by the leasing company. These days, therefore, most leasing companies limit dealerships to specific amounts for add-ons. The leasing company will only finance the true cost of an add-on radio, for instance, not its selling price. The leasing companies' interest there was to protect themselves, not the consumer. Self-interest rules throughout this business.

How Do Leasing Companies Defend Their Services?

First, they deny. They deny primarily any disadvantages to leasing. A famous king without clothes tried that, too, but it didn't work. Second, they proudly proclaim, "We actually help people with less cash because we don't require a down payment." A noble statement, but misleading. Virtually all leasing companies require at least one month's payment as a security deposit to be returned at the end of the lease. They also require the first month's payment in advance. Those two sums would make an adequate down payment in a purchase situation.

And, finally, leasing companies state that "it is always cheaper on a *monthly* basis to lease." A correct statement, especially if you plan to lease for thirty-six months or less. Because leasing companies subtract the projected lease-end value of the car at the beginning of the lease, your payment amount will be less than buying. But are you willing to pay hundreds or a thousand more in the long run for a short-term lower payment? Keep in mind that at the end of three years, you will not own the vehicle and will have to lease or purchase another one. Most owners these days are happily driving their cars for four or five years or more. If you drive your purchased car just one additional year after paying off your thirty-sixth and final car payment, you'll have a year without any payments at all. And even after that *free* year, you've got an asset to trade in.

UNDERSTANDING THE COMPONENTS OF A LEASE

You will be lost if you don't have a basic understanding of lease terms and the components of a lease they describe, and if you don't have a way to compare lease cost at different leasing sources. That's why you should study the following terms and then become very familiar with the *Personal Leasing Checklist.* This special checklist is adapted from **The Reality Checklist for Vehicle Leasing**™, which was developed by twenty-three attorneys general with the help of many other consumer attorneys and consumer groups. The checklist helps you *compare the cost of items at different leasing companies.* However, since we've found that many leasing companies and agents refuse to provide all the information requested on the checklist, the section on how to negotiate a lease the right way provides a leasing strategy that works whether you have been able to complete the checklist or not. Of course, the more information you can get, the better equipped you will be.

Important Leasing Terms

MSRP: Manufacturer's Suggested Retail Price, also known as the manufacturer's or factory sticker. Leasing companies typically acquire vehicles at a cost expressed as percentage of MSRP.

Capitalized cost: The total cost of the vehicle you are leasing; also known as "cap cost." This total cost includes the price the leasing company pays for the car and any options plus any other fees or costs included in the amount you finance. For example, an "acquisition fee," taxes, title and license fees, and charges for optional warranties or insurance may be included in this cap cost.

Although most leasing companies still do not list the costs of items included in the cap cost, under new federal regulations you have a right to request a detailed breakdown of cap costs. *But remember, you won't get it unless you specifically request it.*

Capitalized cost reduction: A down payment. A "cap cost reduction" may be made with cash and/or a trade-in.

Acquisition fee: This fee simply represents additional profit on this lease. The profit may benefit the leasing agent or the leasing company. Not all leases have acquisition fees.

Initial payment: This is the money that you must pay on delivery of the leased vehicle. At a minimum it usually includes a security deposit and the first lease payment. Many leases also require you to pay additional fees up front such as a cap cost reduction, taxes, title and license fees, and acquisition fees. If you are trading in your old vehicle, its true wholesale value should be applied against this initial payment or shown as part of the cap cost reduction. Watch like a hawk how your trade-in is handled on the lease, since as we've said, it's easy for dealerships to hide the fact that they've given you no money for your trade.

Security deposit: A refundable cash deposit required at the beginning of a lease.

Residual value: An estimate of what the vehicle is worth at the end of the lease. A higher residual value should result in lower lease payments since the lease is paying for less of the value of the vehicle. But negotiating this one item alone without understanding how it affects other aspects of the lease (such as cap cost or payments) can be a worthless exercise at best and a very dangerous one at worst since it lulls you into a false sense of victory.

The cost of money: You won't find this term on any lease document. Though leasing companies may tell you that since you are "renting" rather than financing there is no interest, there is a cost to the money which is often called a "monthly lease charge," "service fee," or "service charge." Since you are paying for the cost of this money, I think you have a right to have it presented to you in an understandable and comparable way. The best way is as an "effective annualized percentage rate." Many leasing companies will refuse to give you their rates, claiming the calculation is too complicated. Some will give you a *money factor* which when multiplied by twenty-four will give you an estimate of the interest rate. But two words of caution: first, the cost of money may include more than the amount represented by a "money factor," and second, consumer research has found that many leasing agents may misrepresent a money factor or interest rate because it is hard for you to verify it.

Monthly payment: The amount you pay on the lease each month for the term of the lease.

Excess mileage charge: Charges incurred at the end of the lease for miles driven beyond the maximum allowed mileage under your lease terms. These charges average ten to fifteen cents a mile. Most leases limit your mileage to 12,000 to 15,000 miles per year of the lease. If you anticipate driving more than the mileage indicated in your contract allows, have the lease figured on a realistic mileage allowance or be prepared to pay thousands extra at the end of the lease.

Excess wear and tear: Leasing companies charge you extra at the end of the lease for any wear on the vehicle that the company determines is above and beyond "normal." Be sure that the lease company provides you documentation in the lease agreement about what constitutes excess wear and tear.

GAP insurance: Wreck a leased vehicle before the end of the lease or have it stolen and you are still responsible for the total cost of the lease. This amount can be thousands more than your regular automotive insurance covers. GAP insurance covers the difference. A leasing company may charge for this insurance or provide it as part of the lease. Be sure you know whether or not it is included in your lease and what it costs.

Personal Leasing Checklist

This checklist highlights some of the important components of a lease and gives you a means to compare leasing terms offered by different companies. It is not a lease contract or a legal document. Lease contracts or agreements offered by different companies can vary greatly in the information they provide. Use the information from this checklist to help you study leasing opportunities and agreements very carefully.

I. WHAT IS THE TOTAL COST OF THE VEHICLE TO BE LEASED?

Vehicle Make/Model _____

(Vehicle Identification Number _____)

The MSRP (Manufacturer's Suggested Retail Price) _____

Price paid for basic vehicle by the leasing company: _____

This is _____ % of MSRP.

COST OF OPTIONS:

Item: _____ $_____

Item: _____ $_____

Item: _____ $_____

TOTAL COST OF VEHICLE

(Add basic cost and options)   (1) _____

Acquisition Fee   (2) _____

Taxes, Title, License   (3) _____

Optional Insurance/Warranties   (4) _____

Security Deposit   (5) _____

Total cost of acquiring vehicle   (add 1–5) _____

II. WHAT IS THE INITIAL PAYMENT REQUIRED BEFORE OR AT DELIVERY OF LEASE VEHICLE?

Capitalized Cost Reduction   (6) _____

  composed of Cash   _____

        Trade-In (true wholesale value)   _____

Acquisition Fee (if required)   (7) _____

Security Deposit   (8) _____

Taxes, title, license (if required)   (9) _____

Other   (10) _____

First monthly payment   (11) _____

Total initial payment   (add 6–11) _____

III. WHAT IS THE COST OF MONEY
TO LEASE THE VEHICLE?

The amount to be financed on the vehicle is _____
(the total cost of vehicle minus the initial payment other than the first
monthly payment [items 6–10]). This may also be called "total depreciation" in the lease agreement.

The effective interest rate expressed as an APR is _____
(Alternate: Money factor of _____ × 24= _____ %)

The total cost of money is
the total of your monthly payments _____
minus the "depreciation" or amount financed on the vehicle _____

for a total cost of _____ .

IV. WHAT IS THE RESIDUAL VALUE OF THE
VEHICLE TO BE LEASED?

Residual value is _____

V. WHAT IS THE MONTHLY PAYMENT?

The lease is for a total of _____ months at $_____ per
month.

VI. WHAT ADDITIONAL COSTS MAY BE INCURRED AT THE END OF THE LEASE?

Excess mileage charge: Mileage allowance on this lease is _____ miles per year for a total of _____ for the lease. The charge for miles above this amount is _____ per mile.

What is the definition of excess wear and tear and what is the penalty?

At the end of the lease you may buy the vehicle for $_____ .

If you break the lease early, what costs—lease payments and termination fees—will you be responsible for? Ask the company to estimate the total cost of breaking the lease at twelve, twenty-four, and thirty-six payments (as applicable for your intended lease term).

LEASING THE RIGHT WAY

Sell your old car yourself, if you can. Selling it yourself might put an additional $1000–2000 in your pocket. If you choose not to sell it, you must know its *true wholesale value* before you begin your leasing negotiations. Clean it up, and take it to several larger used-car operations. Tell the boys there you're thinking about selling your car rather than trading it. Write down your highest offer. You're going to fight for that amount when we get around to lease negotiating. Remember that leasing companies love to steal your trade-in. You must know its true value or you will probably give it away as profit.

Do your homework on your budget. Never let a leasing company decide what you can afford to pay per month. Use our budgeting process in Chapter 5 to determine how much you can spend to acquire a vehicle. When you've determined the lease payment that fits your budget—write it down right here, and stick to it!

MY BUDGET SUPPORTS A _____ LEASE PAYMENT

Use the payment you can afford to determine how much vehicle you can afford to lease. If you, for instance, can afford to pay $400 per month on a lease, how much car will that lease payment really get you? It's easy. Use the same steps as in buying a car (discussed in Chapter 7) to determine your leased-vehicle price range.

Do your homework on the vehicles which fit your budget. Are they safe? Are they mechanically reliable?

Choose two leasing sources. There are about 13,000 leasing companies out there, but generally speaking you want to stay with the major national leasing companies. You also want to use the leasing company whose parent company manufactures the vehicle you're planning to lease. For instance, use FMCC for leasing a Ford. If a Ford dealer wants to lease you a car through "Ultra-Oomph Leasing," you can bet there's only one reason: Ultra-Oomph pays the dealer a much fatter profit. And you, of course, are the person who really pays that profit. An Ultra-Oomph, likely as not, has the most onerous lease terms in America.

Compare rates and terms at your two sources. Sound simple? It isn't. Follow these steps carefully.

1. *Determine the number of months you would like to lease a car.* If you drive 20,000 miles a year, don't lease for more than thirty-six months. Relatively new used cars drop dramatically in value if their speedometers show more than 50,000 miles total. If you drive less than 15,000 per year, don't lease for more than forty-eight months. Make these decisions before you visit your sources.

2. *Find a single car that fits your needs at each source.* Remember that shopping for a lease car is like shopping to buy: *Don't* lease on your first visit! This visit is for gathering information only. Drive the vehicle; listen to the sales spiels, but *don't lease!*

3. *At each leasing source, insist that the leasing manager provide you with the information to fill out your "Personal Leasing Checklist."* Some leasing managers won't provide specific an-

swers. Leave those dealerships. At a very minimum, you must insist that these items on your personal checklist are filled in:

- ➤ Selling price of the vehicle to the leasing company
- ➤ MSRP of the vehicle
- ➤ your trade-in's true wholesale value
- ➤ total "rent" or "service charge" or "cost of money"
- ➤ itemized breakdown of Capitalized Cost. *Note: leasing companies are now required to give you a breakdown of capitalized cost.*
- ➤ monthly payment
- ➤ serial number of vehicle
- ➤ residual value of vehicle
- ➤ the amount required as an initial payment

From the safety of your home, determine a payment figure that reflects the approximate cost of the lease. If you could lease a vehicle for a payment based on acquiring a vehicle at cost and at a reasonable interest rate, that payment would come very close to cost or below cost for the leasing company. Unless you're looking at a subsidized lease (more on those in a moment), you won't lease a vehicle for this payment in real life. But in leasing, as in buying, you want to negotiate up from cost, not down from their figure. Determining a payment figure that reflects cost is easy. It takes only a few quick steps using the information you gathered on your Personal Leasing Checklist.

- ➤ First, look up the car you plan to lease in the back of this book, in *Edmund's*, or at an online pricing service. The invoice cost of the vehicle and options is _____ .

- ➤ The residual value quoted for the vehicle is _____ .

- ➤ Subtract the residual value of the vehicle _____ from its base cost _____ to determine the minimum amount to be financed on the lease _____ . For the moment assume that the lease you are considering has no acquisition fee and you are not going to buy any options such as insurance and warranties. Forget taxes, too, for the moment.

- ➤ Figure the monthly payment on this difference for the term of the lease (twenty-four months, thirty-six months, etc). Use the interest rate quoted on your Checklist (or if that rate is too high, use the fair rate you'd like), and the tables in the appendix to figure the payment just as you would if you were buying (chapter 4).

➤ Financing $_____ (cost minus residual value) for _____ months at _____ APR equals a monthly payment of _____.

This payment figure represents an estimate of the cost of the lease. The difference between this payment figure and the figure quoted by the leasing company is profit—your negotiating room.

Before we look at an example of how this works and you dash out to the showroom, here are a couple of cautions. This cost payment is figured without any down payment or cap cost reduction. If your checklist indicates that such a cash amount is required, subtract that figure from the vehicle's base cost before you compute the payment. You will also need to divide the taxes quoted by the amount of months in the lease and add that to your payment figure. We'll cover how to handle any options such as insurance and warranties in a moment.

Now an example: Let's say the vehicle has an MSRP of $16,500 and an invoice cost of $14,000. On a thirty-six-month lease, you've been quoted a residual value of $9000 and an effective interest rate of 10 percent. The monthly payment on the $5000 difference between cost and residual value is $161. The sales/use tax on the vehicle is $720, or $20 a month, bringing your cost payment to $181. The leasing company has quoted you a payment of $390. The closer you can come to your payment figure of $181 the closer to cost you will come, providing the other factors in the lease such as down payment/cap cost reduction (in our example, zero) stay the same.

How low will the leasing company really go? These folks are spoiled. So, no manager is going to like your negotiating the payment figure they've quoted you by even a dollar. But it's your money, so use the principle we've talked about all through this book—negotiate up from cost.

If you choose options such as warranties or insurance, remember that the cost quoted on your Checklist has profit built in and that these options can be negotiated separately. Don't divide their cost and add them to your cost payment until you have negotiated their cost.

Call up your managers and begin to negotiate. Tell them you're comparing payments, and if you're brave, tell them what you'll pay (in our example $181 per month). Start at the actual cost payment. If the manager won't agree to that (and believe me, he won't), then ask the manager to come back to you with one final monthly quote and hang up.

Leasing managers are like any salesman: they want to make a sale even if the profit isn't great. But don't accept their offer. Tell them you'll think about it. Negotiate like this with both of your sources, and *fight for every dollar.*

When to say yes. This is a business of supply and demand, so there is no "bottom" price. But generally speaking, you will be doing wonderfully well if you cut the difference between your cost figure and their quoted payment in half.

Surviving the Minefield at the Dealership

Even though you may have agreed on a monthly lease payment, don't think the dueling is over yet. Because you've been a good bargainer, the lease manager is going to be very anxious to regain some of that nice profit. So take your time and stop whenever you become confused.

1. **Make an appointment to see the lease manager.** If you have a trade, you must know by now how much it's really worth in wholesale dollars. If you haven't shopped it, reread the section "Computing Your Car's Dollar Value" in chapter 3.

   Tell the manager you have now decided to trade in your car, and you already have an idea of its true wholesale value. You'll find the manager will want to know that number, but don't tell him. You may have been offered $4000 for it, for instance, but this dealership may need your trade and offer more.

   Your objective: to make sure that the company gives you at least as much as you have been offered on your pricing trip.

2. **When you have agreed on the value of your old car,** have the manager now draw up your contract. The contract should now contain an entry for your trade.

3. **Check to make sure the manager has given you full credit for your trade-in.** When you arrived at the dealership, you already had an agreed-upon monthly lease payment, but that payment didn't take into account the equity in your trade. Let's say you had finally agreed to a monthly payment of $270 without a trade. With your trade-in, that payment should now be lowered by *a very specific amount.* For instance, if you agreed your trade-in is worth $4000 and you owe nothing on it, your lease payments should be lowered by $4000 spread over the term of your lease: on a thirty-six-month lease, about $111 per month. Your monthly payments should now be no more than $270 minus $111, or $159 per month. If it's higher than that, the folks are playing with the numbers.

4. **Don't let them sell you "add-ons" at this point.** Some companies will at the last minute try to add service agreements, accessories, or other "special value" packages. Ignore them. Stick to your payment.

5. **Check the contract carefully.**

   ➤ Make sure the excess mileage charge is as you had agreed.
   ➤ Make sure the lease was computed on the number of miles you stated.
   ➤ Make sure your trade is shown as a separate item on the lease.
   ➤ Make sure the residual value and initial cash payment are the same as you were quoted (some companies may agree to your lower payment figure while lowering the residual value and raising initial cash payments to make up the difference).

6. **Drive that beauty home.** If you've been careful and thoughtful, you may be one of the few people in America to lease a car right. Do let me know how you did.

How Do I Negotiate Down the Effective Interest Rate?

The "service" or "rent" charge—or whatever your leasing company calls interest—is a complex item for you to negotiate down separately. If you've done your homework and negotiated down the *payment,* you will automatically have negotiated down the effective interest rate.

Why Can't I Save All This Work and Just Lease One of Those "$199 a Month" Cars I Always See on Television?

Generally speaking, these promotional rates are an excellent, excellent deal, if the dealership will actually lease you a vehicle *at* the promotional rate. And *if* you can live with the usually severe mileage limitations. Some lease-promo cars only allow you 10,000 per year rather than the normal 15,000, and charge a hefty penalty if you go over their mileage limit.

Really cheap monthly lease payment promotions usually mean two manufacturers are slugging it out for a sales record—for instance, Ford is trying to outsell Toyota, so the manufacturer throws cars out the window at cheap lease rates to increase sales. Toyota then counterattacks.

Since dealerships make a lot less on these promotions, they don't want you to drive that bargain car. They try to switch you to a car with more options, or say your credit isn't up to snuff. But if a promo car fits your needs and your mileage requirements, slug it out with the dealership and insist on the promo rate.

What About Leasing Used Cars?

If you only need a car for a couple of years, and if you're not planning to put many miles on a car, leasing a late-model used-car can make a lot of sense. Negotiate your lease payment as you would for a new vehicle. And then after you've negotiated your payment, insist that you have the vehicle checked out by a mechanic. If your mechanic says the vehicle needs work, have the work done before you sign any contracts. And don't let the lessor raise your monthly payment to cover the repair.

9

Negotiating the Sale:
Specific Tactics
for Specific Buyers

WHAT IS A "FAIR" DEAL?

One of the best general managers I know says and believes this: "If the customer is happy and we are happy, *that's* a fair deal." Unfortunately, there is a problem with his logic: The house will always *know* what it did to you—how much money it made. The vast majority of customers *think* they are satisfied. And the vast majority of those people would commit murder if they knew the truth. Be wary of your deal if you see the manager pouring your salesman champagne and hear shouts of glee through the walls.

It's a cruel world out there, you've worked hard for your money, and all those dealers are living in fancy houses, so let's define "fair" in the buyer's terms, for a change: *the least dollar amount any particular seller will take for a specific car.* That figure may include a $100 profit or a $1000 profit; you won't know until you bargain a little, but always assume a seller will say "yes" only if the deal benefits him. This chapter on negotiating the sale assumes that fact. It will show you how to negotiate price *until* the seller says "yes." *It's important to approach "fair" from this point of view rather than a fixed percentage of profit,* because most dealers' definitions can also change because of factory incentives and contests. At times, a dealer will happily sell a specific car for less than $100 "profit," and within days, refuse to sell the same car for less than $500 profit. But, regardless of the final figure any seller will take for a specific car, remember he will be making more money than you think.

If you are the type of person who absolutely refuses to dicker over price, if you are determined to offer one firm price only, offer the seller a maximum profit of two percent of the list price. And I said maximum. If the dealer absolutely refuses to take your offer, raise it a percent if you like, but don't go above that figure. Go to another dealership. Car dealerships survive on churning their money, turning cars over quickly. Don't fall prey to sob stories, even in "bad" car years. Smart dealers make money in the worst years—they don't need your sympathy. Car people will attempt to convince you no business can live on very small profits, two or three percent or less, and they are right. But follow this logic for a moment: If you are looking at a $10,000 car, don't think the dealer paid $10,000 for it, or even the invoice cost of $7700. The vast majority of new-car automobile dealerships floor-plan their cars; they do not own them outright. Most dealerships' new cars are owned by their financing institutions, such as Ford Motor Credit or GMAC. When the new car you want to buy was ordered, the car was shipped to the dealer on consignment. The dealer pays only interest on the invoice price of the car. For instance, that $10,000 car will probably cost the dealer $1800 a year in interest, or $150 per month for each month the car sits on his lot.

If the car has been on his lot for three months, the dealer has an investment of $450 in the car. If you pay the dealer three percent profit, and the dealer adds to that three percent the profits built in and hidden in the invoice, his gross will be over $800. Now subtract the $450 interest and $70 commission to the salesman. The dealer has a net cash increase of $280 on an investment of $450. A fifty percent return on his investment—in three months. Can you do that with your money?

So, what's a fair deal? When you know the seller is taking the least amount of money, *that's* a fair deal.

HANDLING HIGH-PRESSURE TECHNIQUES

As we have continually said, dealerships are masters at using sophisticated, high-pressure sales techniques. Salesmen wear you down, curse you out behind your back, and generally don't give a damn about you once you've bought a car from them. Since most of us have

felt many of these pressures before, it's hard to imagine a car transaction that is simple, clean, and to the point. But that's exactly what
your next transaction will be, if you've read this book carefully. And
if you decide to stick with these basic ground rules, right now, before
you enter the negotiation.

1. Have all your facts on paper when you go to the dealership. If
   you know the true wholesale value of your car, the amount of
   your Available Cash, and your financing terms *before* you
   shop, salesmen won't be able to lead you on some mini-safari
   around their lot. If you plan to shop for a new or used car,
   you'll know the dollar range of cars that fit your budget.

2. Don't fall for "if" questions. It may not sound like a high-
   pressure technique, but it's really the *highest*-pressure technique. "If" questions are simply designed to suspend logic. For
   instance, anyone would be inclined to say yes to "If I can sell
   you a $10,000 car for $5000 will you buy it?" Of course you
   would. But logic dictates the reality. No dealership can do
   that. When salesmen use the "if" approach, *take control of the
   conversation* and don't commit. Simply smile and say, "I don't
   know."

3. Insist on straight answers. If you ask the wholesale value of
   your trade, don't accept some mumbled answer about "allowance." Many salesmen will tell you cars "don't have just one
   value. The value of your trade will be determined by the car
   you want to purchase." Say good-bye to people like this and
   leave.

4. Don't be "worked." *All* selling systems are based on working
   you: The salesman brings in reinforcements, or the salesman
   keeps leaving and coming back with sincere-sounding notes
   written by his manager (all malarkey), or the salesman keeps
   picking up the phone as if he's carrying on a sincere conversation with his manager. *Don't put up with any of it.* Break the
   system. Tell the man in no uncertain terms you want definite,
   quick answers or you will leave.

5. Do things in your sequence, not theirs. In order to understand
   a car transaction, you will have to control the order in which
   information is gathered. Many salesmen will tell you, "Oh, no,

before we have your car appraised, we always fill out the buyer's order." Say no. Follow the steps outlined in "Stalking and
the Kill," page 264. If someone insists on changing your order,
thank him and say good-bye.

If you follow these steps, *you* will be in control, not the salesman.
You will probably find that most salesmen and dealerships won't like
your approach, but they will be nice to you. Remember: Any dealership would rather sell you a car on your terms than miss a sale. It's
the most important pressure you can bring to bear.

DEALING WITH THE FINANCE "MANAGER"

The Toughest Sales Gimmicks at the Dealership

Even if you do your homework, even if you do everything right at the
dealership, you'll still pay more than *$3000* in extra profits if you don't
know how to counter the finance manager's smooth but ruthless at-
tacks on your pocketbook.

The basic strategy is simple. After you've agreed to buy a vehicle,
after your defenses are down, they go for the big profits: financing,
"protection" packages, service agreement–warranty packages, alarm-
system packages, etc.

For many dealerships, this is an interesting shift in strategies, too,
starting with *the shrinking of the dealer sticker*. Because so many people have complained about the excess charges on this sticker—and
have learned how to negotiate away these excess profits—the
smartest dealers have removed many charges (such as "protection

packages" and extended warranties) from there and *added them back in the finance officer* after you've agreed to buy.

Two New Very Popular and Very Dangerous Finance Manager Lines
We're going to talk about the normal scams in a minute, but here are two you can certainly expect to hear about.

   "Why don't we just apply that rebate as part of your down payment?" The finance salesperson isn't trying to help you, he's probably getting ready to steal your rebate, as we mentioned earlier: the dealership would like to keep it as profit, rather than credit it against the amount you owe the dealership. *How do you protect yourself?* The dealership flimflam can be hard to catch. The only sure way to make sure the money goes in your pocket rather than theirs is to insist that the rebate check be mailed directly to you. Don't consider it part of the transaction at all. Use your mortgage money, if you have to, as a down payment. When your rebate check comes (in about six weeks), pay yourself back.

   "How would you like it if I can cut that payment in two?" The finance salesperson is, of course, going to try to switch you to leasing. Ignore the spiel. If you're thinking of leasing, come back another day after reading the leasing section.

Protection Packages, Warranties: Should You Buy from the Dealers at Any Price?

   Rustproofing, undercoating, glazing. Don't buy from the dealer. You can buy a better rustproofing and undercoating for hundreds less from other sources. But do you need it? Probably not. Manufacturers are doing an excellent job of both interior and exterior rustproofing these days. And paint protection or "glazing"? Don't waste your money.

   Service agreements and extended warranty packages. I'll give you details on these later, but here's a summary: New cars come with very comprehensive warranties these days, so don't waste your money. If you just have to buy one of these, you shouldn't pay more than $250, and see if your bank or credit union sells one. Many do. *Used car* *warranties:* These can be useful if you can buy a warranty for $250. Many banks and credit unions are offering these, too.

Alarm systems. If saving $300 to $500 is worth anything to you, don't automatically buy from the dealership. Dozens of reputable places will sell and install an alarm system.

The same goes for security registration and other protection system services.

So, what to do if the items are already on the car? If you want the item, pay for it, but negotiate the price. Dealers generally mark up their additions to your car from 100 to 1000 percent. Items like warranties and radios are normally marked up *at least* 100 percent, so consider 50 percent of the asking price as "cost." On a $1000 warranty, offer $600 or so.

A warning: On items like "Protection" packages—some dealerships call these pitiful offerings "Environmental protection packages" to sound fancy—markups are much greater, as we've mentioned. If someone wants to charge you $795 for rustproofing and undercoating, offer them $100, and negotiate up from that. And with some security registration systems, the dealer says that since they've already engraved a registration number on, say, the window of the vehicle, you have to take the service. You don't. Again, if you want the service, negotiate.

What to do if the dealership won't budge. Dealerships generally won't budge at first. They assume your natural excitement over driving out in that new car will overcome your good sense. Have better sense than that. If the dealership won't budge, *you* budge right out of your seat and tell them the deal's off. Stand up and start walking toward your old car, and don't look back. You'll find the price on those overpriced add-ons will fall very quickly.

Where You'll Meet the Finance Salesperson (a.k.a., Your Friend, the Business Manager or "Financial Counselor")

There are lots of places and ways to take you in this area, but here are the main danger spots:

If you've done your homework and plan to finance at a bank or credit

union. You are the prime target for the tough dealerships. They'll first insist that you talk to their "business manager" regardless of your protests. And once you get there, they'll say anything, including lies, to switch you to their financing and then sell you their "add-ons." And that's their real objective: To charge you $600 to $1200 for rustproofing and undercoating that should sell for no more than $200. To charge $600 to $1200 for an extended service agreement that used to sell for $250. To charge you $600 to $900 for an alarm package that could be bought from a specialty company for $300.

Because of their rip-off prices, there's one thing dealerships won't do, though: let you think about or compare their costs with the cost for other financing, credit life and disability insurance, warranty plans, rustproofing and undercoating, or alarm systems. Would you want people to compare if you were charging their prices?

So, how do you handle the pressure? If you want to be tough, refuse to listen to the sales pitches at all. Tell the "business manager" or "financial counselor" you're not interested in talking at all, and if they pressure you, you'll leave.

But if you're not that tough, or if you're curious about the dealership spiel, listen very politely, and expect some of the nicest, most believable lies you've ever heard, and then tell the person this:

"I'll be happy to consider your financing if *you'll give me an exact copy, filled out, of the finance contract you want me to sign so that I can compare it with my other source.*" That's a very simple request. When they hem and haw and eventually refuse, remember how readily your bank and credit union provided you their figures and take the dealership's refusal for what it is—an admission they're trying to take you again. Come back with a check from your other source.

If they say yes, go home and compare the costs between sources for each charge, using the comparison method we showed you in Chapter 4.

If you are financing at the dealership and are a payment buyer. If you are, you haven't read this book carefully enough and are probably already doing two things wrong. But in this case, expect to see the finance manager before you come to terms on the car. At this stage, the finance salesperson will probably quote you a vague (and low) payment simply to get you committed to buy. *What to do:* Make the finance salesperson be specific. What exactly is included in the payment? At exactly what rate? You'll invariably be told "We can't give you a specific rate yet," but that is a lie. Dealership rates generally don't change with your credit. *Caution:* At some point you'll be told the virtues of the dealership's credit life and disability insurance. Don't forget they're dramatically more expensive than from other sources. And then the pitch will come for warranties, protection packages, etc. These two are also much more expensive than from other sources.

If you are financing and the dealership wants to "spot deliver" you. Just say no. Go home and defuse. Refuse to sign any "recission" form or any other document which says the dealership can change your figures or terms. If you think you might be tempted by spot delivery, go back and read the section on this bad sales tactic on page 55.

YOUR HOUR UPON THE STAGE: THE IMPORTANCE OF PLAY-ACTING

Have you ever met someone you really didn't like at a party, but managed to be passably nice to that person? Or, in your own particular job, have you ever said the "right" thing, rather than expressed the thought really on your mind? If you have, you'll have no problem dealing in the car world, for dealerships are the world's greatest arena for amateur actors. Salesmen do it every day—like Joe Girard, "the world's number-one car salesman," as he's fond of claiming in his book. Girard sells more cars than most dealerships and proudly proclaimed in a *Newsweek* article that he would "do anything to make a sale. I'll kiss the baby, hug the wife. It's nothing but an act." Customers do it every day, too. Even the most intimidated Caspar Milquetoast in the world usually forgets to tell his salesman little things that might adversely affect the value of his trade-in.

Rather than condemn the process, however, why not accept it for what it is? Car negotiations are simply polite tugs-of-war. One side is fighting mightily to make lots of money. The other side is trying to conserve money. And neither side has much sympathy with the other's plight.

STALKING AND THE KILL:
THE NEGOTIATIONS

When you were in school, did you ever fudge a little on exams? Perhaps read the Cliff Notes version of some novel rather than the real thing? Or were you the type who memorized answers rather than understood concepts? Well, you may have graduated with honors using those tactics in school, but you can't cheat on the final exam in this game. Unless you've done your homework thoroughly you'll stumble, fumble, generally make an idiot of yourself, and lose money in the process—no fun at all. But:

1. if you've shopped your car,
2. if you've shopped your financing rates,
3. if you're comfortable developing Loan Cash and Available Cash figures, and
4. if you are prepared to develop cost figures—read on. We're going to walk through, step-by-step, each buying situation. Pick the one that fits your particular need and go directly to that section. The Appendix also contains these same steps in much abbreviated form. You may want to refer to them once you are comfortable with the entire buying process. *After you've read your section, turn next to the section on "Warranties: New and Used," page 297.*

If you are planning to finance your next car, review these terms before going to your section:

1. *Loan Cash*
   The lump sum of cash your payment will buy. For instance, 36 payments of $164 at 11 percent APR will buy you $5000 in Loan Cash.

2. *Equity*

The wholesale value of your car minus your payoff. For example, if the wholesale value is $5000 and your payoff is $3500, your equity is $1500.

3. *Available Cash*

Your Loan Cash and equity (or cash down payment) added together. This figure tells you how much car you can buy.

4. *Difference*

The final selling price of their car minus the wholesale value of your car.

Go directly to the section that applies to you:

IF YOU PLAN TO FINANCE

Buying a New Car and Trading the Old	page 267
Buying a New Car Without Trading	271
Buying a Used Car and Trading the Old	275
Buying a Used Car Without Trading	279

IF YOU PLAN TO PAY CASH

Buying a New Car and Trading the Old	page 283
Buying a New Car Without Trading	287
Buying a Used Car and Trading the Old	289
Buying a Used Car Without Trading	294

If You Are Financing, Buying a New Car, and Trading the Old

Let's walk through a typical transaction. We'll say that you've shopped your present car, arriving at a value of $5000. Its payoff is $3500. We'll assume 10.5 percent APR was your best financing rate and that you have decided to finance for three years. You want to pay $260 per month.

1. Compute your Available Cash (Loan Cash plus Equity). For shopping purposes, your Available Cash is the important figure. It tells you the maximum amount of car you can buy, including tax, tag, title, and all other charges. By using this figure while shopping, you won't have to be concerned with the effect of your trade, since its real value is *already included in your Available Cash figure.* Our figure is $9500.

2. Go to two different car stores and look for specific cars that interest you. Find at least two cars at each store and ask your salesman for a demonstration ride. Don't discuss price. Don't be "if-ed" to death; simply find two cars you like and drive them. When you've finished your demonstration ride, copy down all the information from the price sticker on the window. Remember, don't pay any attention to the dealer's sticker. Copy information only from the manufacturer's sticker. Take down the name and price of everything, including freight. Ask your salesman to give you the stock number of the car. Write that down by the name of the dealership and your salesman. Ask him to give you the amount of any miscellaneous charges, such as title fees. Ask him how tax is computed. For instance, is tax paid on the total price of the new car or on the difference figure? Don't be talked into *anything* during this visit; simply thank your man and leave. Once you have visited two stores, go home and relax for a while.

3. At home, write down the price information and stock number of each car on a clean sheet of paper and compute the cost of the car and all its options. We'll assume you've found a car that lists for $9400, and have figured a true cost for the car and options of $8600. When you've done this, total the following:

Cost of the car and options	$8600
Transportation charge	225
Title fees and miscellaneous charges	55
TOTAL COST	$8880

The maximum profit you will pay (for our example, we'll assume $350)	350
YOUR MAXIMUM OFFER WILL BE	$9230

4. Now, check to see if you are over or under budget. Don't forget that tax will need to be added to your offer. But for now, simply check your Available Cash against your offer.

Your Available Cash	$9500
Your offer on the new car	9230
AMOUNT OVER OR UNDER BUDGET	$270 *under*

5. Now compute your *difference* figure. Remember, the difference will be your method of checking their figures.

Your offer on the new car	$9230
Wholesale value of your car	5000
DIFFERENCE	$4230

Use these five steps for each one of the cars you have driven. And then put the following information on your pad. You will need it at the store.

A. Write down the location, stock number, and color of each car. By that, write down your offer on the car and your trading difference on the car.
B. Write down the wholesale value of your car. You'll only need to write this once, since the wholesale value won't change.
C. Write down your Available Cash figure once, too.

DEALING WITH THE STORE

You don't have any reason to be nervous now, for you have more information at your fingertips than your salesman. Go back to the store and see him. Make an appointment if you like. Let him show you the two cars again, and if both cars were in your price range, make an emotional decision on which car you really like the best. Enjoy! This is the only time your heart rate should affect your negotiations. Once you have decided on *the* particular car, head to the salesman's office. Be nice. Smile and laugh. But remember that *you* must control the order of the next few minutes. Do it like this:

1. Tell the salesman to have your car appraised. Don't tell him your wholesale figure either, but review that figure in your mind. When the guy returns, speak before spoken to. Look him in the eye, and think positive thoughts.

2. Ask your salesman for the appraisal on your car. Let him know you want their wholesale offer, *not* an allowance figure. If the figure is lower than your wholesale value, tell him. But don't tell him the amount; give him room to come up as much as he will. If the figure is higher than your figure, smile. You are ahead of the game. If his offer never equals yours, tell him your figure. Tell him who gave you the figure. If necessary, remind your salesman that his used-car boys can sell your car to the same people you would sell it to. If he still won't accept your figure, go to your other dealership. If he finally agrees to your figure or offers you more, write his offer on your pad.

3. Make your offer on the new car. The figure is on your pad. Don't be afraid for him to see your pad, either. Salesmen are invariably thrown off-guard by customers who actually know what they are doing. If you are smart, offer him *less* than your figure; give him room to dicker a little. But don't go over your maximum figure. Once the two of you have agreed on a figure, write it down in your pad. Put it by your original offer for that particular car.

4. Stop and check your difference figure. Deduct *his* offer on your trade from the agreed price of the new car. If this difference figure is more than your difference figure, you are losing money. If the figure is lower than your figure, you are making money. If the figure is an acceptable one to you, go to the next step. If it is not acceptable, continue to negotiate or go to your other dealership.

5. Tell him to write it up. Once the salesman has completely filled in the buyer's order, look at the difference figure on the order. If you don't see it, ask the salesman to point it out to you. That figure must agree with the one you have just computed.

   Most buyer's orders are not designed to show cash offers on a new car and wholesale figures on used cars. Your salesman will probably indicate, for instance, that you are buying the new car at sticker price but receiving more than wholesale on your trade. That's okay *if* the difference figure is the same.

6. If the difference figure is the same, sign the buyer's order, but do not give him a deposit. Tell him you will give him a check *when* the deal is approved by a manager. The salesman will probably insist on a deposit. Tell him it's your way or not at all. Remember: a deposit before you have an approved deal is their way of keeping you there while they work you.

7. If the salesman returns with a signed order, give him a deposit. If he returns with his boss or insists your offer is too low, tell him again you will not be raised. If he keeps insisting, raise your offer $50 if you wish. But don't be raised more than once. If you are determined not to be raised at all, say good-bye. Head to your other dealership.

8. If you're not financing at the dealership, be prepared for pressure. Arrange the time to pick up your car.

9. If you are financing the car at the dealership, be prepared to talk with their finance manager. Remember, you already know the number of months and the interest rate. You have already made a decision on insurance. *Don't let the finance manager change your terms.* Before you leave his office, confirm the amount to be financed, and take that figure home with you. If the amount to be financed is not exactly the same as your projected Loan Cash, compute the payment when you get home and take that figure with you when you pick up the car. It should be within pennies of his payment.

If You Are Financing and Buying a New Car without Trading

You're going to have an easy time of it.

1. Determine your Loan Cash. Let's assume you have shopped financing sources and found 10.5 percent APR money. You plan to pay $248 a month for 48 months. Your Loan Cash would be $9700.

2. Determine how much money you intend to pay down. If you're smart, you'll pay at least twenty-five percent down—in this instance, $2425. If you don't plan to pay twenty-five percent down, you will have to pay a sum equal to or larger than the total of the profit on the new car, your taxes, and other expenses.

3. Now total your Loan Cash and down payment. That figure is your Available Cash, how much car you can buy, including tax, tag, and any other charges. In our example, Available Cash is $12,125.

4. Go to two different car stores and look for specific cars that interest you. Find at least two cars at each store, and ask your salesman for a demonstration ride. Don't discuss price. Don't be "if-ed" to death; simply find two cars you like and drive them. When you've finished your demonstration ride, copy down the item and price of everything on the window sticker. Remember, don't pay attention to the dealer's sticker. Ask your salesman to give you the stock number of the car. Write that down by the name of the dealership and your salesman. Ask the salesman to give you any miscellaneous charges, such as title fees. Also ask him how tax is computed. Is it figured on the *list* price of the new car, or the discounted price? Don't be talked into anything during this visit; simply thank your man and leave. Go home and relax for a while.

5. Once you are home, write down the price information and stock number from each car on a clean sheet of paper. Compute the cost of the cars and all their options. We'll assume you've found a car that lists for $13,500 and have figured a true cost for the car and options of $11,475. When you've done this, add the following:

Cost of the car and options	$11,475
Transportation charge	300
Title fees and other miscellaneous charges	55
TOTAL COST	$11,830
The maximum profit you will pay (for our example, we'll assume $350)	350
YOUR MAXIMUM OFFER WILL BE	$12,180

6. Now, check to see if you are over or under budget.

Your Available Cash is	$12,125
Your offer on the new car is	12,180
AMOUNT OVER OR UNDER BUDGET	$55 *over*

You are over budget. *Plus,* you've still got to pay tax and other fees. If your state charges four percent sales tax on the total selling price, you will owe tax of $487. You are over budget a total of $542. Can you afford that? Can you pay your over-budget figure with your own cash? If not, your payments will go up. If you refigured your payments, they would be $261 rather than $248.

Let's assume that you don't want to spend that much. Remember that this car *listed* for $13,500. You'll need to find a car that lists for about $500 less, if you plan to stay in budget. Let's say that you have found a car listing for $13,000 instead. You have computed the cost to be $10,900. If you use step five to refigure your offer and step six to check your budget, you'll find you are now $520 under budget. Nice! You are under budget enough to pay your taxes. Put $11,605, the new offer, on your pad.

DEALING WITH THE STORE

You really don't have any reason to be nervous now. You know more than your salesman. So, call up the store that's home to your favorite cars, and make an appointment to see your salesman. Go see him.

1. Look at your favorite car again. If you would like, don't feel shy about asking to drive it. Decide if it's the car you really want to own.

2. Tell your salesman you would like to go to his office and talk price. Don't wait for him to drag you to his office, take the initiative. Remember, you must be in control.

3. Pull out your pad once you are in his office. He won't like your pad, but that's okay. The more uncomfortable he is, the more in control you are. Tell your salesman that you are prepared to make an offer on the car. Tell him it is a *firm* offer. Tell him your offer doesn't leave any money on the table. Use that phrase, too.

4. Make your offer and insist that he take it to his manager. Let him write it up, but *don't* give him a deposit. Even if he insists, don't do it. Tell him there are other dealerships down the road that don't require a deposit until both parties have agreed on a figure.

5. Before signing, compare the total sale price to your Available Cash. For instance, using our last example:

Your Available Cash	$12,125
Your offer	11,605
Sales tax (assuming 4 percent)	464
Other miscellaneous charges	50
AMOUNT OVER OR UNDER BUDGET	$6 *under*

You are under budget $6. Not bad at all.

6. If the salesman returns with a signed buyer's order, give him a deposit. If he returns with his boss or insists himself your offer is too low, insist on your offer. If your salesman will actually let you leave on your figure, consider budging a little. But don't budge much. If you make a counteroffer, make only *one*. Tell the salesman it is your final offer. Do not let them "work" you. If your final offer is not accepted, thank the man and say good-bye. Head to your other dealership. If your final offer is accepted, and you're within budget, pat yourself on the back. You have survived.

7. If you are not financing at the dealership, be prepared for pressure. Arrange a time to pick up your car.

8. If you are financing the car at the dealership, be prepared to talk with their finance manager. Remember, you already know the number of months and the interest rate. You have already made a decision on insurance. Don't let the finance manager change your terms. Before you leave his office, confirm the amount to be financed and take that figure home with you. If the amount to be financed is not exactly the same as your projected Loan Cash, compute the payment when you get home and take that figure with you when you pick up the car. It should be within pennies of his payment.

If You Are Financing, Buying a Used Car, and Trading the Old

Before reading any further, tell me the truth: Did you really work through the chapter on used cars, or did you just read the headings? If you cheated, go back and read the chapter carefully—you're a candidate for the slaughterhouse. If you did it right the first time, read on.

Remember that there is no set value on any used car, no accurate book to tell you what a particular car is worth. Remember, also, that you must be prepared to dicker quite a lot. Remember, finally, that "asking price" always includes a very healthy profit. For dickering purposes, always assume a nice used car has a mark-up of $600 to $1000 *regardless* of its wholesale value or asking price.

Now, let's walk through a typical transaction. We will assume you've shopped your car and found that it's worth $1500 wholesale. You owe $500 on the car. We'll also assume your best financing rate is 12.5 percent APR and you plan to pay no more than $147 per month for twenty-four months.

1. Compute your Available Cash (Loan Cash plus equity). For shopping purposes, your Available Cash is the important figure. It tells you the maximum amount of car you can buy, including tax, tag, title, and all other charges. By using this figure while shopping, you won't have to be concerned with the effect of your trade, since its real value is *already included in your Available Cash figure.* In our example, your Available Cash is $4100.

2. Decide on three or four sources, using the guides in the chapter on buying a used car. Include at least one new-car dealership.

3. Visit the lots and look for cars with *asking* prices a few hundred dollars higher than your Available Cash figure. Do *not* tell the salesman you are trading. Used-car operations raise the prices of their cars if they feel you are going to trade. Do not tell them your Available Cash figure. As you find cars with asking prices close to your figure, take time to drive them. Take with you the checklist from the Appendix, and look for

obvious problems with the car. If you still like the car after a test drive, write down the stock number and a description of the car. Write down the asking price, the name of the person you are dealing with, the miles of the car, and any options that may add to loan value, such as a vinyl roof, air-conditioning, power windows, or cruise control. Then thank your salesman and go home.

4. Call a local bank or credit union and ask for a loan officer. Tell the officer the year and model of the car. Then ask him the minimum interest rate and the maximum number of months the car can be financed. Write that information down and keep it in your pad. You'll want to compare it to the rate you need in determining your Loan Cash. Now, accurately describe the car to him. Give him the options and mileage, and then ask for the loan value of that particular car. Put that figure in your pad, too.

5. Compare the seller's asking price to the loan value of the car. We'll assume you've found a car with an asking price of $4600 and a loan value of $3800. The spread is their *probable profit* —in this instance, $800.

6. Compute your "best probable" difference figure. Subtract the wholesale value of your car from the loan value of the seller's car.

The loan value of the seller's car	$3800
The wholesale value of your car	−1500
EQUALS YOUR BEST PROBABLE DIFFERENCE	$2300

When we begin to negotiate, we will be trying to be close to this difference figure or below it. Put the figure in your pad; it's your most important figure.

7. Go back to the lot and tell your salesman you have decided to trade your car. Though it may not do any good, tell him you want the actual wholesale value of your car, *not* an allowance figure. He'll probably be surprised you know the difference. And then tell him you would like to take his car to your mechanic. Leave your car with him for ransom. If your salesman won't agree to this, don't buy the car. If he agrees, take

a clean copy of the Mechanic's Checklist in the Appendix and drive to your mechanic's shop. Don't forget to add to the checklist any specific problems you have noted in your pad. Before leaving the shop, ask for an estimate to repair the car to your satisfaction. Put that figure in your pad, and take a coffee break.

8. Your Available Cash is $4100. But you may now have a repair bill, if you buy the car. Let's assume the repairs were estimated to cost $300. To stay in budget, you will need to *subtract* the estimate from your Available Cash ($4100 minus $300). Your new Available Cash figure is $3800. Make that adjustment and head back to the lot.

9. Don't let your salesman do the figuring when you return, but ask him directly how much he is giving you for your car. Subtract that from his "asking price" and determine his difference figure. We'll assume he actually appraised your car for $1500.

Asking price	$4600
His figure on your car	−1500
HIS DIFFERENCE FIGURE	$3100

10. Now, compare his difference figure to your "best probable" difference figure. The balance will be how much more money he wants for the car than you are planning to spend. That figure is also his profit, most likely.

His difference figure	$3100
Your "best probable" difference figure	−2300
HIS PROBABLE PROFIT	$800

11. If by some act of God, his difference figure is the same as yours, don't automatically agree to buy the car. Every salesman's first offer, regardless of how low it is, has a cushion in it. Offer the man $200 or $300 less. You should be smiling on the inside, too.

   If his figure is close to your figure, only $200 or $300 above, tell him that the figure is $400 or $600 away. Always compromise and split the difference on any offer.

12. At some point in the discussion, your salesman is not going
to budge. When he reaches that point, check these things:

   A. His probable profit. Subtract your difference figure from his.
   We'll assume he agreed to $2650.

His final difference figure	$2650
Your "best probable" difference	2300
HIS PROBABLE PROFIT	$350

For a nice used car, that's a very reasonable profit.

   B. Can you afford it? Add these items together and determine
   how much you will owe the seller.

His final difference figure	$2650
The payoff on your old car	500
Tax (we'll assume 4 percent; use your own state's rate)	106
YOU WILL OWE THE SELLER	$3256

   C. What will be your total expenditure? Subtract what you will
   owe the seller and the repair estimate from your Available
   Cash:

Your Available Cash	$3800
What you owe the seller	−3256
The repair estimate	−300
AMOUNT OVER OR UNDER BUDGET	$244 *under*

   You're in good shape.

13. If you've determined this is the actual car you want to buy,
discuss warranties. Be sure you are familiar with the section
on warranties before opening your mouth, or you'll probably
find your foot resting on your molars.

14. If the salesman's final offer fits your budget and the warranty
is satisfactory, have him write it up. Tell him you'll take the
car at that figure. Once the salesman has completely filled out
the buyer's order, look at the difference figure. If you don't

see it, ask the salesman to point it out to you. That figure must agree with your final difference figure. Make sure the warranty is written. If the figure is the same, sign the buyer's order, but do not give him a deposit. Tell him you will give him a check when the deal is approved by a manager. The salesman will probably insist on a deposit. Tell him it's your way or no way at all. Remember, a deposit before you have an approved deal is their way of keeping you there while they work you. If the salesman returns with his boss or insists himself your offer is too low, tell him you will not be raised. If he insists, and if you really like the car, raise your offer $50, if you wish. But don't be raised more than once. If you are determined not to be raised, say good-bye.

15. If you're not financing with the dealership, be prepared for pressure. Arrange a time to pick up your car.

16. If you are financing with the seller, be prepared to be worked again. Remember, you already know the number of months and the interest rate. You have already made a decision on insurance. Don't be talked into changing your mind. Before leaving, confirm the amount to be financed, and take that figure home with you. If the amount to be financed is not exactly the same as your projected Loan Cash, recompute the payment when you get home and take that figure with you when you pick up the car. It should be within pennies of his payment.

If You Are Financing and Buying a Used Car without Trading

Before reading any further, tell me the truth: Did you really work through the chapter on used cars, or did you just read the headings? If you cheated, go back and read the chapter carefully. You're a candidate for the slaughterhouse. If you did it right the first time, read on.

1. Determine your Loan Cash. Let's assume you have shopped financing sources and found 12.5 percent APR. You plan to pay

$174 per month for twenty-four months. Your Loan Cash would be $5200.

2. Determine your down payment. If possible, plan to pay down thirty percent of your Loan Cash figure. If you can't afford that much cash from your pocket, you will need to pay down a sum equal to the total of the profit on the car, tax, and other charges. In our example, we'll assume you will pay a $300 profit. We'll also assume that your Loan Cash figure is also the loan value of the car. For shopping purposes, you can assume the same thing: Compute your tax on your Loan Cash figure. Then allow $100 for other miscellaneous charges. In this instance, your down payment will need to be $608, figuring four percent tax on your Loan Cash.

3. Now, determine your Available Cash, the total of your down payment and Loan Cash. This figure will be the total amount of money you can spend, including tax, tags, and all other expenses. In our example, your Available Cash is $5808.

4. Decide on three or four car sources, using the guides in the chapter on buying a used car. Include at least one new-car dealership.

5. Visit those lots. Look for cars with asking prices $400 or $500 above your Available Cash figure. Don't tell the salesman your price range. Virtually all used-car salesmen have a very bad habit of raising asking prices up to your figure. When the salesman asks you, "Well, what were you thinking about spending?" just tell him, "Well, it depends on the car," and smile. Let's assume you have found a car with an asking price of $6300. Take it for a drive. Use the checklist in the Appendix, and look for obvious problems with the car. If you still like it after your test drive, write down the stock number and description of the car, the mileage, and the name of the person you are dealing with. Write down any options that may add to loan value, such as automatic transmission, air-conditioning, vinyl roof, or power windows. And then thank your salesman, saying good-bye in the process.

6. Call a local bank or credit union and ask for a loan officer. Tell the officer the year and model of the car. Then ask him the minimum interest rate and maximum number of months the

car can be financed. Write that information down and keep it in your pad. You'll want to compare it to the rate you used in determining your Loan Cash. Now, accurately describe the car to him. Give him the options and mileage, and then ask for the loan value of that particular car. Put the figure in your pad, too.

7. Now, compare the seller's asking price to the loan value of the car. We'll assume loan value was $3200. The spread is their probable profit.

Asking price	$6300
Loan value	−5000
PROBABLE PROFIT	$1300

You want to pay as little of that profit as possible. You want to buy the car for a figure as close to loan value as possible.

8. Determine your offer. Since you would ideally like to buy the car for loan value or less, decide the *maximum* amount you are willing to pay over loan value and add the two figures. In our example, the maximum profit will be $300, loan value is $5000, and your maximum offer will be $5300. Remember that tax and other charges must be added to that figure.

9. Now, head back to the lot and tell your salesman you would like to take his car to your mechanic. Leave whatever car you are driving as ransom. If your salesman won't agree to this, don't buy the car. If he agrees, take a clean copy of the Mechanic's Checklist and drive to your mechanic's shop. Don't forget to add to his list any specific problems you have noted in your pad. Before leaving, ask your mechanic for an estimate to repair the car to your satisfaction. Put that figure in your pad and take a coffee break.

10. Your Available Cash is $5808. But you may now have a repair bill, if you buy the car. To stay in budget, you will need to *subtract* the estimate from your Available Cash. Let's assume your repair bill was $300. Your new Available Cash figure is $5508. Make that adjustment and head back to the lot.

11. Lead the salesman to his office. Don't be led, take the initiative. Offer the man *less* than the loan value. When the man

counteroffers, don't accept his figure. Compromise; offer to split the difference with him.

12. At some point in the discussion, your salesman is not going to budge. When he reaches that point, compare his final offer to your Available Cash. Let's assume his final offer is $5200.

Your Available Cash	$5508
His final offer	−5200
AMOUNT OVER OR UNDER BUDGET	$308 *under*

You're in pretty good shape. Don't forget that tax will need to be added to that figure. Can you afford the car?

Now, compare his final offer to the loan value of the car. The answer, in this instance $200, is his probable profit. Is that figure satisfactory? It should be, Jesse James.

13. If you've determined this is the actual car you want to buy, discuss warranties. Be sure you are familiar with the section on warranties before opening your mouth, or you'll probably find your foot resting on your molars.

14. If the salesman's final offer fits your budget and the warranty is satisfactory, have him write it up. Tell him you'll take the car at that figure. Once the salesman has completely filled out the buyer's order, check the figures. Make sure the warranty is written. Sign the buyer's order, but do not give him a deposit. Tell him it's your way or not at all. Remember, a deposit before you have an approved deal is their way of keeping you there while they work you. If the salesman returns with his boss or insists himself your offer is too low, tell him you will not be raised. If he still insists, and if you really like the car, raise your offer $50, if you wish. But don't be raised more than once. If you are determined not to be raised, say good-bye.

15. If you're not financing at the dealership, be prepared for pressure. Arrange a time to pick up your car.

16. If you are financing with the seller, be prepared to be worked again. Remember, you already know the number of months and the interest rate. You have already made a decision on insurance. Don't be talked into changing your mind. Before leaving, confirm the amount to be financed and take that figure

home with you. If the amount to be financed is not exactly the same as your projected Loan Cash, recompute the payment when you get home and take that figure with you when you pick up the car. It should be within pennies of his payment.

If You Are Paying Cash, Buying a New Car, and Trading the Old

Let's walk through a typical transaction. We'll say that you've shopped your present car, arriving at a value of $7000.

1. Compute your Available Cash (your cash plus the value of your trade). We'll assume you're flush this year and have allocated $8000 in cash. Your Available Cash is $15,000. For shopping purposes, that figure is an important one. It tells you the maximum amount of car you can buy, including tax, tags, title, and all other charges. By using this figure while shopping, you won't have to be concerned with the effect of your trade, since its value is included in your Available Cash.

2. Go to two different car stores and look for specific cars that interest you. Find at least two cars at each store, and ask your salesman for a demonstration ride. Don't discuss price. Don't be "if-ed" to death; simply find two cars you like and drive them. When you've finished your demonstration ride, copy down all the information from the price sticker on the window. Remember, don't pay any attention to the dealer's sticker. Take down the name and price of everything, including freight, and ask your salesman to give you the stock number of the car. Write that down by the name of the dealership and your salesman. Ask him to give you the amount of any miscellaneous charges, such as title fees. Ask him how tax is computed. For instance, is tax paid on the total price of the new car or on the difference figure? Don't be talked into anything during this visit; simply thank your man and leave. Once you have visited two stores, go home and relax for a while.

3. At home, write down the price information and stock number of each car on separate sheets of paper and compute the cost

of each car and their options. We'll assume one car lists for $17,500 and costs $14,100. When you have figured the cost, total the following:

Cost of the car and options	$14,100
Transportation charge	375
Title fees and miscellaneous charges	50
TOTAL COST	$14,525

The maximum profit you will pay (in our example, we'll assume $500—you make the real decision)	500
YOUR MAXIMUM OFFER WILL BE	$15,025

4. Now, check to see if you are over or under budget. Don't forget that tax will need to be added later. But for now, simply check your Available Cash against your offer:

Your Available Cash	$15,000
Your offer	15,025
AMOUNT OVER OR UNDER BUDGET	$25 *over*

After taxes, you're going to be hundreds over budget. Can you afford that? Since you are the flush type, we'll assume you don't worry about things like taxes and will happily pay it.

5. Now compute your *difference* figure. Remember, the difference will be your method of checking their figures.

Your offer on the new car	$15,025
Wholesale value of your car	−7,000
DIFFERENCE	$8,025

Use these five steps for each one of the cars you have driven. And then put the following information in your pad. You will need it at the store.

A. Write down the location, stock number, and color of each car. By that, write down your offer on the car and your trading difference figure.

B. Write down the wholesale value of your car. You'll only need to write this once, since the wholesale value won't change.

C. Write down your Available Cash figure once, too.

DEALING WITH THE STORE

You don't have any reason to be nervous now, for you have more information at your fingertips than your salesman. Go back to the store and see him. Make an appointment if you like. Let him show you the two cars again, and if both cars are in your price range, make an emotional decision on which car you really like the best. Enjoy! This is the only time your heart rate should affect your negotiations. Once you have decided on *the* particular car, head to the salesman's office. Be nice. Smile and laugh. But remember that *you* must control the order of the next few minutes. Do it like this:

1. Tell the salesman to have your car appraised. Don't tell him your wholesale figure, either, but review that figure in your mind. When the guy returns, speak before spoken to. Look him in the eye, and think positive thoughts.

2. Ask your salesman for the appraisal on your car. Let him know you want their wholesale offer, *not* an allowance figure. If the figure is lower than your wholesale value, tell him. But don't tell him the amount; give him room to come up as much as he will. If the figure is higher than yours, smile. You are ahead of the game. If his offer never equals yours, tell him your figure. If necessary, remind your salesman that his used-car boys can sell your car to the same people you would sell it to. If he still won't accept your figure, go to your other dealership. If he finally agrees to your figure or offers you more, write his offer on your pad.

3. Make your offer on the new car. The figure is on your pad. Don't be afraid for him to see your pad, either. Salesmen are invariably thrown off guard by customers who actually know what they are doing. If you are smart, offer him *less* than your actual figure; give him room to dicker a little. But don't go over your maximum figure. Once the two of you have agreed

on a figure, write it down in your pad. Put it by your original offer for that particular car.

4. Stop and check your difference figure. Deduct *his* offer on your trade from the agreed price of the new car. If this difference figure is more than your difference figure, you are losing money. If the figure is lower than your figure, you are making money. If the figure is an acceptable one to you, go to the next step. If it is not acceptable, continue to negotiate or go to your other dealership.

5. Tell him to write it up. Once the salesman has completely filled in the buyer's order, look at the difference figure on the order. If you don't see it, ask the salesman to point it out to you. That figure must agree with the one you have just computed.

    Most buyer's orders are not designed to show cash offers on a new car and wholesale figures on trades. Your salesman will probably indicate, for instance, that you are buying the new car at sticker price but receiving more than wholesale on your trade. That's okay *if* the difference figure is the same.

6. If the difference figure is the same, sign the buyer's order, but do not give him a deposit. Tell him you will give him a check *when* the deal is approved by a manager. The salesman will probably insist on a deposit. Tell him it's your way or not at all. Remember: A deposit before you have an approved deal is their way of keeping you there while they work you.

7. If the salesman returns with a signed order, give him a deposit. If he returns with his boss or insists himself your offer is too low, tell him again you will not be raised. If he keeps insisting, raise your offer $50, if you wish. But don't be raised more than once. If you are determined not to be raised at all, say good-bye. Head to your other dealership.

8. Expect the dealership to try to convert you to their financing, but resist.

If You Are Paying Cash and Buying a New Car without Trading

You're going to have a very easy time of it.

1. Decide just how much money you plan to spend on a car. Let's say you would like to spend $16,000. That figure, obviously, is your Available Cash.

2. Go to two different car stores and look for specific cars that interest you. Find at least two cars at each store, and ask your salesman for a demonstration ride. Don't discuss price. Don't be "if-ed" to death; simply find two cars you like and drive them. When you've finished your demonstration ride, copy down the items and prices of everything on the window sticker. Remember, don't pay attention to the dealer's sticker. Ask your salesman to give you the stock number of the car. Write that down by the name of the dealership and your salesman. Ask the salesman to give you any miscellaneous charges, such as title fees. Also ask him how tax is computed. Is it figured on the *list* price of the new car or the discounted price? Don't be talked into anything during this visit; simply thank your man and leave. Go home and relax for a while.

3. Once you are home, write down the price information and stock number from each car on a clean sheet of paper. Compute the cost of the cars and all their options. We'll assume you've found a car that lists for $18,000 and have figured a true cost for the car and options of $15,500 dollars. When you've done this, add the following:

Cost of the car and options	$15,500
Transportation charge	275
Title fees and other miscellaneous charges	55
TOTAL COST	$15,830

The maximum profit you will pay (in our example, we assume $350—you decide the real profit)	350
YOUR MAXIMUM OFFER WILL BE	$16,180

4. Now, check to see if you are over or under budget.

Your Available Cash is	$16,000
Your offer on the new car is	$16,180
AMOUNT OVER OR UNDER BUDGET	$180 *over*

You are over budget. *Plus,* you've still got to pay tax and other fees. If your state charges 4 percent sales tax on the total selling price, you will owe tax of $647. You are over budget a total of $827. Can you afford that?

Let's assume that you don't want to spend that much. Remember that this car listed for $18,000. You'll need to find a car that lists for about $800 less, if you plan to stay in budget. Let's say that you have found a car listing for $17,250 instead. You have computed the cost to be $14,850. If you use step three to refigure your offer and step four to check your budget, you'll find you are now $470 under budget. Nice! You are under budget almost enough to pay your taxes. Put $15,530, the new maximum offer, on your pad.

DEALING WITH THE STORE

You really don't have any reason to be nervous, now. You know more than your salesman. So, call up the store that's home to your favorite cars and make an appointment to see your salesman. Go see him.

1. Look at your favorite car again. If you would like, don't feel shy about asking to drive it. Decide if it's the car you really want to own.

2. Tell your salesman you would like to go to his office and talk price. Don't wait for him to drag you to his office; take the initiative. Remember, you must be in control.

3. Pull out your pad once you are in his office. He won't like your pad, but that's okay. The more uncomfortable he is, the more in control you are. Tell your salesman that you are prepared to make him an offer on the car. Tell him it is a *firm* offer. Tell him your offer leaves no money on the table. Use that phrase, too.

4. Make your offer and insist that he take it to his manager. Let him write it up, but *don't* give him a deposit. Even if he insists, don't do it. Tell him there are other dealerships down the road that don't require a deposit until both parties have agreed on a figure.

5. Before signing, compare the total sales price to your Available Cash. For instance, if your Available Cash were $16,000 and your final offer on this car were $15,300, the comparison would look like this:

Your Available Cash	$16,000
Your final offer	−15,300
Sales tax (assuming 4 percent)	−612
Other miscellaneous charges	−50
AMOUNT OVER OR UNDER BUDGET	$38 *under*

You are in good shape. Let the man take the buyer's order to his boss.

6. If the salesman returns with a signed buyer's order, give him a deposit. If he returns with his boss or insists himself your offer is too low, insist on your offer. If your salesman will actually let you leave on your figure, consider budging a little. But don't budge much. If you make a counteroffer, make only *one*. Tell the salesman it is your final offer. Do not let them "work" you. If your final offer is accepted, and you're within budget, pat yourself on the back. You have survived.

7. Expect pressure to finance at the dealership, but resist it.

If You Are Paying Cash, Buying a Used Car, and Trading the Old

Before reading any further, tell me the truth: Did you really work through the chapter on used cars, or did you just read the headings? If you cheated, go back and read the chapter carefully—you're a candidate for the slaughterhouse. If you did it right the first time, read on.

Remember that there is no set value on any used car, no accurate book to tell you what a particular car is worth. Remember, also, that you must be prepared to dicker quite a lot. Remember, finally, that "asking price" always includes a very healthy profit: for dickering purposes, always assume a nice used car has a mark-up of $600 to $1000 *regardless* of its wholesale value or asking price.

Now let's walk through a typical transaction. We will assume you've shopped your car and found that it's worth $1500 wholesale. You have decided to spend $3100 cash.

1. Compute your Available Cash (your cash plus the value of your trade). For shopping purposes, your Available Cash is the important figure. It tells you the maximum amount of car you can buy, including tax, tag, title, and all other charges. By using this figure while shopping, you won't have to be concerned with the effect of your trade, since its real value is included in the figure. In our example, your Available Cash is $4600.

2. Decide on three or four sources, using the guides in the chapter on buying a used car. Include at least one new-car dealership.

3. Visit the lots and look for cars with *asking* prices a few hundred dollars higher than your Available Cash figure. Do *not* tell the salesman you are trading. Used-car operations raise the prices of their cars if they feel you are going to trade. Do not tell them your Available Cash figure. As you find cars with asking prices close to your figure, take time to drive them. Take with you the checklist from the Appendix, and look for obvious problems with the car. If you still like the car after a test drive, write down the stock number and a description of the car. Write down the asking price, the name of the person you are dealing with, the miles on the car, and any options that may add to loan value, such as a vinyl roof, air-conditioning, power windows, or cruise control. Then thank your salesman and go home.

4. Call a local bank or credit union, and ask for a loan officer. Tell the officer the year and model of the car. Accurately de-

scribe the car to him. Give him the options and mileage, and then ask for the loan value of that particular car. Put the figure on your pad.

5. Compare the seller's asking price to the loan price of the car. We'll assume you've found a car with an asking price of $4800 and a loan value of $3800. The spread is their *probable profit* —in this instance, $1000.

6. Compute your "best probable" difference figure. Subtract the wholesale value of your car from the loan value of the seller's car.

The loan value of the seller's car	$3800
The wholesale value of your car	−1500
EQUALS YOUR BEST PROBABLE DIFFERENCE	$2300

When we begin to negotiate, we will be trying to be close to this difference figure or below it. Put the figure on your pad; it's your most important figure.

7. Go back to the lot, and tell your salesman you have decided to trade your car. Though it may not do any good, tell him you want the actual wholesale value of your car, *not* an allowance figure. He'll probably be surprised you know the difference. And then tell him you would like to take his car to your mechanic. Leave your car with him for ransom. If your salesman won't agree to this, don't buy the car. If he agrees, take a clean copy of the Mechanic's Checklist in the Appendix and drive to your mechanic's shop. Don't forget to add to the checklist any specific problems you have noted on your pad. Before leaving the shop, ask for an estimate to repair the car to your satisfaction. Put that figure on your pad, and take a coffee break.

8. Your Available Cash is $4600. But you may now have a repair bill, if you buy the car. Let's assume the repairs were estimated to cost $300. To stay in budget, you will need to *subtract* the estimate from your Available Cash ($4600 minus $300). Your new Available Cash figure is $4300. Make that adjustment and head back to the lot.

9. Don't let the salesman do the figuring when you return, but ask him directly how much he is giving you for your car. Subtract that from his "asking price," and determine his difference figure. We'll assume he actually appraised your car for $1500.

$$
\begin{array}{ll}
\text{Asking price} & \$4800 \\
\text{His figure on your car} & \underline{-1500} \\
\text{HIS DIFFERENCE FIGURE} & \$3300
\end{array}
$$

10. Now, compare his figure to your "best probable" difference figure. The balance will be how much more money he wants for the car than you are planning to spend. That figure is also his profit, most likely.

$$
\begin{array}{ll}
\text{His difference figure} & \$3300 \\
\text{Your "best probable" difference figure} & \underline{-2300} \\
\text{HIS PROBABLE PROFIT} & \$1000
\end{array}
$$

11. If by some act of God his difference figure is the same as yours, don't automatically agree to buy the car. Every salesman's first offer, regardless of how low it is, has a cushion in it. Offer the man $200 or $300 less. You should be smiling on the inside, too.

    If his figure is close to your figure, only $200 or $300 above, tell him that the figure is $400 or $600 away. Always compromise, split the difference on any offer.

12. At some point in the discussion, your salesman is not going to budge. When he reaches that point, check these things:

    A. His probable profit. Subtract your difference figure from his. We'll assume he agreed to $2850.

$$
\begin{array}{ll}
\text{His final difference figure} & \$2850 \\
\text{Your "best probable" difference} & \underline{-2300} \\
\text{HIS PROBABLE PROFIT} & \$550
\end{array}
$$

For a nice used car, that's a very reasonable profit.

B. Can you afford it? Add these items together and determine how much you will owe the seller.

His final difference figure	$2850
Tax (we'll assume 4 percent; use your own state's rate)	114
Miscellaneous charges	50
YOU WILL OWE THE SELLER	$3014

C. What will your total expenditure be? Subtract what you owe the seller and the repair estimate from your Available Cash:

Your Available Cash	$4300
What you owe the seller	−3014
The repair estimate	−300
AMOUNT OVER OR UNDER BUDGET	$986
	under

If you can bargain that well, you should go into the car business.

13. If you've determined this is the actual car you want to buy, discuss warranties. Be sure you are familiar with the section on warranties before opening your mouth, or you'll probably find your foot resting on your molars.

14. If the salesman's final offer fits your budget and the warranty is satisfactory, have him write it up. Tell him you'll take the car at that figure. Once the salesman has completely filled out the buyer's order, look at the difference figure. If you don't see it, ask the salesman to point it out to you. That figure must agree with your final difference figure. Make sure the warranty is written. If the figure is the same, sign the buyer's order, but do not give him a deposit. Tell him you will give him a check when the deal is approved by a manager. The salesman will probably insist on a deposit. Tell him it's your way or no way at all. Remember, a deposit before you have an approved deal is their way of keeping you there while they work you. If the salesman returns with his boss or insists himself your offer is

too low, tell him you will not be raised. If he insists, and if you really like the car, raise your offer $50, if you wish. Don't be raised more than once.

15. Expect the dealership to try to convert you to their financing, but resist it.

If You Are Paying Cash and Buying a Used Car without Trading

Before reading any further, tell me the truth: Did you really work through the chapter on used cars, or did you just read the headings? If you cheated, go back and read the chapter carefully. You're a candidate for the slaughterhouse. If you did it right the first time, read on.

1. Determine how much you plan to spend. Let's say, for example, $3700.

2. Decide on three or four car sources, using the guides in the chapter on buying a used car. Include at least one new-car dealership.

3. Visit those lots. Look for cars with asking prices $400 or $500 above your cash figure. Don't tell the salesman your price range. Virtually all used-car salesmen have a very bad habit of raising asking prices up to your figure. When the salesman asks you, "Well, what were you thinking of spending?" just tell him, "Well, it depends on the car," and smile.

   Let's assume you have found a car with an asking price of $4200. Take the car for a drive. Use the checklist in the Appendix and look for obvious problems with the car. If you still like it after your test drive, write down the stock number and description of the car, the mileage, and the name of the person you are dealing with. Write down any options which may add to loan value, such as automatic transmission, air-conditioning, vinyl roof, or power windows. And then thank your salesman, saying good-bye in the process.

4. Call a local bank or credit union and ask for a loan officer. Tell the officer the year and model of the car. Accurately describe the car to him. Give him the options and mileage, and then ask for the loan value of that particular car. Put that figure on your pad.

5. Compare the seller's asking price to the loan value of the car. We'll assume loan value was $3200. The spread is their probable profit.

Asking price	$4200
Loan value	−3200
PROBABLE PROFIT	$1000

You want to pay as little of that profit as possible. You want to buy the car for a figure as close to loan value as possible.

6. Determine your offer. Since you would ideally like to buy the car for loan value or less, decide the *maximum* amount you are willing to pay over loan value, and add the two figures. In our example, the maximum profit will be $300, loan value is $3200, and your maximum offer will be $3500. Remember that tax and other charges must be added to that figure.

7. Now head back to the lot and tell your salesman you would like to take his car to your mechanic. Leave whatever car you are driving as ransom. If your salesman won't agree to this, don't buy the car. If he agrees, take a clean copy of the Mechanic's Checklist, and drive to your mechanic's shop. Don't forget to add to this list any specific problems you have noted on your pad. Before leaving, ask your mechanic for an estimate to repair the car to your satisfaction. Put that figure on your pad and take a coffee break.

8. You have $3700 to spend. But you may now have a repair bill, if you buy the car. To stay in budget, you will need to *subtract* the estimate from your cash. Let's assume your repair bill was $300. You now have only $3400 to spend, if you plan to stay in budget. Make that adjustment and head back to the lot.

9. Lead the salesman to his office. Don't be led, take the initiative. Offer the man *less* than loan value. When the man counteroffers, don't accept his offer. Compromise; offer to split the difference with him.

10. At some point in the discussion, your salesman is not going to budge. When he reaches that point, compare his final offer to your cash. Let's assume his final offer is $3300.

Your cash	$3400
His final offer	−3300
AMOUNT OVER OR UNDER BUDGET	$100 *under*

You're in pretty good shape. Don't forget that tax will be added to that figure. Now, compare his final offer to the loan value of the car. The answer, in this instance, $100, is his probable profit. Is that figure satisfactory? It should be, Jesse James.

11. If you've determined this is the actual car you want to buy, discuss warranties. Be sure you are familiar with the section on warranties before opening your mouth, or you'll probably find your foot resting on your molars.

12. If the salesman's final offer fits your budget and the warranty is satisfactory, have him write it up. Tell him you'll take the car at that figure. Once the salesman has completely filled out the buyer's order, check the figures. Make sure the warranty is in writing. Sign the buyer's order, but do not give him a deposit. Tell him you will give him a check when the deal is approved by a manager. The salesman will probably insist on a deposit. Tell him it's your way or not at all. Remember, a deposit before you have an approved deal is their way of keeping you there while they work you.

If the salesman returns with his boss or insists himself your offer is too low, tell him you will not be raised. If he still insists, and if you really like the car, raise your offer $50 if you wish. But don't be raised more than once. If you are determined not to be raised, say good-bye.

13. Expect the dealership to try to convert you to their financing. Resist it.

WARRANTIES, NEW AND USED

New-Car Warranties

Three specific "free" warranties apply to just about every new car sold in America. One is the "adjustment warranty." Adjustment warranties are provided by the selling dealer, not the manufacturer, and supposedly cover items such as squeaks and rattles, air leaks, alignment, and other minor annoyances. Because the selling dealer provides this warranty and pays for the work himself, many dealers are loath to spend much time correcting those little problems that affect most new cars. Dealers also limit the time period for minor adjustments—usually no more than ninety days. If you are concerned with rattles, you will do well to talk with a dealership's service department before purchasing a car. Ask the service manager specifically if *all* problems with your new car will be fixed for free. Note the time limit on these repairs. Smart car buyers keep a small note pad in their new cars and list each problem the moment it develops. You would be wise to do the same and provide your service department with a written list of all minor adjustments.

All new cars in America also provide a basic manufacturer's warranty. Most of these warranties protect the major components of each car for a minimum of twelve months or twelve thousand miles up to 5 years or 100,000 miles. Should your car need repairs under the manufacturer's warranty plan, these repairs will be paid for by the manufacturer—and that's the rub. Most manufacturers pay a lower hourly service rate for warranty repairs than the service department charges individuals; consequently, the service department makes less money on this work. So, which cars normally are serviced first? The paying customers, of course. Warranty work is shuttled to the end of the line, and you are left sitting in "the customer's lounge"—a nice name for the best imitation of the Black Hole of Calcutta—reading a six-year-old copy of *Modern Bride*. You can do something to lessen this problem, but you will need to act *before* you sign anyone's buyer's order. Make it clear to your salesman and his manager, if necessary, that you plan to sit in *their* offices—unshaven and undeodorized—wasting the time of everyone in sight should you be detained in the service line.

There is one other "free" warranty no dealer will volunteer to discuss, the "secret warranties" provided by virtually all manufacturers. Both dealers and manufacturers even deny that such warranties exist, but they do. Called "policy adjustments" or "goodwill service," they apply to most cars sold here, including the best. Dealers and manufacturers like to keep these little free services from the general public to save money, as usual. But, should you have a major problem with your car after the normal factory warranty expires, be loud and visible in your complaints. If your selling dealer refuses to help you with a problem, write the manufacturer's customer service office. The address of these offices are located in the owner's manuals for cars produced after 1979.

A hot tip: The National Highway Traffic Safety Administration maintains a really useful 800 number if you want to know about recalls, want to report a problem, or even want to know about "secret" warranties. The menu on this service is always changing, but call if you're thinking *used cars:* 1-800-424-9393 (for the hearing impaired, TDD 1-800-424-9153). You can also check out NHTSA's information online at http://www.nhtsa.dot.gov.

WHAT ABOUT NEW-CAR SERVICE CONTRACTS?

Service contracts, or extended warranties, have replaced accident and health insurance as a dealership's favorite trinket to sell you in the finance office. They have replaced credit insurance because they can be sold to cash and finance customers alike, and because they are so much more profitable—at their current very funny prices and markups—than insurance. For instance, an average dealership might sell you insurance that costs $2000 over the course of your loan. Dealerships *only* make about 55 percent on insurance, $1100 in our example.

Service contracts sell for up to $1800. But guess what the claims over the course of an average contract actually cost the dealer? *Sixty dollars.* Let's see: that's a profit of *$1740,* per contract.

The profit for the dealer is so great because claims are very small because coverage is really very limited. For instance, read the average policy carefully and you'll find a version of this language: "Though we say this is a five-year contract, this policy doesn't go into effect until your car's regular warranty expires in three years." Which means you're really paying a fortune for a two-year warranty, not a five-year.

Dealers get rich on these agreements for another reason they don't tell you: Rather than sell you a national service agreement such as GMAC, they usually sell you a questionable agreement from no-name companies located in states with few consumer protection laws. Why? The dealers own the companies.

The message: Service contracts are a waste of time for most people. But if you buy one, insist on a contract from a national brand, and negotiate that price down to under $350. Don't waste your money if you can't win on both counts.

The Biggest Joke: Used-Car Warranties

If you are buying a used car, the negotiation of a proper warranty is something you'll need to do before you sign anything. But negotiate for the warranty *after* you have agreed on a price. Many people insist on something approaching real protection before agreeing on price and are unknowingly stuck with a "service pack." For instance, if you should insist on a full ninety-day warranty, your seller will be happy to provide that. But you will pay a higher price for the car. The seller will give you a $4000 car for $4400 and bank the extra $400 as "insurance" against future repairs. Since the seller has neglected to tell you he's raised the price, he is covered on both ends: If the car needs repairs, you have paid for them in advance; and if the car doesn't need repairs, he has an extra $400 in profit. You want to buy that car for $4000 *and* receive the best warranty.

USED CAR WARRANTIES, FROM BEST TO WORST

After agreeing on price, begin your battle by asking for the best of the following warranties first; negotiate downward only after long and intense discussions.

1. One hundred percent warranty on all mechanical parts. This warranty won't cover your radio, squeaks and rattles, or leaks, but it will cover just about everything else. Try for a ninety-day, one hundred percent warranty. Be happy if you get a thirty-day or sixty-day warranty. If your used car has major problems, they'll usually show up within thirty days. This is a hard warranty to get any seller to agree to, but try for it. The mere fact you are just asking for the best warranty means the seller will be less likely to offer you some of the really rotten "warranties."

2. One hundred percent drive-train warranty. The drive train encompasses your engine, transmission, and rear axle. It does not include your braking system or air conditioner. Drive-train warranties are fairly common in the business, but most sellers will try to give you a fifty-fifty drive-train warranty. Say no; it's a lesser option. Aim for a one hundred percent drive-train warranty as your minimum coverage. Again, try for ninety days, but accept thirty or sixty.

3. Fifty-fifty warranties. If sellers were honest, fifty-fifty warranties would be acceptable under most circumstances. But many dealers will agree to provide this coverage, then simply raise the price of the repair one hundred percent. You, friend, are left paying the full bill. Another version of the fifty-fifty warranty is the "parts and labor" split: You agree to pay for the labor, and the seller agrees to pay for the parts. Unfortunately, the price for labor is conveniently raised far above its normal cost, in most instances. And since labor is the largest portion of most repair bills, you are doubly stuck—nice. Sellers can do this because they require you to have service work done in their shops or in places of their choosing.

   If a fifty-fifty warranty is your only choice, consider doing this before actually taking your car to the seller's shop for repair: Take the car to some other shop and ask them for a written estimate for the same work that needs to be done. Then take your car to the seller's shop and ask for an estimate before the work is done. If there is a substantial difference in the two estimates, you are being taken again. If you don't really cotton to confrontations with the service manager, show him your other estimate up front. You might make the guy a little more honest. On any fifty-fifty warranties, insist on coverage for at least ninety days.

4. Repairs "at cost." This type of warranty is worthless, because who defines cost? How can you check the definition of "cost"? Don't accept this favor.

5. "As is." Unless you are deliberately buying a piece of junk, don't buy any car "as is." Most dealers will actually attempt to make you sign a statement acknowledging your stupidity when you agree to "as is" purchases. Your signature waives virtually every single right of recourse, even if the car blows up *before* you drive it off the lot.

   Regardless of the type of warranty you finally negotiate, insist that the full conditions of the warranty be placed in writing, either on the buyer's order or on a separate sheet of paper **signed by the manager, not by the salesman.** Salesmen can promise you anything, even sign their personal guarantee in blood, but they cannot obligate the seller to honor their promises.

IMPLIED WARRANTIES

For both new and used cars, many courts are beginning to enforce the principle of "implied" warranties. New cars are more strongly protected by the principle, but you should consider *any* car to be covered by implied warranty. This principle states that any car you buy can be safely purchased on the assumption that it is roadworthy and will perform for a reasonable amount of time without undue expense or trouble on your part. Some states have developed specific implied warranty definitions, but most are developing guidelines slowly. Should you purchase a car that honestly fails to give reasonable service, first have a talk with your seller. Mention the implied warranty concept. If the seller is uncooperative, tell him you are filing a written complaint with one or all of the organizations or officials listed in the Appendix. Normally, a seller will help you with your problem rather than enter into sticky ethical battles with the various agencies responsible for consumer protection.

USED-CAR SERVICE AGREEMENTS

These will normally cost you more than service agreements on new cars, and they invariably cover less. But if your mechanic has indicated that major problems could develop down the road with your purchase, consider buying a service agreement. If you purchase one of these insurance policies, still insist that the seller provide his own warranty for the longest period of time possible. In all likelihood, the seller will tell you this is a duplication of warranty and will not be inclined to provide his own protection. Don't accept that answer. If the seller's warranty does duplicate your service agreement, he will be protected. But if problems should develop that are not covered by the service agreement, you may still be protected. *Price:* Don't pay more than $250 for a used car service contract.

Whether given by the seller or paid for by you, warranties are no better than determination to receive a fair shake during each visit to the service department. Be a nice person, be an honest person, but especially be an insistent person when it comes to your rights.

A NOTE ON DEPOSITS

Regardless of the car you plan to purchase, don't give the dealer a big deposit. Car people are like the rest of us; they need incentive. Let's assume you signed up last night for the perfect car and gave the man a check for the total purchase price. You return to the dealership the next day to pick up your car and notice a funny noise in the air conditioner and a small scratch on the hood. The salesman says they will, of course, take care of both, but the body shop is busy for two weeks, and the mechanics are busy right now. Can you bring the car back at six in the morning sometime next month?

What can you do? You've paid for the car. Don't think you can stop payment on the check, either. They've probably "hammered" it, taken it to the bank for certification. If you had paid a $100 deposit instead, your car would be in the plant before the eye can blink, and mechanics would be swarming over the air conditioner. To car people, a car isn't sold until all the money is paid. Keep your deposit low, and turn over the rest of your hard-earned dough or sign that contract when you are satisfied the car is right.

SIGNING THINGS

Most dealerships are very smart when it comes to the moment of signing. They seem to invariably pick the very second your heart is beating wildly, your lips are smacking in anticipation, and your common sense is visiting in a neighboring state; *then,* and only then, will your salesman or finance manager stealthily slide the large mound of papers under your quivering hand and say, "Sign here, and here, and here." Most of us could be signing away our inheritance or rights to conjugal visits and never know the difference.

Dealerships call this rapidfire signing of dozens of documents "fanning." And though the routine may vary a bit, the first two documents you will be asked to sign are usually the most disquieting. The first sheet normally states "I have read all of the documents put before me very carefully before I signed them." Don't you think that's an interesting document to put in front of you *before* you sign anything?

The next document says, in effect, "I agree that the dealership may have made mistakes on these papers. I also agree that, even though the dealership has told me I am financed, they could be telling a little white lie. So I agree that none of this paperwork means anything if the dealership wants to change its mind. I'll be glad to pay more."

If you have survived to the signing stage, if you've really followed the steps carefully, don't blow it now. Sober up quickly and consider each of these points carefully. Most dealerships won't alter things you sign—but many will put things in front of you that shouldn't be signed and put in figures without telling you.

1. The buyer's order. Your buyer's order shouldn't be a scratched-up piece of paper, it should be a clean, neat sheet of paper

with every important piece of information filled in. It's important: Many customers have been taken because the major record of their sale was too scratched over and through to stand up in court. Remember, this is a *contract*. If you are not financing at the dealership, it is the only contract. If you are financing at the dealership it is a conditional sales contract that will be replaced by the financing contract—but it is still the only record containing important information about warranties and a few other tidbits.

Make sure your buyer's order contains the following information. Take this list with you to the dealership, if necessary.

a. The date

b. Year of cars (yours, too, if you're trading)

c. Make and model of cars

d. Serial number of cars

e. Asking price

f. Trade allowance (if you're trading)

g. "Difference" figure (if you're trading)

h. Amount of your payoff

i. Taxes

j. Amount to be financed

k. Other fees

l. Complete warranty statement (if a used car, if no other warranty statement is provided)

m. Number and amount of payments (if you are financing at the dealer)

n. APR (if you are financing)

If the buyer's order is completely filled out, *check it.* Do the figures match those on your pad? Are the financing figures as you have agreed? Are the years and makes of cars right? Are the serial numbers right? The serial number on the car you are purchasing is important. Remember Killer's little trick. Then, and only then, sign the buyer's order. Be sure you have an *exact copy,* and *keep that copy* with your other car papers. You'll need it soon to check the financing contract, if you finance, and you may need it later if you have problems.

2. Mileage statements. You will be asked to sign a mileage statement for your trade-in. The statement should be completely
filled out, *including* the mileage. Many salesmen will leave the
mileage blank and happily inform you the figure will be filled
out later. Baloney. You go to the car and write down the figure.
Your mileage statement makes *you* liable for the actual mileage
on your trade. If you let the salesman leave this figure blank,
a sneaky salesman or store could run the miles on your car
back, enter the false figure, and sell the car. If the new buyer
should discover this, *you* can be sued, not the dealer—because you signed it blank, dummy.

The seller will also provide you a mileage statement on his
car. If you are buying a new car, the mileage should obviously
be low. It should also match the figure on the odometer. Again,
insist that the statement be filled out completely. If you are
buying a used car, the seller is obligated to give you a copy
of a statement signed by the previous owner. If there is no
mileage statement from the previous owner, *don't* buy the car.
Insist that copies of both mileage statements be given to you.

3. Powers of attorney. You will be required to sign "limited powers of attorney." Normally, you will be asked to sign two of
these, one for the car you are purchasing and one for the car
you are trading. These powers of attorney simply give the
seller the legal authority to change titles. If you have already
signed the buyer's order, it's okay to sign the powers of attorney form—many dealerships must type these up to satisfy
state law—but at least ask that they be filled out before you
sign, especially if the people you are dealing with make you
feel a little "greasy."

4. Finance contracts. All finance contracts, especially those used
by dealers, will remind you of *War and Peace*. The back of
every single page is just loaded with all types of unusual protection for the financing institution. For instance, most contracts say your car can be repossessed even if you pay your
payments on time—the institution simply needs to feel that
their loan is in jeopardy. Most of these contracts also state
that your car cannot be driven or "domiciled" out of your
state without the permission of the financing institution.
Friendly people you are dealing with, right? They really trust

you. Unfortunately, you can't do much about all this fine print, but you do need to check several things on the front of the contract. *Take your buyer's order with you* when you go for the actual signing, and check the following things:

a. Is the serial number the same as the car on the buyer's order?

b. Is the "amount financed" the same?

c. Look at the "finance charge" section. This section contains the total amount of interest, the charges for insurance, if you wanted it, and other charges such as state documentary fees. If there are any charges here you don't understand, ask what they are.

d. Look at the APR. Is it the same rate you agreed to?

e. Look at the amount and number of payments. Do they agree with your buyer's order? Be sure this section does not contain a "pickup payment." Some dealers will attempt to make a little extra money by adding an extra payment due within a week or two. For instance, if you have agreed to pay thirty-six payments of $100, their contract will read "thirty-six payments of $100 and one payment of $80." Unless you have agreed to a pickup payment, stop doing business with these people—they are trying to cheat you. Get your money, tear up all the paperwork, and run to your Better Business Bureau.

f. *Important:* Make sure the dealership hasn't automatically added charges for such things as warranties or "protection packages."

5. **Warranty agreements.** If you are purchasing a service agreement on a new or used car, you will probably be required to sign the agreement. Most of these agreements are *not* transferable to the next owner of your car. Before signing, review again the coverage that is supposedly being provided.

   If you are buying a used car, many dealers will provide you a separate piece of paper detailing their particular warranty for that car. Many times, this paper will not detail any specific agreements you may have made with the seller. For instance, your salesman may have told you air-conditioning is covered under the warranty. But your sheet of paper may simply state, "One hundred percent drive-train warranty for ninety days." Air conditioners are not covered on drive-train warranties. Make sure the seller writes down specifically such exceptions. Make sure the warranty is signed, too, by the manager, *not* by the salesman.

10

Lomax

It began as the sweetest of dreams. Killer had fallen in the bed, rolled on his back, and sighed, his fall rocking the bed like some giant jelly bean making hard contact with a bowl of Jell-O.

"Honey, are you okay?" Killer's better two-thirds asked.

"Lilly, I feel fine, just fine. Guess what's happened?"

"What?"

"J. C. and Davies have bought the Chevy store in Lomax. And honey . . . ?"

"Yes?"

"I'm going to be the new sales manager there, or at least I'm going to ask to be. What do you think of that!"

"Bob, why do we want to move to a small town? And can't we talk about this tomorrow?"

"Lilly, I'm tired of the rat race. And I hear the people in small towns are really nice." Killer's definition of nice is "easily taken," but Lilly didn't know that. She is much like some Mafia don's wife who thinks her husband sells olive oil for a living. At the moment, however, she was a sleepy don's wife.

"That's fine, honey, whatever you say. Oh, does the Dead End have a branch there?"

"Lilly, that isn't fair! You know I work there. Now good night, princess."

Lomax. Robert DeMarco, Sales Manager. His dream took him quickly to the big office overlooking the showroom. Killer was holding his first sales meeting with the six young men hired to become the mirror of the master. "Now, men, we're going to work *my* system here, like I said. It's all so simple. We use niceness and logic, and we win every time. I'm even going to show you how to do it with the first

308

customer who comes in this morning. When I finally get that customer in my office, all of you head in the next room. I'll leave my intercom on, so you can hear." Killer dismissed the men and walked on the lot, a satisfied smile marking his career as a manager.

Within minutes an older Chevy pulled up. The driver was a woman in her mid-thirties—blond, slender, breathtaking, and friendly. Oh, God, what a way to start a career, Killer thought.

"Hello, ma'am, I'm Robert DeMarco, the sales manager. How can I help you today?" Killer said "sales manager" as if the title meant "I'm the greatest thing since canned heat." The lady was obviously impressed.

"Well, isn't this nice," she said. "I was so nervous coming here—it's the first time I've bought a car by myself—and who should help me but the manager himself. I hope it won't bother you that I'm a rookie buyer."

"Oh no, ma'am, that won't bother me at all," Killer replied quickly—an understatement, to say the least. "I'm sorry, ma'am, but I missed your name."

"Oh, Mr. DeMarco, *do* forgive me. My name is Jo Wright."

At that point in the dream, Killer should have awakened. But he didn't, and some creature hidden away in his brain quickly pushed the "bad dream" button. But not before Killer's last remark. "Well, Jo, I hope it's okay if I call you Jo—well, I'll tell you what. You are our first customer at the *new* Lomax Chevrolet. And I *personally* want you to know that you have been treated fairly. If we don't I'll *give* you the car!"

She quickly found the perfect car and just as quickly drove it. Killer appraised her old Chevy and walked casually to his office with the beautiful lady at his side. He noticed that the door to the adjoining room was closed and thought, Good, the guys are in there.

Jo sat quietly across from him, right leg resting comfortably on left, watching as he began to fill out a buyer's order.

"Well, Mr. DeMarco, what do we do now?" Jo volunteered cheerily.

Killer wrote "$1500" on the "trade" line of the order and pushed it around to face her. He was smiling. The car had been appraised at $2200. "Jo, as you can see, I'm going to give you a really enormous allowance on your car." He smiled again. But Jo wasn't returning the gesture.

"Allowance! Mr. DeMarco, I'm not interested in allowance! I want to know what my trade is worth in wholesale dollars, and it's certainly worth more than $1500. As a matter of fact, it's worth $2200, isn't it?

What are you going to do next? Try to fool me with the cost figure of your car?"

Killer was stunned. He looked back at the buyer's order, Jo's last name jumping from the page like a dagger to the heart. He stuttered, "You . . . you . . . are you by any chance . . . ?" He looked up and saw a couple standing by her. They looked too familiar. Jim and Gloria Wright.

Lilly DeMarco opened her eyes and listened. Killer, still sleeping, was emitting the moan of some wounded animal. Beads of sweat were popping on his forehead. "Bob? Bob!" Lilly reached over and shook him gently. But the dream was not to end that quickly.

"Mr. DeMarco," Jo said, "do you remember these people, my aunt and uncle?" She was smiling now. But the eyes that had appeared so beautiful moments ago were red and glaring, the teeth sharply pointed. "Do you remember these people, MR. MONSOON!"

Killer's office quickly filled with perhaps twenty customers, the only buyers during Killer's entire career who had really defeated him in car transactions. Each carried a placard emblazoned, "K.O. Killer" or "Kill Him! Kill Him!" All were chanting, "Killer! Killer! Killer!"

Jim Wright leaned across the desk, pounding his fist just under Killer's running nose and drippy eyes, and yelling, "We know your name, Killer Monsoon! We know your game! And we've all moved to Lomax!"

Killer's moans sounded like the dying rumbles of the army of evil, and Lilly began to shake him violently, a shake that coincided with the joggling Jo was administering at that moment.

"A free car! A free car!" Jo yelled, grabbing the keys for the new Chevrolet and running from the office. Killer tried to run too, but he was blocked by the twenty maddened buyers, and then his own salesmen, who were yelling, "Rotten! Rotten! Rotten!"

"Stop!" Killer bounced awake in the bed, sweat pouring from his body as from a broken pipe. He rubbed his neck.

"Honey, are you okay?" Lilly asked.

Killer looked around the room, slipped his feet to the floor, and headed to the kitchen. "Yeah, yeah, I'm okay," he said over his shoulder. "Lilly, forget what I said about Lomax, okay? I don't think small towns are for me."

Scraps of the nightmare roiling in his head, Killer paused with his hand on the refrigerator door, staring at its blank white front. Surely *that* hadn't been scrawled on the back window of the fleeing Chevy. Surely not. Not TAKEN AT LAST.

Appendix

Checking Out a Used Car or Used Truck

Objectivity and honesty aren't qualities you'll find very often when you talk with used-car people about their wares. Used-car dealers will tell you their vehicles have "been checked out from top to bottom," place fancy stickers on many car windows proclaiming their top-notch condition, and then head for the hills the moment you drive back in with your first problem. Invariably, your problem just isn't one of the things their "service specialists" checked out. Tsk, tsk.

If you will adhere to the first checklist carefully yourself, and have your mechanic adhere to the second, you won't need these folks' help, and will discover just about every skeleton in any vehicle's closet. The first checklist will require some judgment calls and a good amount of objectivity on your part. Copy the items and take them with you as you shop. Take a flashlight, too.

THINGS TO CHECK OUT YOURSELF

1. The name of the previous owner. Insist on a name and number. If the seller resists, ask to see the title. If he still resists, don't buy. The previous owner's name and address should be on the title. Call the owner and ask specifically, "What were the major problems with the vehicle when you owned it?" Don't

ask the owner *if* he or she had problems, assume there were problems. You'll get a more direct answer. Note the problems, if any, and add them to your Mechanic's Checklist.

2. Check the exterior. Kneel down by each front fender and look down each side. Look for ripples in the metal or dull paint. Either could indicate that there's been body damage. If the ripples or bad paint cover an area larger than twelve inches, make a note for your mechanic to check the frame. Also look directly at the damaged area and check for the match of the paint. Are you satisfied with the paint job? When you call the owner, ask him, "How badly was the car wrecked?" Again, don't ask him *if* the vehicle was wrecked. If it had damage to the frame or engine compartment, you would do well to look for another vehicle. If you are still interested in the car, plan to drive it at least half a day.

3. Check the moldings around the bumpers, grill, wheel wells, and windows. Are any missing or damaged? Cosmetically, is the vehicle well-kept? Are there signs of small paint bubbles accumulating around the moldings? If you see these small rust bubbles, ask the seller to punch through them firmly with a screwdriver. If the screwdriver continues through the entire piece of metal, the body is rusting from the inside out, and will probably require major work. If the bubbles are only surface bubbles, repairs will be less costly. *Any* rust indicates the presence of salt. Be conscious of other rust as you check the vehicle.

4. Open and close all doors. Do they open and close properly? If a door needs to be forced to close, the door may have been hit in an accident. Look carefully at all metal on the bottom and inside of the doors. Are paint bubbles present, or are other signs of rust evident? Many doors begin to rust through along the bottom first. If rust is present there, ask the seller to use his screwdriver again. Normally doors with rusted-through bottom edges will continue to rust even after repairs. If you buy such a vehicle, you may eventually need to replace the doors. Look at all rubber moldings on the doors and adjacent surfaces. Are they brittle or cracked? Rubber moldings are expensive to replace. Make a note.

5. If it's a car, open the trunk. Look carefully at all inside edges. Is there rust present? If so, check it with the screwdriver. Look at the interior walls of the trunk. Are there stains present? Stains are an indication of leaks. If possible, lift up the trunk mat and check for rust. Check the spare tire. Does it match the other tires—i.e., is it a radial if the others are radials? Or, is it the proper small spare for that vehicle? Will the tire make a satisfactory spare? If the tire doesn't match or is barely serviceable, make a note and insist on a different spare. Make sure a jack is in the trunk.

6. Check the wheel wells and undercarriage. Turn the steering wheel completely to the right and look in the left well. Do the opposite for the right well. Are there signs of rust? Are there signs of fresh undercoating? Many sellers will simply spray over rust. Take a screwdriver or knife and scrape away a small portion of the undercoating. If rust is mixed in with the undercoating, don't buy the vehicle—you are probably dealing with a shyster. Check the rear wheel wells, too. Then look under the car with your flashlight. Check the muffler system with the engine running. Are fumes escaping at any point along the system? Are the holes larger than a pinpoint? If so, the system will probably need to be replaced rather than repaired. Has the underside been freshly undercoated? If so, forget the vehicle or plan to spend an hour or so scratching undercoating from the various surfaces. Used-car sellers have absolutely no incentive to undercoat their vehicles other than to hide things. Most rustproofing and undercoating companies won't guarantee or perform their work on used models because the product actually seals in rust; it does not stop it.

   If the vehicle is a front-wheel-drive model, look for welding seams along the frame or underbody. Welds can indicate a wrecked vehicle, or worse, *two* wrecked vehicles. Some less-than-reputable dealers are actually taking two wrecked cars and welding them together—and not telling the potential customer. Don't buy a vehicle with extensive welding seams *unless* it's checked out first by a body shop. If the seller has failed to inform you of welding work, do the rest of us a favor and report the incident to your local Better Business Bureau.

7. Check all glass and plastic. Is any broken or cracked? In many states, a cracked front windshield must be replaced. The seller should be responsible for the expense. Check the headlights, parking lights, and taillights. Are they cracked or broken? All broken light covers will need to be replaced.

8. Check the wiper blades. Are they cracked or pitted? They are cheap to replace, but make a note and determine who will replace them.

9. Check any vinyl roof for lumps. Under every lump is a mountain of rust. If the lumps are really numerous, don't buy the car unless the seller will pull the roof and repair the rust. Rust under vinyl roofs can be serious and can actually rust through the roof of the vehicle quickly. Check for tears in the roof. Do they appear large enough to allow water to enter? If so, they must be repaired. Note this and determine with the seller who will bear the expense.

10. Check brake lights, turn signal, hazard lights, parking lights, interior lights, and headlights. Have someone sit in the vehicle and use each one as you watch. Note problems. If any systems are not working properly, don't just assume that a bulb is burnt out. Have the bulb replaced then and check again. Bulbs are cheap to replace. Repairs to electrical systems are normally very expensive.

11. Check for ease of starting. Start the engine cold, and then start it several times after you test drive. Race the engine under both circumstances, and look for blue smoke shooting from the exhaust. Many sellers will tell you that smoke "simply means the carbon is burning off the rings." Don't believe them. Make a note for your mechanic to test to determine the cause.

12. Open the hood and check the following with the engine *off*:
    A. ALL BELTS AND HOSES. Look on the inside of the belts, not the outside. Are they cracked and dry? They will need to be replaced. Make a note.
    B. LOOK FOR CORROSION AND RUST ON THE RADIATOR. If there is any, the radiator probably leaks. Make a note for your mechanic to check it.

C. LOOK AT THE RADIATOR COOLANT. If the coolant is rusty, the cooling system has probably not been maintained. Make a note for your mechanic to determine if the radiator needs to be recored or replaced.

D. LOOK AT THE BATTERY. Are the terminals corroded? Are the wires wearing through? If so, the battery probably has not been maintained. Check the battery case. Is it cracked? If so, the battery will probably need to be replaced. Look at the battery levels. If even one of the cells is dry, the seller obviously doesn't service his vehicle—or the battery is definitely in need of replacement.

13. Leave the hood open and have someone start the engine. Have him push the accelerator down gently, slowly increasing pressure. Do you hear knocks? Knocking sounds can indicate valve problems. Make a note. Do you see any signs of leakage on the engine block or attached parts? Leakage can indicate bad seals. Do you hear any clicking or grinding? Both can indicate problems. Let the engine run at idle for at least five minutes, and then pull the vehicle forward. Are there pools of liquid? Many sellers will tell you, "Oh, that's only the air-conditioner condensation." Likely story. Rub your fingers in the pools. If they are red or brown or clear and slippery, you have problems with the transmission, engine seals, or block. While the engine is running, walk back to the exhaust. Is it pulsing? If so, you could have a bad valve. Check this by holding a dollar bill over the end of the exhaust pipe. If the bill is pulled to the pipe, you have *serious* valve problems. Rub your finger inside the pipe. Is there oil on your pinkie? If so, the engine is burning oil.

14. Check the interior:
    A. LOOK UNDER MATS AND CARPETS. Are there signs of rust or excess wear? You can live with the wear, but rust indicates both leakage and rust coming through from the underside, which is very expensive and at times impossible to repair.

    Again, look for welding seams on both sides of the floorboard. Seams can indicate a wrecked vehicle at best, two pieced together at the worst.

B. LOOK UNDER THE SEAT COVERS. Are they just soiled, or are the seats tearing apart?

C. LOOK ALONG THE WINDOWS AND AT THE HEADLINER. Are there signs of stain? Stains always indicate leakage.

D. LOOK FOR MISSING DOOR HANDLES OR CONTROL KNOBS. Are the missing parts important to the operation of the vehicle?

E. CHECK THE HORN, RADIO, WIPERS, AND OTHER ELECTRICAL GADGETS, SUCH AS POWER WINDOWS AND SEATS. Are any inoperative things important to the operation of the vehicle? If so, make a note.

F. START THE ENGINE, CHECK THE OPERATION OF THE AIR CONDITIONER, HEATER, AND DEFROSTER. CHECK ALL GAUGES. If any systems are inoperative, make a note for your mechanic.

G. CHECK THE BRAKES. Don't move the vehicle, but apply strong pressure to the pedal and hold it for at least thirty seconds. If the pedal continues toward the floor, you probably have leakage in your braking system.

H. CHECK THE CLUTCH (for standard transmission). Start the engine, set the parking brake, put the transmission in first gear, and let the clutch out as you slowly press on the gas pedal. The engine should stall when the clutch pedal is one-half to three-quarters of the way up. If it doesn't, you probably need clutch work. Make a note.

I. CHECK THE AUTOMATIC TRANSMISSION. With the engine idling, and your foot on the brake, slip the transmission from neutral to reverse. If you hear a loud "clunk," the transmission bands probably need tightening, at the minimum. Make a note. Slip the transmission from neutral to drive, and listen for the same sound.

J. LOOK AT THE SPEEDOMETER. Are the miles reasonable for the age of the vehicle, no more than fifteen thousand miles per year? If the miles are unreasonably low, ask the *owner* what the mileage was when he traded the car in. If the vehicle has a conventional odometer, see if the numbers line up evenly; if they don't, the mileage may have been altered. If the vehicle has an electronic speedometer, you will have to rely on the previous owner to confirm its true mileage.

15. The test drive. Tell the seller you will be happy to buy the gas, and you will be happy to have him go with you, but that you would like to drive the vehicle thirty to forty-five minutes. Plan to drive on crowded streets and on uncrowded ones; on bumpy roads and smooth; up and down hills, if there are any in your neck of the woods. Don't be satisfied with a drive around the block. Too many problems with used vehicles don't surface during quick test drives.

A. CHECK THE ENGINE PERFORMANCE. The vehicle should be responsive when cold and warm. There should be no grinding or humming sounds in the rear end or transmission. If there are, make a note for your mechanic.

B. CHECK THE BRAKES. The brakes should stop you without pulling, fading, or making unusual noises. Listen for a grinding sound when the brakes are applied. Grinding can indicate worn-out brake pads or worse. At an appropriate place on the highway, slow the car to five miles per hour, and apply the emergency brake. If the vehicle does not come to a complete stop immediately, the emergency system is faulty.

C. CHECK THE STEERING. Is there lost motion when you turn the wheel back and forth? The vehicle could have linkage problems. Does the steering wheel jerk and resist when you turn it? There are probably power-steering pump problems.

D. CHECK THE TRANSMISSION. *If the vehicle is an automatic,* speed up gradually until the gears shift. Is there a clunking sound or a second of hesitation before shifting? Hesitation or jerky shifts could indicate problems with a gear mechanism. Slow down to ten miles per hour and then press firmly on the accelerator. Do the gears shift quickly? If you are driving a three-speed automatic, the vehicle should shift two times. If it doesn't, this could indicate gear problems, too. *If the vehicle is a standard shift,* shift several times through all gears from a standstill. Are some gears hard to enter? Is there a grinding sound? Either could indicate linkage problems.

E. CHECK THE SUSPENSION. Drive over bumpy roads at slow and fast speeds. At a safe point on the road, "veer" hard right and left. If either action causes a large amount of bouncing or sway, your shocks may be defective. Make a note for your mechanic. Now, drive back to the lot and check under the hood again. Is there any fluid on the engine? Is steam or any other vapor rising from the engine? Is the radiator hissing? Make notes.

16. Finally, check the tires. Do they match, four radials or four polyester? If they don't, the tires will have to be changed. Driving with mixed tires can cause excessive tire wear and heating, handling problems, and accidents. Are the tires worn evenly? Look at the rear tires. Are the edges of the tires badly or unevenly worn? If so, your seller has probably placed the front tires on the rear. That's okay, but if any of the four tires show unnecessary wear along the edges, your vehicle is probably out of alignment. Make a note.

These sixteen steps obviously take a good deal of time and attention, but take the time. And don't be self-conscious. Look over each vehicle as if you were going to marry it. If you buy it, that's what you will be doing: living with the thing, warts and all.

Now, look over your checklist. If there are many minor things wrong with the vehicle, don't scratch it from your list. If there is an indication of major things, make sure each of those items is added to the following checklist for your mechanic. Make out a clean, neat sheet for him, and leave room for his notations concerning each item. Leave room also for his cost estimate to repair the car to your satisfaction.

Mechanic's Checklist

1. **CHECK THE ENGINE**
    inspect transmission
      fluid
    check points, con-
      denser, and rotor
    check spark plugs and
      ignition wire

2. **CHECK FAN AND BELTS**
    charging system
    power steering
    air conditioner

3. **CHECK COOLING SYSTEM**
    radiator
    heater
    bypass hose

4. **CHECK BATTERY**

5. **CHECK BRAKING SYSTEM**
    lining
    wheel and master
      cylinders
    drums and front disks
    hoses, bearings,
      grease seals

6. **CHECK EXHAUST SYSTEM**

7. **CHECK SUSPENSION**
    ball joints
    tie rod end
    idler arm

8. **REMOVE DIFFERENTIAL PLUG AND CHECK LUBRICANT**

9. **TEST-DRIVE VEHICLE**

IN YOUR OPINION

➤ Should engine compression be checked with gauge?
➤ What are the specific problems, if any, with this vehicle?
➤ What is your estimated repair cost?

What They Cost: Minus the Profit

NOTE: Remember that the definition of "cost" we're using here includes a hidden profit for the dealers on all American cars and many foreign cars—the holdback.

Use these figures for shopping purposes only. For the latest figures and greatest accuracy use a current pricing guide such as *Edmund's*.

Remember that American cars and some imports, in addition to these profits, have a 2 percent to 3 percent profit built into the base cost as "dealer holdbacks." For an explanation of dealer holdbacks, see page 00.

If a number has an A by it, the profit margin on the base vehicle or on the options may vary by half a percent or so. Use these figures for shopping purposes, but use a new copy of *Edmund's* or other guide if you really want to be accurate.

The base price of the car and total cost of its options are listed on the window of every car sold in America. (Remember that trucks and full-size vans are not required by law to post the Manufacturer's Suggested Retail Price; you may need to consult a buying guide such as *Edmund's* to be sure that the price on the sticker is the true MSRP.)

To determine the cost of the vehicle, multiply the base cost of the vehicle by the number in the column "% of base vehicle" and the total cost of options by the number in the column "% of options." Add the two resulting figures together to determine the profit built into the price. Subtract away the profit to determine the true cost of the vehicle.

PERCENTAGE OF PROFIT
CARS AND MINIVANS: AMERICAN AND IMPORTED

	% of base vehicle	% of options		% of base vehicle	% of options
ACCURA			**CHEVROLET**		
2.2 CL	.11	Not available; dealer installed	Camaro	.085	.14
			Cavalier base	.055	.11
			RS, LS	.075	.11
Integra	.12		Z24	.085	.11
NSX, RL	.14		Corvette	.145	.16
TL	.13		Lumina	.095	.11
			Monte Carlo	.095	.11
AUDI					
A4, A6,	.12	.13	**CHRYSLER**		
Cabriolet			Cirrus	.085	.11
			Concorde	.085	.11
BMW			LHS	.085	.11
318ti	.115	varies for all models	Sebring LX, JX	.08	.11
			LXi, JXi	.085	.11
318is, 328i,		.14	Town and	.09	.15
328is			Country SX,		
318i, 328i	.135		LX	.095	.15
M3	.135		LX AWD, LXi	.10	.15
528i	.125		LXi AWD		
540i	.14				
740i	.12		**DODGE**		
740iL	.145		Avenger	.08	.11
750iL	.14		LS	.085	.11
840Ci	.135		Caravan,	.09	.15
850Ci	.155		Grand Caravan		
Z3	.15		SE	.095	.15
			LE, ES, AWD	.10	.15
BUICK			Intrepid	.085	.11
LeSabre	.085	.14	Neon	.06	varies
Park Avenue	.095	.14	Highline	.085	varies
Regal	.085	.14	Stratus	.08	.11
Riviera	.095	.14	ES	.085	.11
Skylark	.055	.14			
			EAGLE		
CADILLAC			Talon	.75A	.15
Catera	.045	.15A	Vision	.85	.11
w/leather	.075	.15A			
DeVille	.085	.15A	**FORD**		
Eldorado base	.85	.15A	Aspire	.07A	.11
Touring	.135	.15A	Contour GL, LX	.85	.11
coupe			SE	.09	.11
Seville	.85	.15A			

PERCENTAGE OF PROFIT
CARS AND MINIVANS: AMERICAN AND IMPORTED, CONT.

	% of base vehicle	% of options		% of base vehicle	% of options
Ford, cont.			Other models	.08	
Crown Victoria	.065	.11	Elantra base	.09	
LX	.07	.11	GLS	.11	
Escort	.065	.11	Sonata base	.09	
Mustang	.08	.11	(auto)		
Coupe		.11	base	.095	
GT Coupe	.085	.11	(5-speed)		
Convert., GT	.09	.11	GL	.105	
Convert.			GLS	.125	
Cobra	.095	.11	Tiburon	.10	
Probe	.085	.11	FX	.12	
GT	.09				
Taurus G	.075	.11	**INFINITI**		
GL sedan	.08	.11	130 standard	.10	.12A
GL wagon	.085	.11	other models	.12	.12A
LX	.09	.11	J30	.11	.11
SHO	.095	.11	Q45	.11	.12A
Thunderbird	.09	.11			
Windstar	.07	.11	**ISUZU**		
GL	.095	.11	Oasis	.08	.21A
LX	.12	.11			
		.15	**JAGUAR**		
GEO		.15	XJ6, Vanden	.155	.18
Metro base	.06	.15	Plas		
LSi sedan	.065		XJR, XJ12	.16	.18
LSi	.07				
hatchback		.11	**KIA**		
Prizm base	.05	.11	Sephia RS	.10	varies for all models
LSi	.08	.11			
			LS	.105	
HONDA		.14	GS	.12	
Accord	.115	.14			
			LEXUS		
			ES300	.13	varies for all models
Civic CX	.06	Not available; dealer installed			
DX, HX, EX	.105		GS300	.14	
Del Sol	.105		LS400	.15	
LX	.12		SC300	.15	
Odyssey	.115		SC400	.16	
Prelude	.115				
			LINCOLN		
HYUNDAI			Continental	.09	.14
Accent L	.06	Not available	Mark VIII	.09	.14
			Town Car	.12	.14

PERCENTAGE OF PROFIT
CARS AND MINIVANS: AMERICAN AND IMPORTED, CONT.

	% of base vehicle	% of options		% of base vehicle	% of options
MAZDA			Galant DE	.11	varies
626 DX	.08	varies for all models	ES	.12	varies
LX	.10		LS	.15	varies
ES	.11		Mirage DE (5-speed)	.08	varies
Miata base	.095		DE (auto)	.085	varies
other	.115		LS	.10	varies
Millenia	.115				
w/leather	.125		**NISSAN**		
S	.135		200SX	.05	varies for all models
MVP	.095A				
Protege DX	.055		SE, SE-R	.09	
LX	.075		240SX	.105	
ES	.085		Altima XE	.10	
			GXE	.105	
MERCEDES-BENZ			SE, GLE	.11	
C-Class	.13	.13A	Maxima GXE (5-speed)	.095	
E-Class	.13	.13A	GXE (auto)	.105	
S-Class	.13	.13	SE, GLE	.11	
SL-Class	.13	.13	Quest	.11	
			Sentra	.05	
MERCURY			XE	.07	
Cougar XR7	.085	.11	GXE, GLE	.095	
Grand Marquis GS	.065	.11			
LS	.07	.11	**OLDSMOBILE**		
Mystique	.085	.11	Achieva	.85	.11
Sable G	.075	.11	Aurora	.95	.11
GS	.085	.11	Cutlass Supreme	.85	.11
LS	.09	.11	Eighty-Eighty	.85	.11
Tracer	.065	.11	LSS	.85	.11
Villager GS	.095	.15	Regency	.85	.11
LS, Nautica	.10	.15	Silhouette	.95	.14
MITSUBISHI			**PLYMOUTH**		
3000GT base	.15	.18	Breeze	.85	.11
other models	.18	.18	Neon	.06	.11
Diamante	.15	varies	Highline	.85	.11
Eclipse RS, Gs, GST	.18	varies	Voyager, Grand Voyager	.09	.15
GSX	.14	varies	SE, Grand V. SE	.95	.15
Eclipse Spyder	.13	varies			

PERCENTAGE OF PROFIT
CARS AND MINIVANS: AMERICAN AND IMPORTED, CONT.

	% of base vehicle	% of options		% of base vehicle	% of options
PONTIAC			**TOYOTA**		
Bonneville	.095	.11	Avalaon XL	.125	varies for all models
Firebird	.085	.11	XLS	.135	
Grand Am	.085	.11	Camry CE	.115	
Grand Prix	.085	.11	LE, XLE	.125	
Sunfire	.075	.11	Celica ST	.12	
Trans Sport	.095	.11	GT	.115	
			convertible		
PORSCHE			GT liftback	.125	
911 Carrera	.14	.20	Corolla standard, CE	.085	
911 Turbo	.14	.20	DX	.115	
			Paseo	.08	
SAAB			convertible		
900 S	.105	.145	coupe	.105	
SE 2-door	.125	.145	Previa 2WD DX	.12	
SE other models	.105	.145	LE, All Trac	.125	
9000			Supra	.06	
			(5-speed)		
SATURN			(auto)	.065	
SC	.10	.10	Turbo, Sport Roof	.08	
SL	.10	.10	Tercel coupe	.06	
SW	.10	.10	sedan	.075	
SUBARU			**VOLKSWAGEN**		
Impreza Brighton	.07	varies for all models	Cabrio	.95	.125A
L	.09		Highline	.09	
Outback Sport	.095		Golf GL, GT1	.075	
Legacy Brighton	.063		GT1 VR6	.08	
L	.10		Jetta GLX	.075	
LSi, 2.5GT, Outback	.105		GL, GLS	.095	
SVXL	.09		GT	.09	
LSi	.10		Passat	.10	
SUZUKI					
Esteem	.05	Not available; dealer installed			
Swift	.07				

PERCENTAGE OF PROFIT
CARS AND MINIVANS: AMERICAN AND IMPORTED, CONT.

	% of base vehicle	% of options		% of base vehicle	% of options
VOLVO		varies for	T-5 Wagon	.08	
850 GLT wagon	.07	all	T-5 Sedan	.085	
		models	R Wagon	.09	
GLT sedan,	.075		R Sedan	.095	
Wagon (auto)	.075		960 Wagon	.075	
Sedan,			Sedan	.08	
Wagon	.08				
(5-speed)					

PERCENTAGE OF PROFIT
VANS, SPORT UTILITY VEHICLES, AND TRUCKS
AMERICAN AND IMPORTED

	% of base vehicle	% of options
ACCURA		
SLX	.125	Not available; dealer installed
CHEVROLET		
Astro	.095	.14
Blazer	.095	.14
Chevy Van	.125	.14
Express Van	.125	.14
C/K 1500	.095	.14
Pickup Reg. Cab		
Fleetside,	.125	.14
Sportside		
C/K 2500	.125	.14
Pickup		
C/K 3500	.125	.14
Pickup		
S-10 Pickup	.055	.14
Fleetside		
LS Fleetside	.095	.14
Suburban	.125	.14
Tahoe	.125	.14
DODGE		
Dakota Reg. 2WD	.09	.15
Reg, 4WD, Club Cab	.095	.15
Ram BR1500 Pickup		
WS Shortbed	.085	.15
WS Longbed	.09	.15
LT & ST 2WD	.12	.15
LT & ST 4WD	.125	.15
Ram BR2500 Pickup	.125	.15
Ram BR3500 Pickup	.125A	.15
Ram Van		
1500 109"	.09	.15

	% of base vehicle	% of options
wheelbase 2500 109"	.12	.15
wheelbase Other models	.125	.15
Ram Wagon		.15
1500	.095	
2500, 3500	.125	.15
3500	.135	.15
Maxiwagon		.15
FORD		
Club Wagon XL	.125	
Reg		.15
XL HD, XL	.13	
Super Club		.15
XLT	.13	
Econoline Van	.125	.15
E150, E250		.15
E350	.13	
Expedition XLT	.125	.15
2 WD		.15
All 4WD	.13	
models		.15
Expolorer		
XL 2-door	.09	
2WD		.15
Sport 2WD	.09	
Sport 4WD	.095	.15
XL 4WD, XLT	.09	.15
Eddie Bauer	.10	.15
edition		.15
2WD, AWD	.10	
Ltd. edition		.15
4WD	.105	
F150 Pickup		.15
Standard	.085-.10	.15
XL2WD	.12-.125	.15
XL4WD	.125-.13	.15
XLT 2WD	.12-.13	.15
XLT 4WD	.13-.145	.15
Lariat	.13-.135	.15

	% of base vehicle	% of options		% of base vehicle	% of options
FORD, *cont.*			**GMC**		
F250 Pickup			Jimmy	.095	.14
Standard	.09-.095	.15	Safari	.095	.14
Standard Super Cab 4WD	.10		Savana	.125	.14
			Sierra 1500		
XL, XLT	.125-.13	.15	Special Reg Cab	.095	.14
Lariat	.13-.135	.15	Reg Cab, X-Cab	.125	.14
F250 Heavy Duty Pickup			Sierra 2500	.125	.14
Reg. 2WD	.12	.15	Sierra 3500	.125	.14
Reg. 4WD	.125	.15	Sonoma SL	.055	.14
Super Cab Crew Cab 2WD	.125	.15	SLS	.095	.14
			Suburban	.125	.14
Crew Cab 4WD	.13	.15	Yukon	.125	.14
F350 Pickup			**HONDA**		
Reg. 2WD	.12	.15	Passport	.115	Not available; dealer installed
Reg. 4WD	.125	.15			
Crew Cab 2WD	.125	.15			
Crew Cab 4WD	.13	.15			
Ranger			**ISUZU**		
XL Reg 2WD	.05	.15	Hombre S	.08	.11A
XL Reg 4WD	.06	.15	XS	.09	.11A
XL Super Cab 2WD	.095	.15	Rodeo		
			S 2WD 5-speed	.06	.11A
XL Super Cab 4WD	.10	.15	S & LS 2WD V-6	.085	.11A
XLT, Splash Reg 2WD	.095	.15	S & LS 4WD	.09	.11A
			Trooper S	.13	.11A
XLT Reg 4WD	.10	.15	LS, LTD	.145	.11A
XLT 4WD Super Cab	.105	.15	**JEEP**		
STX	.10-.105	.15	Cherokee SE	.06	.15
Splash 2WD	.095-.10	.15	Sport, Country 2WD	.095	.15
Splash 4WD	.105	.15	Country 4WD	.10	.15
			Grand Cherokee Larado	.095	.15
GEO					
Tracker	.05	.11	Limited	.10	.15

PERCENTAGE OF PROFIT
VANS, SPORT UTILITY VEHICLES, AND TRUCKS
AMERICAN AND IMPORTED, CONT.

	% of base vehicle	% of options
JEEP, *cont.*		
Wrangler SE	.04	.15
Sport	.095	.15
Saraha	.10	.15
KIA		
Sportage 2WD	.09	Not available
Wagon	.09	
4WD	.10	
Wagon EX	.10	
EX 4WD	.105	
LAND ROVER		
Discovery	.11	.16
Range Rover	.115	N/A
LEXUS		
LX450	.14	varies
MERCURY		
Mountaineer 2WD	.095	.15
4WD	.10	.15
MITSUBISHI		
Montero LS	.145	varies
NISSAN		
Pathfinder	.165	
Truck 2WD SR	.10	.14A

	% of base vehicle	% of options
Standard	.04	.14A
XE Reg Cab	.05	.14A
XE King Cab	.08	.14A
SE 5-speed	.09	.14A
SE auto	.095	.14A
Truck 4WD		
XE Reg Cab	.08	.14A
XE King Cab	.095	.14A
SE	.10	.14A
OLDSMOBILE		
Bravada	.095	.14
SUZUKI		
Sidekick	.09	N/A
X-90 2WD	.06	varies
4WD	.07	
TOYOTA		
4Runner	.125	varies for all models
Land Cruiser	.14	
RAV4 2WD	.09	
4WD	.105	
T100 Standard	.075	
DX 2WD	.105	
DX 4WD	.115	
SR5 2WD	.11	
SR5 2WD	.12	
Tacoma		
Reg Cab 2WD	.085	
Xtra Cab 2WD	.095A	
4WD models	.105A	

CHART FOR USE IN FIGURING LOAN CASH OR MONTHLY PAYMENTS

MONTHLY PAYMENTS FOR $1000						
3%	**4%**	**5%**	**6%**	**7%**	**8%**	**8.5%**
2 yr 42.98	43.42	43.87	44.32	44.77	45.23	45.46
3 yr 29.08	29.52	29.97	30.42	30.88	31.34	31.57
4 yr 22.13	22.58	23.03	23.49	23.95	24.41	24.65
5 yr 17.19	18.42	18.87	19.33	19.80	20.28	20.52
6 yr		16.10	16.57	17.05	17.53	17.78
9%	**9.5%**	**10%**	**10.5%**	**11%**	**11.5%**	**12%**
2 yr 45.68	45.91	46.14	46.38	46.61	48.84	47.07
3 yr 31.80	32.03	32.27	32.50	32.74	32.98	33.21
4 yr 24.89	25.12	25.36	25.60	25.85	26.09	26.33
5 yr 20.76	21.00	21.25	21.49	21.74	21.99	22.24
6 yr 18.03	18.27	18.53	18.78	19.03	19.29	19.55
12.5%	**13%**	**13.5%**	**14%**	**14.5%**	**15%**	**15.5%**
2 yr 47.31	47.54	47.78	48.01	48.25	48.49	48.72
3 yr 33.45	33.69	33.94	34.18	34.42	34.67	34.91
4 yr 26.58	26.83	27.08	27.33	27.58	27.83	28.08
5 yr 22.50	22.75	23.01	23.27	23.53	23.79	24.05
6 yr 19.81	20.07	20.34	20.61	20.87	21.15	21.42
16%	**16.5%**	**17%**	**17.5%**	**18%**	**18.5%**	**19%**
2 yr 48.96	49.20	49.44	49.68	49.92	50.17	50.41
3 yr 35.16	35.40	35.65	35.90	36.15	36.40	36.66
4 yr 28.34	28.60	28.86	29.11	29.37	29.64	29.90
5 yr 24.32	24.58	24.85	25.12	25.39	25.67	25.94
6 yr 21.69	21.97	22.25	22.53	22.81	23.09	23.38
19.5%	**20%**	**20.5%**	**21%**			
2 yr 50.65	50.90	51.14	51.39			
3 yr 36.91	37.16	37.42	37.68			
4 yr 30.16	30.43	30.70	30.97			
5 yr 26.22	26.49	26.77	27.05			
6 yr 23.66	23.95	24.24	24.54			

"The Negotiation" in Abbreviated Form

IF YOU ARE FINANCING, BUYING A NEW CAR, AND TRADING THE OLD

1. Compute your Available Cash (Loan Cash plus equity in your trade).

2. At the store, copy down all information on the particular cars which interest you.

3. At home, develop the cost and your maximum offer for each car.

4. Check your budget: Compare your maximum offer to your Available Cash.

5. Compute your "best probable" difference figure (your maximum offer minus the wholesale value of your trade).

Dealing with the Store—

Take the following information with you:

➤ the location, stock number, and color of each car
➤ your maximum offer and "best probable" difference figure on each car
➤ the wholesale value of your car
➤ your Available Cash figure

6. Have your car appraised.

7. Agree on the wholesale value of your trade.

8. When you have agreed, make your offer on the car.

9. Check dealer's difference figure (his offer on your car minus the agreed price of his car): Compare it to your "best probable" difference figure.

10. Let dealer write it up; check the buyer's order for accuracy.

11. Sign the order, but do not give a deposit.

12. Give a deposit when your offer is accepted. Recheck your difference figure, if necessary.

13. If you are financing at the dealership, confirm the amount to be financed and the APR.

14. Expect finance pressure!

IF YOU ARE FINANCING AND BUYING A NEW CAR WITHOUT TRADING

1. Determine your Loan Cash.

2. Determine your down payment.

3. Compute your Available Cash (Loan Cash plus down payment).

4. At the store, copy down all information on the particular cars which interest you.

5. At home, develop the cost and your maximum offer for each car.

6. Check your budget: Compare your Available Cash to your maximum offer.

Dealing with the Store—

Take the following information with you:

➤ the location, stock number, and color of each car
➤ your maximum offer on each car
➤ your Available Cash figure

7. Go to the lot that is home to your favorite car.

8. Take the salesman to his office.

9. Tell the salesman you are prepared to make a firm offer.

10. Make your offer and insist it be taken to management.

11. Check the buyer's order: Compare the figure on the order to your Available Cash. If the figure is satisfactory, sign the order, but do not give a deposit.

12. Give a deposit when your offer is approved. Compare the final accepted offer to your Available Cash, if necessary.

13. If you are financing at the dealership, check the amount to be financed and the APR.

14. Expect finance pressure!

IF YOU ARE FINANCING, BUYING A USED CAR, AND TRADING THE OLD

1. Compute your Available Cash (Loan Cash plus the equity in your trade).

2. Decide on three or four used-car sources.

3a. Look for cars with asking prices higher than your Available Cash figure.

3b. Drive each car; use your checklist to inspect each car.

3c. Write down all items that may affect loan value.

4. Call your bank or credit union and ask for

➤ the loan value of the car
➤ the lowest interest rate and number of months the car can be financed.

5. Determine their "probable profit": Compare their asking price to the loan value of the car.

6. Compute your "best probable" difference figure (loan value of their car minus wholesale value of your car).

Dealing with the Store—

Take the following information with you:

➤ the location, stock number, and color of each car
➤ your "best probable" difference figure on each car
➤ the loan value of each car
➤ the wholesale value of your car
➤ your Available Cash figure

7. Leave your car to be appraised and take their car to your mechanic. Take your Mechanic's Checklist and note on the list any problems with the car. Ask your mechanic for an estimate to repair the car to your satisfaction.

8. Subtract the repair estimate from your Available Cash figure and put the new figure on your pad.

9. Return to the lot and compute his difference figure: Subtract his figure on your car from his asking price.

10. Compare his difference figure to your "best probable" difference figure.

11. Always negotiate, even if his difference figure is a good one.

12. When the salesman will not budge

> ➤ check his probable profit: Subtract your "best probable" difference figure from his final difference figure
> ➤ decide if you can afford it: Add his final difference figure, tax, and the payoff on your car
> ➤ compare this total to your Available Cash.

13. After agreeing on a price, discuss warranties.

14. Let him write it up. Check the buyer's order, sign it, but do not give him a deposit.

15. If you are financing with the seller, check the amount to be financed and the APR.

16. Expect finance pressure!

IF YOU ARE FINANCING AND BUYING A USED CAR WITHOUT TRADING

1. Determine your Loan Cash.

2. Determine your down payment.

3. Determine your Available Cash (Loan Cash plus down payment).

4. Decide on three or four used-car sources.

5a. Look for cars with asking prices higher than your Available Cash figure.

5b. Drive each car; use your checklist to inspect each car.

5c. Write down all items that may affect loan value.

6. Call your bank or credit union and ask for

> ➤ the loan value of the car
> ➤ the lowest interest rate and number of months the car can be financed.

7. Determine their "probable profit": Compare their asking price to the loan value of the car.

8. Determine your maximum offer.

Dealing with the Store—

Take the following information with you:

➤ the location, stock number, and color of each car
➤ your maximum offer on each car
➤ the loan value of each car
➤ your Available Cash figure

9. Take their car to your mechanic. Take your Mechanic's Checklist, and note on the list any problems with the car. Ask your mechanic for an estimate to repair the car to your satisfaction.

10. Subtract the repair estimate from your Available Cash figure and put the new figure on your pad.

11. At the lot, offer your salesman *less* than loan value. Negotiate.

12. When the salesman will not budge

➤ compare his final offer to your Available Cash figure
➤ determine his "probable profit" figure: Subtract the loan value of the car from his final offer.

13. After agreeing on price, discuss warranties.

14. Let him write it up. Check the buyer's order, sign it, but don't give the salesman a deposit.

15. Negotiate; compromise; give a deposit when your offer is approved. If necessary, compare the final figure to your Available Cash figure.

16. If you are financing with the seller, check the amount to be financed and the APR.

17. Expect finance pressure!

IF YOU ARE PAYING CASH, BUYING A NEW CAR, AND TRADING THE OLD

1. Compute your Available Cash (your cash plus the equity in your trade).

2. At the store, copy down all information on the particular cars that interest you.

3. At home, develop the cost and your maximum offer for each car.

4. Check your budget: Compare your maximum offer to your Available Cash.

5. Compute your "best probable" difference figure (your maximum offer minus the wholesale value of your trade).

Dealing with the Store—

Take the following information with you:

➤ the location, stock number, and color of each car
➤ your maximum offer and "best probable" difference figure on each car
➤ the wholesale value of your car
➤ your Available Cash figure

6. Have your car appraised.

7. Agree on the wholesale value of your trade.

8. When you have agreed, make your offer on their car.

9. Check dealer's difference figure (his offer on your car minus the agreed price on the new car); compare it to your "best probable" difference figure.

10. Let him write it up. Check the buyer's order for accuracy.

11. Sign the order, but do not give a deposit.

12. Give a deposit once your offer is accepted. Recheck your difference figure, if necessary.

13. Expect finance pressure!

IF YOU ARE PAYING CASH AND BUYING A NEW CAR WITHOUT TRADING

1. Determine your Available Cash.

2. At the store, copy down all information on the particular cars that interest you.

3. At home, develop the cost and your maximum offer for each car.

4. Check your budget: Compare your Available Cash to your maximum offer.

Dealing with the Store—

Take your Available Cash and maximum offer figures with you.

5. Go to the lot that is home to your favorite car.

6. Take the salesman to his office.

7. Tell your salesman you are prepared to make a firm offer.

8. Make your offer and insist it be taken to management.

9. Check the buyer's order: Compare the figure on the order to your Available Cash. If the figure is satisfactory, sign the order but do not give a deposit.

10. Give a deposit when your offer is approved. Compare the final offer to your Available Cash figure, if necessary.

11. Expect finance pressure!

IF YOU ARE PAYING CASH, BUYING A USED CAR, AND TRADING THE OLD

1. Compute your Available Cash (your cash plus the equity in your trade).

2. Decide on three or four used-car sources.

3a. Look for cars with higher asking prices than your Available Cash figure.

3b. Drive each car: use your checklist to inspect each car.

3c. Write down all the items that may affect loan value.

4. Call your bank or credit union and ask for the loan value of the cars which interest you.

5. Determine their "probable profit": Compare their asking price to the loan value of the car.

6. Compute your "best probable" difference figure (loan value of their car minus wholesale value of your car).

Dealing with the Store—

Take the following information with you:

➤ the location, stock number, and color of each car
➤ your "best probable" difference figure on each car
➤ the loan value of each car

➤ the wholesale value of your car
➤ your Available Cash figure

7. Leave your car to be appraised and take their car to your mechanic. Take your Mechanic's Checklist and note on the list any problems with the car. Ask your mechanic for an estimate to repair the car to your satisfaction.

8. Subtract the repair estimate from your Available Cash figure and put the new figure on your pad.

9. Return to the lot and compute dealer's difference figure: Subtract his figure on your car from his asking price.

10. Compare his difference figure to your "best probable" difference figure.

11. Always negotiate, even if his difference figure is a good one.

12. When the salesman will not budge

➤ check his probable profit: Subtract your "best probable" difference figure from his final difference figure
➤ decide if you can afford it: Add his final difference figure, tax, and the payoff on your car
➤ compare this total to your Available Cash.

13. After agreeing on a price, discuss warranties.

14. Let him write it up. Check the buyer's order, sign it, but do not give him a deposit until your offer is approved.

15. Expect finance pressure!

IF YOU ARE PAYING CASH AND BUYING A USED CAR WITHOUT TRADING

1. Determine how much you plan to spend (your Available Cash).

2. Decide on three or four used-car sources.

3a. Look for cars with asking prices higher than your Available Cash figure.

3b. Drive each car; use your checklist to inspect each car.

3c. Write down all items which may affect loan value.

 4. Call your bank or credit union and ask for the loan value of the cars which interest you.

 5. Determine their "probable profit": Compare their asking price to the loan value of the car.

 6. Determine your maximum offer.

Dealing with the Store—

Take the following information with you:

➤ the location, stock number, and color of each car
➤ your maximum offer on each car
➤ the loan value of each car
➤ your Available Cash figure

 7. Take their car to your mechanic. Take your Mechanic's Checklist and note on the list any problems with the car. Ask your mechanic for an estimate to repair the car to your satisfaction.

 8. Subtract the repair estimate from your Available Cash figure and put the new figure on your pad.

 9. At the lot, offer your salesman *less* than loan value. Negotiate.

10. When the salesman will not budge

➤ compare his final offer to your Available Cash figure
➤ determine his "probable profit" figure: Subtract the loan value of the car from his final offer.

11. After agreeing on price, discuss warranties.

12. Let him write it up. Check the buyer's order, sign it, but don't give him a deposit.

13. Negotiate; compromise; give a deposit when your offer is approved. If necessary, compare the final figure to your Available Cash figure.

14. Expect finance pressure!

Glossary

Add-Ons: High-profit items added to cars by the seller, not installed at the factory.

Allowance Buyers: Customers who care only about the amount of money given them for their trade. Also referred to as wienies.

Asking Price: The maximum amount of money sellers wish to attain; an imaginary figure used by sellers to snare imbeciles.

Available Cash: The total amount of money available to an individual buyer, including equity, Loan Cash, and out-of-pocket cash.

"Be-Backs": Customers who tell a salesman, "Oh, don't worry, I'll be back tomorrow." Sure.

"Best Probable" Difference Figure: The lowest price a customer will probably pay when trading.

Bird-Dogs: People who send customers to a particular salesman, usually for money.

Bonus Cars: Slow-selling cars that pay extra commission to salesmen.

Bumblebees: Folks who flit from dealership to dealership, looking at every new car in sight but never buying.

Bumping: Getting a customer to raise his offer on a particular car. Also called "raising."

Car Queers: People who dream constantly about buying a new car and enjoy hanging out at car stores.

The Chart: When a customer is paying the highest interest rate for financing allowed by law and also buying life and accident and health insurance.

Chopped Car: A car reconstructed from two wrecked and/or stolen cars. This procedure, also called clipping, is a specialty of "chop shops."

The Christmas Club: A technique designed to convince the customer his or her first payment is being paid by the dealership when it is actually being paid by the customer.

"Clocking": Turning the car's speedometer back to register lower mileage.

The Close: When a customer is finally convinced to sign the buyer's order.

Closer: A dealership employee whose only job is getting customers to sign a buyer's order.

Cream Puffs: Extremely nice used cars; also referred to as "cherries."

Curbstones: A person paid by a used-car dealership who tells potential buyers that he or she is the owner.

Demos: New cars driven by salesmen and other dealership employees. Seldom a good buy.

Detail Man: A person who cleans new or used cars, especially a person who "doctors" minor problems with cars.

"Difference": The selling price of a new or used car minus the actual wholesale value of a trade-in.

Difference Buyers: Customers who care only about the difference between their present car and the newer car. Also referred to as jerks.

"Dipping": Borrowing a down payment for a customer, usually from a small loan company.

Double-Dipping: Borrowing a down payment for a customer from two lending institutions. Persons who are double-dipped are also referred to as spastics.

Down Stroke: The total amount of the down payment, including cash and equity in your trade.

Equity: The amount of value left in a used car when the car's payoff is subtracted from its true wholesale value.

Fairies: Rainy-day buyers, invariably pipe smokers and other weird types, who actually seem to understand the car-buying process and are not intimidated by salesmen.

Finance Charge: The total of all charges customers incur when they finance a car rather than pay cash; includes interest, documentary stamps, insurance, and credit fees.

Floor-Planning: When cars are owned by financing institutions rather than dealerships. The vast majority of automobile dealerships floor-plan their cars.

Floor Whores: Salesmen who don't work by appointment but simply tackle any unattached customer on the lot.

Gross, Back-End: The profit to the dealership on the sale of financing, insurance, and "add-ons," such as rust-proofing.

Gross, Front-End: The profit to the dealership on the sale of a new or used car.

Holdbacks: Profits built into each new-car invoice but considered "cost" by the dealership.

"In the Bucket": When a car owner has a net payoff that is higher than the true wholesale value of that car, he is said to be "in the bucket."

Lepers: New or used cars avoided even by the salesmen due to their physical condition or length of stay at the dealership.

Loan Cash: The lump sum of cash an installment loan will buy; the actual sum of an installment loan that is applied to the purchase, not interest.

Loan Value: The average amount of money lending institutions will lend on a particular car; usually refers to used cars.

Negative Equity: When you owe more on your car than its true wholesale value.

Net Payoff: The amount owed on a car minus any prepaid interest or insurance premiums.

A Nickel: Five hundred dollars.

"Nickels": Small dents and scratches on a car.

The Pack: Extra profit added to the invoice cost of cars by dealers; packs are used to confuse both customers and salesmen.

Paper Men: Used-car sellers who finance their own cars regardless of the credit of the buyers.

Payment Buyers: Buyers who care only about their payment. Also referred to as suckers.

Peacocks: Persons who must drive the newest cars, regardless of the price penalty they must pay for the privilege.

Retail Value: The wholesale value of a car plus the anticipated profit gained from reselling the car.

Road Hogs: Used-car wholesalers who travel from dealership to dealership peddling their wares.

Skating: When a salesman deliberately sells another salesman's customer.

"Spiffs": Cash bonuses paid to salesmen—tax-free, of course.

The Store: The dealership.

"Switching": The automobile version of sadism: convincing a customer to buy a car with a larger profit margin; convincing a customer to buy a car with a bonus to the salesman.

Tanks: Unpopular cars or station wagons.

"Tissue": The actual invoice price of a new car.

"T.O.": To turn a customer over to another salesman or manager in order to close or raise the profit on a sale.

Trading Down: Buying a smaller or less expensive car than your present one; trading a newer car for an older one.

"Ups": Customers.

The "Up" System: When "ups" are assigned to salesmen by numbers, viz., "Okay, Killer, you're up next."

Water: What remains when the value of a used car is less than the amount the seller has in the car. For instance, if a seller has $1000 in a car with a true wholesale value of $600, the dealership has $400 in "water."

Wholesale Value: The value of a used car to someone who plans to resell it.

Write-Downs: When the value of a used car is lowered on a dealership's book.

Index

A

acquisition fee, 246
adjustment warranties, 208, 297
advertisements, classified:
  buying a car through, 193–94,
    231–32
  selling your car through, 112
advertising, dealership, 185–92
  gimmicks in, 189–92
affordability, 79–80, 132–51
agents, leasing, 242
alarm systems, 263
allowance buyers, 130–31
annualized percentage rate (APR),
  134, 140–41, 150–51, 157
auctions, 234
AutoSearch, 235
available cash, 133, 138, 143, 144,
  157
  determining, 146–51

B

bait and switch, 188, 190
banks, 125–26, 132, 135, 136
  life insurance from, 154
  see also financing
Better Business Bureau, 233
book value, 104–5
"brass hat" cars, 219–20
business managers (finance managers), 261–65
buyers, 65–91
  finance categories of, 130–32

impulse, 75–76
naïveté in, 75
traits of, to cultivate, 88–91
see also buying a car; selling
buyer's order, 303–4
"buy here, pay here" dealers, 129,
  234
buying a car, 76–88
  affordability and, 79–80, 132–51
  American vs. foreign, 86–87
  articles and books on, 183–85
  car-buying services and, 217–18,
    223–24
  and cost of cars, *see* cost of cars
  demos and special vehicles, 219–
    220
  financing and, *see* financing
  need vs. want in, 76–79
  negotiating in, *see* negotiating
  new vs. used, 80–85
  ordering, 218–19
  shopping, *see* shopping
  timing of, 195–97
  trading down, 87–88
  see also buyers; selling

C

capitalized cost (cap cost), 245–46
capitalized cost reduction, 246
car, buying of, *see* buying a car
car, present, 92–114
  book value of, 104–5
  cleanliness of, 96–97

car, present (*cont.*)
  mileage on, 98–99, 305
  popularity of, 97–98
  wholesale value of, 99–104, 112,
    146–47, 250
  see also selling your car yourself;
    trade-ins
car buyers, *see* buyers
car-buying services, 217–18
  Internet, 223–24
car dealerships, *see* dealerships
car manufacturers, Internet sites of,
  222
car pricing services, 222
carryover allowance, 196
cash payment, negotiating and,
  283–96, 339–43
Christmas, 197
cost of cars, 209–17, 322–30
  by car line, 212–13
  dealer's invoice and, 189, 209–10
  dealer's sticker and, 210–12
  Edmund's pricing services and,
    214–16, 220, 222, 322
  manufacturer's suggested retail
    price (MSRP) and, 190, 210
  specific, 213–17
credit, home equity lines of, 121–
  122
credit checks, 60–61
  welcome centers and, 59
credit disability insurance, 152–56,
  157
credit life insurance, 152–56, 157
credit problems, 59
  credit doctor scams and, 56–57,
    58, 59
  dealership advertising and,
    191
  dealership financing and, 128
  and dealerships catering to
    poorer customers, 57–59
credit unions, 122–25, 132, 135,
  136
  life insurance from, 154
  see also financing
customers, *see* buyers

D

dealer invoices, 189, 209–10
dealerships, 22–39, 63–64, 160–61
  advertising by, 185–92
  chain and multiple-car-line (mega-
    dealers), 9–11
  financing at, 126–28, 136, 138,
    139
  Internet sites of, 223
  leasing companies and, 242–44
  for poorer customers, 57–59
  profits of, 38–39
  sales at, 194, 197
  used-car, 232–34
  see also selling
dealer's sticker, 210–12
demo cars, 219
deposits, 60, 302–3
  credit checks and, 60–61
  security, 246
difference buyers, 130
dipping, 67–70, 148
disability insurance, 152–56, 157
down payments, 144–45

E

Edmund's pricing services, 214–16,
  220, 222, 322
enthusiasm, 89–90
equity, in present car, 147–48
  lack of, 147
  negative, 148–51
equity loans, 121–22
"executive" cars, 219–20

F

finance charge, 134–35
finance companies, 129
finance managers, 261–65
financing, 11, 115–59
  affordability and, 132–51
  applying for, 138–39
  APR in, 134, 140–41, 150–51, 157
  available cash in, *see* available
    cash
  from banks, 125–26, 132
  buyer categories and, 130–32

at "buy here, pay here" dealers, 129, 234
contracts in, 305–6
from credit unions, 122–25, 132
from dealership, 126–28, 136, 138, 139
determining best source of, 156–159
down payments in, 144–45
from finance companies, 129
identifying cheapest source of, 138
insurance and, 152–56
Internet and, 222, 223–24
loan cash in, *see* loan cash
monthly payments in, *see* payments, monthly
negotiating in, 267–83, 333–38; *see also* negotiating
rate sales and, 137–38, 191
rebates and, 11, 137–38, 143, 190, 262
shopping for rates and terms in, 132, 134–36, 156–59
sources of, 121–29, 132
for used cars, 230
foreign cars, 86–87
four-square system, 51–52

G
GAP insurance, 247
glazing, 262
glossary, 345–48

H
home equity loan, 121–22
honesty, 35

I
impatience, 91
indecision, 89
initial payment, on leased vehicle, 246
insurance, 152–56, 157
cash value in, 121
GAP, 247
Internet, 214, 221–24

"in the bucket," 67, 147, 148–51
invoices, dealer, 189, 209–10

K
kickbacks, 209–10
knowledge, 90

L
leasing, leases, 12, 238–57, 262
checklist for, 247–50
choosing sources of, 251
closed-end, 241
comparing rates and terms of, 251–52
components of, 245–50
cost of, 252–53
dealerships and, 242–44
deciding about, 239–40
determining price range in, 251
dishonest, 49–50
Internet services for, 223–24
monthly payments in, 247, 250–251, 255, 256
negotiating of, 253–54, 256
open-ended, 241–42
parties in, 242
promotional rates in, 256
right way of, 250–57
service charge in, 246–47, 256
terms used in, 245–47
types of, 241–42
of used cars, 256–57
wrong way of, consequences of, 240–41
lessee, 242
lessor, 242
life insurance, 121, 152–56, 157
loan cash, 133, 138, 140–43, 157
in buying a car with debt-free trade, 146–47
in buying a car with money owed on trade, 147, 150–51
in buying a car without trading, 146
chart for figuring, 331
equity and, 147–48
figuring from a payment, 140–43

loans, *see* financing
lowballing, 62–63

M
Manufacturer's Suggested Retail
 Price (MSRP), 190, 210, 245
mechanic's checklist, 321
mileage:
 on leased vehicle, 247
 on present car, 98–99, 305

N
National Highway Traffic Safety Administration (NHTSA), 298
negotiating, 258–307
 abbreviated guide to, 333–43
 deposits and, 302–3
 "fair" deal and, 258–59
 finance manager and, 261–65
 in financing, buying a new car,
  and trading the old, 267–71,
  333–34
 in financing, buying a used car,
  and trading the old, 275–79,
  335–37
 in financing and buying a new
  car without trading, 271–74,
  334–35
 in financing and buying a used
  car without trading, 279–83,
  337–38
 high-pressure techniques and,
  259–61
 of leasing terms, 253–54, 256
 in paying cash, buying a new car,
  and trading the old, 283–86,
  339–40
 in paying cash, buying a used
  car, and trading the old, 289–
  294, 341–42
 in paying cash and buying a new
  car without trading, 287–89,
  340–41
 in paying cash and buying a used
  car without trading, 294–96,
  342–43
 play-acting in, 265

 of protection packages and warranties, 262–63, 297–302
 sales gimmicks and, 261–62
 signing and, 303–7
net payoff, 147
note system, 52–53

O
"one price, no hassle" systems, 54–
 55
ordering a car, 218–19

P
patience, 91
payment buyers, 131–32, 139
payments:
 down, 144–45
 initial, on leased vehicle, 246
payments, monthly, 79–80, 131–32,
 132–33, 139
 chart for figuring, 331
 dealership advertising and, 190–
  191
 determining from lump sum,
  151–52
 figuring loan cash from, 140–43
 on leased vehicle, 247, 250–51,
  255, 256
powers of attorney, 305
price of cars, *see* cost of cars
"program" cars, 219–20
protection packages, 262–63

R
raise, 61–62
rate sales, 137–38, 191
rebates, 11, 137–38, 143, 190, 262
recission forms, 56, 265
rental company cars, 184, 219–20,
 234
residual value, 246
romance of car buying, 91
rustproofing, 262

S
sales, 194, 197
sales managers, 22–39

salespeople, 22–39, 63–64, 160–61
    after-the-sale, 11–12
    buyer traits and, 88–91
    favorite targets of, 37–38
    see also selling
security deposit, 246
selling, 17–64
    credit and, *see* credit checks;
        credit problems
    honesty and, 35
    lowballing in, 62–63
    negotiating in, *see* negotiating
    raise in, 61–62
    sales managers in, 22–39
    systems in, 10–11, 50–59,
        161–79
    techniques in, 40–50, 259–61
    see also buyers; dealerships;
        salespeople
selling your car yourself, 105–14,
    250
    classified ads and, 112
    dickering in, 113–14
    payoff and financing in, 113–14
    wholesale value and, 112
service agreements, 262, 298–99,
    302, 306
service charge, on lease, 246–47,
    256
service departments, 208–9
shopping, 198–237
    articles and books on, 183–85
    dealership advertising and, 185–
        192
    Internet and, 214, 221–24
    for new car, 207–20
    preliminaries to, 183–97
    for trucks and vans, 220, 225–37
    for used vehicles, 225–37
    see also buying a car
signing, 303–7
spot delivery, 55–56, 265
supply and demand, 39

T
timing, 195–97
T. O. system, 50–51, 164–65

tower system, 54
trade-ins, 233
    book value in, 104–5
    and cleanliness of car, 96–97
    equity in, 147–48
    and knowing your car, 92–
        114
    leasing and, 254–55
    loan cash and available cash in,
        146–47
    mileage and, 98–99, 305
    money owed on, 147, 148–51
    negotiating and, 267–71, 275–79,
        283–86, 289–94, 333–34, 335–
        337, 339–40, 341–42
    and popularity of car, 97–98
    trading down, 87–88
    wholesale value in, 99–104, 146–
        147
trucks:
    checking out, 313–20, 321
    shopping for, 220, 225–37
truth in lending, 187–88

U
undercoating, 262
used vehicles, 80–85
    auctions of, 234
    checking out, 235–37, 313–20,
        321
    dealerships for, 232–34
    down payments on, 144–45
    leasing of, 256–57
    loan value and, 230
    negotiating in buying of, 275–83,
        289–96, 335–38, 341–43
    rental-company, 184, 219–20,
        234
    shopping for, 225–37
    sources of, 231–34
    specific, locating of, 235
    trucks, 225–37
    warranties and service agree-
        ments on, 299–302

V
vans, shopping for, 220

W

warranties, 208, 262–63, 297–302,
306–7
adjustment, 208, 297
implied, 301
manufacturer's, 297–98
new-car, 297–99
secret (policy adjustments; goodwill service), 298

service contracts, 262, 298–99,
302, 306
used-car, 299–302
wear and tear, 247
wholesale value, 99–101, 112, 146–
147
in buying a used car, 230
determining of, 101–4
leasing and, 250